Richard Girling is a senior feature writer for the *Sunday Times Magazine*. He has been awarded the title Journalist of the Year for two years in a row at the Press Gazette Environmental Press Awards in 2008 and 2009. He has also been named Specialist Writer of the Year at the UK Press Awards in 2002 and was also shortlisted for this award in 2005 and 2006. He has been a consultant to the former Department of the Environment and the Department of Culture, Media and Sport and author of campaigns for the Campaign to Protect Rural England (CPRE). He is currently a trustee of the Tree Council.

Richard Girling is also the author of *Rubbish! – Dirt on Our Hands and Crisis Ahead* ('A tour de force' – *Country Life*) and *Sea Change – Britain's Coastal Catastrophe* ('Brilliant and devastating' – *Daily Mail*). He lives and works in north Norfolk.

GREED

RICHARD GIRLING

CORGI BOOKS

TRANSWORLD PUBLISHERS
61–63 Uxbridge Road, London W5 5SA
A Random House Group Company
www.rbooks.co.uk

GREED
A CORGI BOOK: 9780552156486

First published in Great Britain
in 2009 by Doubleday
an imprint of Transworld Publishers
Corgi edition published 2010

Addresses for Random House Group Ltd companies outside the UK
can be found at: www.randomhouse.co.uk
The Random House Group Ltd Reg. No. 954009

The Random House Group Limited supports The Forest Stewardship Council
(FSC), the leading international forest certification organisation. All our titles
that are printed on Greenpeace approved FSC certified paper carry the FSC
logo. Our paper procurement policy can be found at
www.rbooks.co.uk/environment

Typeset in Sabon by Falcon Oast Graphic Art Ltd.
Printed in the UK by CPI Cox & Wyman, Reading, RG1 8EX.

2 4 6 8 10 9 7 5 3 1

For Caroline

Contents

Author's Note

This was not supposed to be an angry book. My aim was not to excoriate 'greedy' people. I wanted rather to explore the ways in which greed and its cousins – selfishness, jealousy, ambition – have contributed not just to the socially disfiguring excesses of people for whom too much is never enough, but also to our well-being, enjoyment of life and survival as a species. The original working title was *Greed: the Biography*, and this is what I have tried to deliver – the full story, from genetics through sexual incontinence and acquisitiveness to the economic mis-adventures of globalism; from peaks of genius to sink-holes of temptation.

When I began, few people had much idea of what a sub-prime mortgage was, or what 'short-selling' meant. Executives from Lehman Brothers were still being paraded before students at Harvard Business School as exemplars of all they should aspire to become. In England, Northern Rock was as solid as its name implied and HBOS was a moated castle of economic prudence. Hardly anyone outside the US had heard of Freddie Mac or Fannie Mae.

How times change. It was in my mind that a book about greed would be unlikely to heap praise on the International Monetary Fund or the World Bank. It was not in my mind that, before I had finished it, the British prime minister would have declared them 'unfit for purpose'. I knew very well (for who did not?) that econ-omists were inclined to false prophecy, but I had not realised the extent to which they would mistake arithmetic for alchemy, or ideology for justice.

I have done my best not to sound sanctimonious. My suitability to write about the subject may be indicated by the fact that my editor was reluctant to believe a paragraph in which I listed all that I had eaten and drunk over a holiday weekend. Like so many manifestations of our baser instincts, our diets not only provide comfort and pleasure but are also badges of status and vectors of moral weakness. The economic crisis has given a jolt to our confidence but done nothing to refine our instincts. For the City's bonus boys, it's business as usual. Not even the promise of catastrophic climate change has done much to dampen our passion for the riches of a high-carbon economy – new cars, bigger houses, smarter clothes, holidays in faraway places – while the world's poor struggle to be heard. We place great store in the way others see us. We might better concentrate on more clearly seeing ourselves.

Richard Girling
Norfolk, December 2009

Part One

The Self

1

Lunch at The Pigs

My palate can't work out the sauce. It's deep and meaty with a pile of red beans rising from its auburn depths, and more notes in it than a peal of bells. On the beans rests a tranche of slow-roasted belly-pork, honeyed, soft as fudge and crowned with a slice of black pudding and a dab of apple sauce. Artfully laid across the top is a slender twig of crackling. Its arrival at the table, alongside my companions' confit of duck, punches a hole in the conversation. All four of us stare at our plates and swallow, saliva glands spurting like geysers.

Yet none of us is hungry in a sense that any truly hungry person would recognize. We all have enjoyed breakfast. We all ate supper the night before, and lunch and breakfast in the hours before that. Our lunch is a spur-of-the-moment thing, inspired by conviviality rather than by any physiological need for depleted bodies to be re-energized. Under our waistbands, pig and duck will splash in spicy baths of red wine from the Rhone, and white from New Zealand's Marlborough Valley. After the briefest of intervals they will blend with creamy English puddings, French cheeses, Italian coffee. I feel virtuous – a Zen-like master of restraint – because I say no to the brandy and the chocolate. Our talk, once revived, is too bookish to register the irony. The East Anglian gastropub in which this extempore feast takes place is called The Pigs.

Afterwards, with all the vast weight of meat and pudding now dragging us towards sleep, we ask ourselves why we have done it. There is something *driven* about such behaviour – something genetic and immutable – that overrides the governance of our conscious minds. It's nothing to do with our supposed gourmet tastes (which, anyway, are just greed with a collar and tie on). We meet our equivalents in a nearby seaside town where amply proportioned tourists – so fat, they could be Americans – have the utmost difficulty in dragging their limbs past the fish-and-chip shop. You'll see it again at any supermarket checkout; in any hamburger joint or school canteen. It's woven into the balance sheets of confectionery manufacturers; in the pages of magazines and on television, where 'food porn' taunts our resistance to excess. Every week I see it in my shopping list. My least favourite guests are the (mercifully few) self-denying neurotics who are morally outraged by the sight of gravy. I with my well-greased chin am normal; they are weird.

Martin Jones, professor of archaeological science at Cambridge, describes in *Feast*, his wise and wonderful book on human eating habits, a great Neanderthal horse-roast held 46,000 years ago in a cave in southern Spain. Did the diners, I wonder, drool in anticipation of barbecued meat? Were they connoisseurs who took particular pleasure in the tenderest muscles and ripest offal? Did they nibble sparingly, no more than they needed, or pack their gullets until they were sick? These are not questions that the dusts and ashes of archaeology can answer, but the huge teeth of our human precursors suggest they were anything but dainty eaters. Bone analysis of early humans shows, too, that they were heavy consumers of meat, not the proto-vegetarians that idealists would prefer. If they could be resurrected and offered the menu at The Pigs, they would gulp the lot from soup to custard. Greed is the one characteristic we share with every living thing, from intestinal parasites to the Nobel laureates they might inhabit. To find its origins we have to scroll back across the billennia, through ever-simpler life forms, shedding backbones, flippers and eyes, losing our very sense of being, until we slip back into the primal soup and become blobs of insensate matter blindly sharing our genes.

The theory of the selfish gene has been around for a while now. It surprises me to find that William Hamilton's two groundbreaking papers, 'The Genetical Evolution of Social Behaviour I and II', were published as long ago as 1964, and that it is more than thirty years since Richard Dawkins's best-selling book, *The Selfish Gene*, transformed the public's understanding of evolutionary science (it was first published in 1976). *The Selfish Gene* ages well, and none of the great men of science who endorsed it at the time has any reason to regret his hyperbole (though Dawkins himself now wonders whether 'Immortal Gene' might have been better than 'Selfish'). His gene's-eye view of evolution, in which whole-body organisms serve only as vehicles, or 'survival machines', for tyrannical genes, exposed as a myth the prevailing orthodoxy that organisms behaved selfishly 'for the good of the species'. Dawkins over the telephone once gave me a ferocious ear-bashing for some careless deviation from the evolutionary high road, and I remain fearful of imprecision. Nevertheless, having a family to feed, I am genetically driven to take the risk . . .

Selfish-gene theory says that genes are both subtly programmed and savagely determined to ensure their own survival. Sometimes, but not always, this means genetically programming the host organism to look after itself, have babies and hang on to life until the last available lungful of breath. 'Not always' because Dawkins constructs an elegant case for the evolutionary benefits of altruism. The self-sacrifice of an individual for the benefit of others (by a parent defending its young, for example) may preserve more copies of its genes than it wastes. This is especially so when the relationship between martyr and beneficiaries is close, and the level of gene-sharing is high (an idea to which we shall return in a moment). 'The gene,' he writes, 'is the basic unit of selfishness.' To some people this has looked like a scientific validation of cynicism, as if there really is no such thing as a self-less act – 'nature' simply drives us to do what is most expedient for it, which may not always conform to our idea of what is 'moral'. But again Dawkins is smooth. Unlike any other species on earth, *Homo sapiens* has the capacity to defy its genes and be driven by intelligence rather than instinct. Nurture, too, has its part to play.

As might already be obvious, I am no scientist. I know what it feels like to be me, however, and I know that my intelligence sometimes can work as little more than a heightened form of animal cunning. In The Pigs, my genes tell me to covet the crusty bread roll that my neighbour has left uneaten. My intelligence tells me not to snaffle it until she is looking the other way. Dogs and cats, I have noticed, behave in much the same way. So do foxes, rats, polar bears and children. This is not to take issue with Dawkins – who would dare? – but rather to set aside his subtleties and put the matter crudely. It doesn't matter whether the primary unit of selfishness is the individual or the gene. We do not need scientific footnotes to conclude that most organisms, most of the time, are intrinsically greedy. We know it from a lifetime's experience of other creatures, our families and other people; we know it from the pit of our bellies.

All the same, we must be careful. One of the risks of studying animals is the temptation to draw parallels with our own species. Far-out political philosophies, of left and right alike, have been extrapolated from the hierarchical behaviour of insects and chimpanzees. 'Anthropomorphism' is a favourite smear-word to deploy against scientists who extrapolate too freely. Another of science's irritating habits is to hijack good, useful words from the English language – 'fitness' and 'function', for example – assign new, narrow meanings to them and then dismiss with grand hauteur any 'scientific illiterate' who uses them in their original sense. This is exacerbated by the necessity for scientists to keep on nudging the boundaries, and for each generation, like tomcats scent-marking their territories, to signal its progress with new vocabulary. Whole areas of study can rename themselves, and do so usually on steepling waves of pomposity, esotericism and self-importance. The study of animal behaviour used to be called 'ethology' and was conducted by zoologists in the field; now it is 'evolutionary psychology', studied by white-coats in the lab.

Whatever you call it, it is a science barely out of its diapers. Darwin put down a marker in *The Origin of Species*, making perfectly understandable use of the word 'instinct' to describe the innate behaviour of animals. It is a word still favoured by non-scientists, who use it to describe the non-thinking, 'instinctive' behaviour of humans and other species – 'Be a good animal,' as D. H. Lawrence put it in *The White Peacock*, 'true to your instincts' – but it has been discarded by the professionals. One reason for this was a clash of cultures. The so-called 'European school' of ethology crystallized in the 1930s around the work of two men who would go on to win the Nobel Prize for physiology – the Austrian zoologist Konrad Lorenz and the Dutch-born Niko Tinbergen, who defined his discipline as 'the biological study of behaviour'. Along with Karl von Frisch, director of the Zoological Institute at Munich, famous for his discovery of the 'waggle dance' that worker bees use to direct each other to pollen, they were happy to be called 'naturalists' – patient, slow-moving observers of the wild whose methods placed them in direct line of descent from Aristotle, through Gilbert White and the legions of Victorian clerics and physicians who followed him. They watched how birds, fish, animals and insects behaved, and tried to understand their motives. What made a herring gull roll a stray egg back into its nest? Why did a male stickleback perform its characteristic zig-zag dance in front of a prospective mate? What were the biological advantages of such a palaver? The assumption was that behaviour – *all* behaviour – was genetically programmed and innate. In terms of its actions as much as the colour of its fur and the arrangement of its limbs, an animal was what evolution had made it. It could no more alter its response to, say, a ripe banana, the sight of a female bottom or the sudden appearance of a rattlesnake, than it could change the size of its head. 'Nature' was everything; 'environment' meant nothing at all.

This opinion was challenged, fiercely and with prolonged intensity, by a new breed of American scientist – not zoologists or ethologists this time, but 'comparative psychologists'. These people had no interest in skulking about the countryside, crouching behind bushes with twigs in their ears and keeping field-diaries. Their habitat was the laboratory, where they devised clinically precise experiments to test animals' ability to learn. How easily could rats or pigeons learn to associate cause with effect, find their way through a maze, operate a machine, recognize a friend? Could their innate, supposedly inflexible patterns of behaviour be modified by teaching? The great-grandfather of such experiments was Ivan Pavlov's demonstration of 'conditioned responses' in dogs (which were taught to salivate at the sound of a bell). Rats duly learned to press the right levers; doves pecked the right keys; blackbirds were taught to mob detergent bottles instead of owls. Outdoors, Konrad Lorenz himself persuaded goslings to believe they owed filial duty to watering cans or Wellington boots. 'Nature' was stood on its head; 'instincts' were supplanted by 'drives', and 'nurture' was all.

Both sides had grenades to lob. The psychologists had shown that supposedly immutable patterns of behaviour could adjust to different environments. The ethologists could show examples of behaviour that were ineradicable. Squirrels, for example, would go on trying to bury their nuts even when they lived on concrete floors. It looked like a stalemate. But any observer of a non-human species locked in such an impasse would predict rapprochement, and so it happened. The ethologists recognized that behaviour was not simply innate; the comparative psychologists recognized that it was not entirely learnt. From the consensual union of the two formerly competing theories was born the new discipline of evolutionary psychology. It recognized that there was no behaviour without inheritance, and none without learning either.

Thus were scientists brought, if not kicking and screaming then at least mouthing and gesticulating, to the point of understanding reached by our remotest grandmothers an infinity of generations ago. Even Christian fundamentalists who rejected Darwin could look at events in the Garden of Eden and see what was planted there. Instincts, drives, urges, needs . . . call them what you will, they had Creation in their grip. Without them, temptation would have no meaning. When I consult a glossary of animal behaviour in a university textbook I find no entry for 'appetite'. I do, however, find one for 'appetitive behaviour', defined as 'active searching behaviour shown by animals seeking a goal, contrasted with the consummatory behaviour they show when they reach it'. This is not the kind of language we use when grazing a menu or talking someone into bed, but we get the point. Like every other species we are driven to pursue goals – food, drink, shelter, sexual partners, heirs, status. Like every other species we are adaptable as well as determined and, given the chance, will take all we can get rather than what we need. I ought to make clear, having just used a relative of 'adaptation', that words throughout this book are employed in their popular rather than their scientific senses. My old *Collins English Dictionary* is the reference point, not the science glossary. I know there is no 'purpose' to evolution, but it won't stop me admiring the ingenuity of its products.

The textbook offers some striking examples. Although I live in a rural part of England where farmers and cottagers have always lived in competition with the rat, until recently I had not heard of the 'Garcia effect'. Contrary to what I had always believed, when a rat comes across unfamiliar food it will not immediately pile in, gung-ho, and eat its fill. Rather, it will nibble a bit, then wait and see how it feels. If it's OK, it will come back later and enjoy the feast. If it feels poorly, it will not only fail to return but will avoid that particular food for the rest of its life. This is why rat-poisoning is not as straightforward as it looks. The human response – using slow-acting anti-coagulants that don't produce symptoms until the animals have had a good feed – is a classic example of one brilliant piece of adaptive behaviour being trumped by another. Where this occurs in nature it is almost always in the service of food and sex, for it's not just *Homo sapiens* that recognizes and exploits the connection. The absolute masters – or perhaps I should say mistresses – of the food/sex interface are fireflies of the species *Photuris*. Like other fireflies, males advertise for females with a sequence of light-flashes which (a bit like birdsong) is peculiarly their own. Females respond with an answering pattern, and the scene is set for romance. But madam is not altogether a cosy piece of work. She replies not only to males of her own species, whom she will receive with fond embrace, but also to males of three other species whose semaphore codes she knows and mimics. When one of these poor saps is lured in, the result is not the longed-for moment of passion for the male but a lavish supper for the lady.

America's zone-tailed hawk, which hunts ground-dwelling prey – ground squirrels, chipmunks, etc. – is cleverer even than that. Small animals and birds generally set up a chorus of alarms as soon as a bird of prey appears in the sky. But they will take no more notice of a vulture than they would of a dove. Vultures are carrion-eaters, not killers, and it is easy to tell a vulture from a hawk. At least, it usually is . . .

There is no reason to believe zone-tailed hawks have any more conscious awareness of their particularity than do, say, wombats or weevils; and yet evolution has handed them an advantage they cannot help but exploit. Their silhouette in flight – short of tail, long and narrow of wing – is such a convincing mimic of the turkey vulture's that even human birdwatchers don't always believe their binoculars. Down below, smaller birds and rodents continue to peck and nibble unperturbed. If the nature of the mistake ever dawns, it is too late. A shadow falls, then all is darkness and silence.

These are just two examples of numberless adaptations made by evolution in pursuit of food. The selfish gene sets no higher priority than feeding yourself, feeding your young and, if necessary, feeding your sexual partner. Where there is food, sex is never very far away. Martin Jones in *Feast* describes chimpanzees literally trading meat for sex during the share-out of monkey-meat in Tanzania. In an imagined reconstruction of early humans killing, butchering and eating a raw horse near the south coast of England 500,000 million years ago, on the basis of archaeological and ethnological evidence, he envisages men and women behaving in much the same way. These particular debauchees were members of the species *Homo heidelbergiensis*, larger-limbed and smaller-brained than *Homo sapiens* but, nevertheless, ancestors of recognizably human form and behaviour. How this translates into the lives of modern men and women is a question to be kept for Chapter 3, though few people who've benefited from a lover's favours will need the food–sex connection spelling out to them.

Back at The Pigs (where we dine with our wives), I allow my friend to order the food and choose the wine. It's a deference thing: he is older than me and was once my editor. In this particular social grouping therefore he is alpha and I am subordinate. Next time I eat in a restaurant, my companions will be younger than me and the privilege will be mine. Look around any restaurant at lunchtime in the business district of a city. I did so recently in Barcelona, where – speaking no Catalan and very little Spanish – I could get no verbal clues from eavesdropping. And yet it was as easy as ABC to 'read' the tables – not only which groups were business lunchers but also which man (it was always a man) was enjoying the ultimate privilege of status and power: paying the bill. It's the same in families. Despite the erosion of standards in domestic kitchens caused by factory-made alternatives to home-cooked food, the family meal remains integral to our cultural identity. Birthdays, weddings, festivals, funerals and anniversaries are celebrated with knife and fork in hand, and father or grandfather at the head of the table. The conspicuous, almost ritualistic, carving of meat by the senior male, says Martin Jones, may be 'an allusion to a distant heritage of Palaeolithic hunting', and a habit which the behaviour of alpha-male chimpanzees suggests must have begun somewhere altogether more primitive, raw and animalistic than even the blood-feasts of early hominids. This is the very point of confluence between nature and nurture, where biological organism and social person meet. Once in a newspaper column – jokingly, not realizing I might be making a serious point – I compared shopping and cooking for my family to the roaming and homing of ancient hunters. In place of a spear I held a bank card; in place of an open hearth I had a German high-tech oven; in place of chipped flints I had hollow-ground Sheffield steel. These things were precisely analogous.

I suppose I was trying to be ironic – always a danger, especially where self-mockery is involved. The result was an outpouring of double-underlined satire from female readers whose encounters with Tesco, frozen lasagne and the washing-up bowl apparently did not summon images of the noble savage. ('You're welcome to paint your face blue and come and hunt for the Baxter tribe whenever you like,' said one.) A dozen years later, I am inclined to advance the same point more seriously. It is not just sex that is bought with the distribution of spoils: power and status – the very rocket-launchers of the selfish gene – come with it too.

The alpha male probably is as old as sexual differentiation. Throughout nature you see him roaring, rutting, first to the kill. Depending on the species he'll be the biggest, strongest, fittest, fastest, fiercest, brightest (in both senses), loudest or richest in his family, tribal or social gathering. He'll sit at the apex of his hierarchy until death, defeat or emergence of an heir dislodges him. He is the product *par excellence* of the selfish gene. Being preferred by females seeking the best genetic material for their young, he is in a position himself to choose the fittest females and to create, through their progeny, the fittest possible vehicles for his genes. As animal breeders will testify, the strategy is brilliantly effective. In the field, the most aggressive individuals always shoulder their way to the food source first, and thus become even bigger, more assertive and territorial. Thus if you selectively breed food animals from the meatiest individuals, you select also for aggression. It's why the 'best' bulls are not the easiest to handle; nor are the heaviest pigs. For this is how evolution and its clumsier simulacrum, selective breeding, work. The dominant animals get the most to eat; the best and biggest territory; the fittest mates; the best chance of survival. Modesty and diffidence, like all the other ingredients of niceness, convey no evolutionary advantage. Greed most certainly does.

Can we translate this into human terms? Not without risking an argument, perhaps, but the parallels are too obvious, and nature too consistent, for us to let them pass. If we're honest, we can recognize it in our own behaviour – all the ways we've tried to create advantages for ourselves and our kin. What is the ingenuity of fireflies and hawks to set against the genius of people who have been cooking since they were Neanderthals? Alpha males throughout history have been characterized by ruthless suppression of everything that does not serve their purpose. Genghis Khan may have been the greatest leader ever to straddle a horse, but he would never have been a candidate for the Nobel Peace Prize. If he had been a pig, he would have been first to the teat and last to make way for the runt, which he would have been more than happy to let die.

This of course makes perfect evolutionary sense. The gene pool is not enhanced by the survival of weaklings, though this is not a rule of nature that has survived in *Homo sapiens*. We remember Richard Dawkins's caution that we have the intelligence to disobey our genes – and of course we do. We assign moral value to human life above all others (an inconsistency that underpins the philosophy of the animal rights movement, for whom all 'possessors of a life' are of equal value). Selective breeding, or 'eugenics', and the culling of supposed inferiors, for most people – we must accept not all – belong with cannibalism on the far side of an unbridgeable moral gulf (though even cannibalism for some of our forebears seems to have been less of a taboo than fish). But a litter of pigs is well worth lingering over. It is striking, for example, that their essential pigginess can survive the attentions of the breeding industry with so little damage to their natures. When domestic pigs escape into the wild they quickly revert to the lifestyle of wild boars. Contrast this, for example, with battery hens, whose resemblance to their wild progenitors – red jungle fowl – is as distant as, say, the Queen of England is from *Homo heidelbergiensis*. In the wild, they wouldn't have a clue.

The use of 'pig' as an abusive sobriquet for a greedy human nevertheless is not entirely misplaced; nor was George Orwell's characterization of the species in *Animal Farm*. Piglets are precociously assertive and greedy. Within hours of birth the dominant individuals will have imposed themselves and a hierarchy will have been fixed from Napoleon all the way down to the runt. Once settled, it remains stable and there is little further need for fighting. Animal communities typically behave like this, with each individual established in the pecking order, lording it over those below and deferring to those above. It is this that gives them the appearance of an ordered society, and persuades theorists to believe they can extrapolate a perfect political system from the conduct of monkeys. You can have common ownership *and* a privileged elite (and pigs will fly at the end of the five-year plan). It's loopy, but not so loopy that it loses all traction with human nature.

Consider, for example, the English, and the weirdness of our attitude to royalty. Like Americans, we pride ourselves on living and flourishing within a competitive meritocracy. Outside our immediate family, and excluding a very few Edwardian throw-backs in the shires, we do not base our expectations or valuations of other people on accidents of birth. Democracy forbids it. And yet look what happens when we meet a Windsor. All that bobbing and curtseying; all that speak-when-you're-spoken-to; all that ma'am and majesty . . . I remember, many years ago, the Queen Mother opening a newly built hospital a few miles north of London. Everyone was lined up for her inspection – civic dignitaries, management and medical staffs, nurses, technicians, architects, builders. Among the last was an Irish trade union official who declared himself to be a militant republican. Under no circumstances, he said, would he bow to any member of this puffed-up, gin-swilling, bloodsucking clan that wouldn't know a day's work if it jumped out of a cake. True to his word, when the tiny figure with its hat and handbag paused before him he did not bow. He *curtseyed*. Eyes down, blushing, like an old-fashioned virgin at a coming-out ball. 'Very well, thank you, ma'am.' It's easily done – I've done it myself, nodding and sirring the Prince of Wales, nodding and ma'aming the late Princess Diana. I am glad only that the trajectory of my life is unlikely to cross the paths of Charles's sister or brothers.

It's a peculiar thing, this obsession with pedigree. Every strand of social and economic policy is aimed at flattening the social pyramid. The English Parliament has fought hard to strip its upper chamber, the House of Lords, of unelected noblemen, and yet each new session is marked by a formal, tiaras-and-ermine State Opening of Parliament in which the supreme champion of human bloodstock, Queen Elizabeth II, sets out the legislative business in a speech marked by multiple repetitions of the words 'my government'. To American eyes the medieval costumes and bizarre ceremonial – Yeomen of the Guard searching the cellars for gunpowder plotters (last seen in 1605); Black Rod summoning the Commons and having the door slammed in his face as a mark of the House's independence – is a quaint reminder of all that the New World fought to get away from. And yet the pavements outside Buckingham Palace are thick with American visitors who, back home, compensate for the absence of Yankee royals with exaggerated respect for the office of president, and who have little to learn from the English about the nuances of speech, dress and manner (never mind race) that mark each person's position on the anthill. Deep inside us, it seems, is some inextinguishable need for the comfort of 'knowing our place', of being clear about whom to look up to and whom to look down upon. It places us in the company of chimpanzees, lions, dogs, pigs, every kind of social animal whose survival depends upon peaceful coexistence with others.

Let us stay for a moment with pigs, as they are the ones, however unfairly, that bear the stigma. The UK's Department for Environment, Food and Rural Affairs (Defra) publishes a Code of Recommendations for the welfare of pigs, from which Recommendations 48 and 49 read as follows:

> Pigs shall be placed in groups as soon as possible after weaning. They shall be kept in stable groups with as little mixing as possible.

> If pigs unfamiliar with each other have to be mixed, this should be done at as young an age as possible . . . When pigs are mixed they shall be provided with adequate opportunities to escape and hide from other pigs.

What is being emphasized here is the importance of settled communities. When pigs meet each other as strangers, they straight away want to settle the hierarchy, just as newborns do in a litter. They do this by displays of aggression and fighting until the pecking order emerges and everyone knows what's what.

Once this has happened, disputes usually can be settled with minimal aggression and violence, but if things do turn nasty, or if there is bullying, victims need somewhere to retreat. The parallels between this and the organization of human societies, at every level from families to nation states, are too obvious to need spelling out. Look what happens – in tribal Africa, Palestine and the former Yugoslavia, for example – when alien groups are penned in, willy-nilly, by political map-makers. What we have, therefore, is a paradox. The impact of alpha males on their subordinates, and the effect of their subordinates on each other, is in one sense a morally deplorable hierarchy of lust and greed. There are parallels with the ganglands of Chicago, London and New York, where expediency, or what in pigs is known as 'avoidance order', keeps the gun barrels cool until a new face appears on the block or a godfather croaks his last. The usefulness of the alpha male – paterfamilias, line manager, chancellor of the exchequer, tyrant, dictator, whatever – is that the whole thrust of his behaviour is to create and maintain a status quo. It may be favourable to him and his heirs, but it is favourable also to the common herd and their own selfish genes which, in a stable environment, will enjoy a greatly improved chance of survival. Perhaps this may explain our own need to locate ourselves within the social order, our nods and ma'ams, our suspicion of non-conformity and rejection of strangers. Perhaps if he *had* successfully brought the entire world to heel, Genghis Khan might have had his Peace Prize after all.

The earliest expression of animal language, whether by sight or by sound – the bleating of lambs, the 'gape' of nestlings, the whimpering of puppies and the squalling of human babies – is 'find me, feed me', and the instinct of many parents is to enslave themselves to their offspring's voracity (an instinct seen at its most extreme in the frantic efforts of exhausted dunnocks to keep pace with the cavernous appetites of cuckoos). Later in life we may see other examples of altruistic or supportive behaviour between members of families or wider social groups – in hunting, food-sharing, watch-keeping, nannying and mutual defence, for example. Again the human parallels are obvious. This brings us to a rather useful theory known as 'kin selection'. It is another way in which a very young science is running to keep up with ancient verities. Your grandmother knows all about kin selection. So did her grandmother, and every other grandmother back to *Homo heidelbergiensis* and beyond. They just didn't have a name for it, or understand that loving their families, showing favouritism to their nearest and dearest, made them agents of the selfish gene. It was William Hamilton himself who translated instinct into maths. The selfish gene, let us remember, is selfish precisely because it aims to maximize the transmission of itself from each generation to the next. The closer the relationship between individuals, the more genes they have in common, and the more the selfish gene will benefit if the individuals support each other. This is why parents favour their own children and other blood relatives, but do so decreasingly as relationships become more distant.

As we have passed from grandmotherly common sense into textbook science, there has to be a scale of measurement – the Coefficient of Relatedness, as it is called, measures the extent to which it is useful for gene-sharers to co-operate, and does so on a scale of 0 to 1. Identical twins sharing a full set of genes score 1; unrelated individuals score 0. A parent and child will have half their genes in common; so will siblings. For them, therefore, the score is 0.5. I won't trouble you with the maths, but you can work out that the coefficient of relatedness for a first cousin is 0.125, a second cousin 0.03125 and a third cousin 0.0078125. Here there-fore we find the genetic root not just of nepotism and altruism, but also of cynicism. The unconscious question an organism puts to itself before helping another is: what's in it for my genes? In other words, the benefit to the recipient must exceed the cost to the donor. In the extreme case of suicidal self-sacrifice, the survivors must have a higher coefficient of relatedness, and so be in a position to replicate more of the genes they share, than the deceased. This is the bottom line. Richard Dawkins in *The Selfish Gene* explains that a gene for suicidally saving five cousins would not make evolutionary sense (the cost would be higher than the gain), but saving five brothers would. 'The minimum requirement for a suicidal altruistic gene to be successful,' he writes, 'is that it should save more than two siblings (or children or parents), or more than four half-siblings (or uncles, aunts, nephews, nieces, grandparents, grandchildren), or more than eight first cousins, etc.' In the natural world, this can explain, for example, the evolution of spiders and mantises in which the males are eaten by the females after mating. Their oats safely sown, the father's last duty to its multiple children is to provide a good, sustaining meal for their mother.

In the human world such extremes are rarer. There is no coefficient of relatedness for the non-lethal sacrifices we are prepared to make, and the loyalties we feel, in the wider community. By consulting the nearest sentient grandmother, however, I am led to the rather obvious conclusion that it works in much the same way. *What's in it for me?* 'You only get out of life what you put into it,' Granny says with biblical authority. Apostles, humanists and philosophers all take the same line. 'Do to others as you would have them do to you,' says the gospel of Matthew (7:12). 'Do as you would be done by,' echoes the humanists' Golden Rule. 'Individuals seek their own interests at all times,' say the psychological egoists. 'There is no such thing as an unselfish act.' We can argue all we like about the terminology and provenance of our thoughts, and trim them in the language of science, religion, philosophy or common sense, but we recognize as clearly as Granny does that banality knows best: charity begins at home.

Greed is embedded deep within us, below the horizon of our consciousness, grabbing what it can and prompting us, the vehicles in which it travels, to do the same. From our corporeal wholes our self-interest floods outward in ever-widening bands – through our families to our streets, villages, towns or cities; to our county, state or region; to the corporations we work for and the industries to which they belong; to religions, trade unions, political parties, special interest groups, teams and sports; to nationalities, countries and, if it ever came to it, to our planet. At varying levels of intensity and rationality, our predisposition to advance our own interests – let us call it the worm – works on behalf of them all.

Like real worms, it can throw up a rich compost. Greed always wants more and better. Sheepdogs are trained by the expectation of reward, and humans are no different. Without it there would be no incentive for self-improvement; no creative energy; no civilization. Everything we value, from the spiritual uplift of art and religion to the queasy gratification of cheeseburger and fries, is born of an impulse we all share but profess to despise. Through its various simulacra – *power*, *aspiration*, *success* – greed crystallizes every ambition; shapes every prayer; fills every stomach, pocket and treasury.

When finance ministers applaud 'growth', they celebrate a process of material gain that reaches far beyond anything we need to fulfil our procreative function or to enjoy the 'equal and unalienable human rights' prescribed for us by the United Nations. Evolution has given us an instinct that is as crucial to our survival as fear or sex. But we have developed no balancing urge to moderate or control our appetites. It has brought us to a tipping point. Greed in the third millennium is a juggernaut without brakes, running out of control. We are defined by what we possess, and are incapable of being satisfied. Individually, collectively, nationally, we are locked in pursuit of *more*. With the exception of body fat, and discounting the malign influence of jealousy (which after all is just our own greed bouncing back at us), we admire the trappings of excess and the superlatives that go with them. The world's most expensive sandwich (Wagyu beef, foie gras, black truffle mayonnaise, Brie de Meaux and salad; £85, London) and most expensive dinner (foie gras, Kobi beef, scallops, Périgord truffles, lobster and too much else to mention; £17,563, Bangkok) are received as amusing follies, not offences against decency. A sacked national football coach waiting out his contract on £6,000 a day; City bonuses bigger than the lifetime earnings of a production worker; carbon released into the atmosphere a million times faster than it was sequestered in the Cretaceous – all these are ribbons and bows on the same package that brings us WAP phones, Pot Noodles and all-year suntans. We know the world cannot go on fulfilling the demands we make of it; we recognize the fantasy of infinite growth; and yet the juggernaut will not slow down.

But we recognize, too, the self-gratifying genius of men and women whose ambitions over the millennia have created a world of infinite possibility that feeds, comforts and entertains us. Our human intelligence means we perceive self-interest in a multiplicity of ways. The coefficient of relatedness takes us only so far: we are more than the sum of our genes. When family duty conflicts with, say, professional opportunity or creativity, it is by no means certain the family will win. The attachments we form, the ideals and loyalties we serve, are wide-ranging and various. We may feed our grandmother to our children; we may sacrifice all duties and comforts for the sake of a symphony, a poem or a creed. The only thing we cannot separate from is the unstoppable drive, the appetites and desires of our most intimate selves. This book therefore is not just a lament for lost innocence or an assault on fat cats (though the fat cats will get their due). It is as much a *celebration* of self-interest and all that it has driven us to achieve, from cave-art to YouTube, eolith to space lab, mammoth haunch to *poulet à l'estragon*, and so on *ad infinitum*. In the beginning, greed is an inchoate, genetic component of organisms too primitive to realize their own existence. In the end it is the driving force of organisms so powerful that they override every obstacle in their path, including governments, other people's lives and their own moral identity.

2

Raiding the Fridge

Greed in its most animalistic form is a demon roosting in the belly. With varying degrees of guilt or regret, we all give in to it, yet we show little sign of understanding what our bodies are saying to us. We fret over the chemistry of greed as if it were one of nature's deepest mysteries, like consciousness or the origin of matter. Psychologists, sociologists, neuroscientists, bio-chemists, cranks, rogues and bishops all strive to explain, and to excuse or condemn, our fatal attraction to fats and sugars. Supermarkets, food manufacturers and the advertising industry don't bother. Temptation is the tool of their trade; greed and indolence the pillars of their economy. 'Naughty but nice' (attributed to the then advertising copywriter Salman Rushdie) was the slogan that sold us cream cakes in the 1970s. The underlying truism – that the saliva glands speak louder than the calorie chart – is as much as any salesman needs to know.

For all of us, unless we are bread-and-water ascetics aiming for sainthood, it's part of the common experience: we've all held up our plates for sticky toffee pudding. As a result, many of us weigh more than the 'experts' say we should (I put 'experts' in inverts because, in matters of diet, today's top tip tends to be tomorrow's laugh-line). And yet, somehow, we can't be sanguine. Body weight, like ugliness and earning power, is on one of those linear scales that we seem to think entitle us to look down on those of inferior rank. We do it openly and guiltlessly. Sizeism is the one form of generalized abuse not proscribed by political correctness.

A cartoon on an internet site shows two women introducing themselves. 'I can never remember names,' says the thin one. 'Do you mind if I just call you Fat Bastard?' Try to imagine the outrage that would follow if 'fat' were substituted by almost any other physical characteristic. Bulimic bastard? Black/brown/yellow bastard? Muslim bastard? You don't have to accept the lamp-jawed prohibitions of the mirth police – you might even find the joke funny – to recognize the victimhood of the chronically overweight. Even a newspaper as fastidiously 'correct' as the *Guardian* can condemn sports fans for their beery girth as much as for their gross behaviour. Overweight politicians are mercilessly lampooned, just as they were 200 years ago by Gillray, as if overweightness itself were evidence of malfeasance. When the well-covered but not exactly lard-arsed Gordon Brown took over from Tony Blair as British prime minister in June 2007, cartoonists drew him as grotesquely fat and farting. The implication was moral dubiety, weakness and a brand of hypocrisy ill-befitting a child of the manse.

It is an easy trap to fall into. A reader complaining to the editor about something I'd written for the *Sunday Times* rounded off his squib with the worst insult he could think of: 'Girling is FAT'. I laughed (a bit comfy around the middle, maybe, but not *fat*); then a few days later I caught myself making an ungallant remark about a woman bending over in a garden. If you are looking for skewed values, look no further than this: a big car is easier to forgive than a big backside. So in most cases is a big libido. An insatiable hunger for sex is less likely to incite ridicule than an uncontrolled appetite for biscuits – unless, of course, the lothario is fat, like Tony Blair's much-mocked deputy John Prescott, in which case, by comparison with ordeal by tabloid newspaper, the pillory would have seemed like a place of refuge.

In societies that inherited their morals from the Christian Church, this is a warping of historical values. Although gluttony to Roman Catholics is a venial sin, the Ten Commandments have nothing to say about big dinners or snacking between meals. Sex, on the other hand, gets a double whammy. Adultery is a shalt-not; so is coveting your neighbour's wife. It might not score quite so highly on the register of sin, but coveting the man's dinner must have accounted for just as much jealousy and lust. We can't fix the exact moment at which some grunted equivalent of 'yum-yum' entered the human vocabulary, but I'd bet it did not long post-date the wolf-whistle. Fire would have been at the heart of it. The consumption of the first cooked meal was the point at which our natural inheritance, life in the raw, passed through a filter of creativity and came out the other side as 'culture'. This was the birth-date of self-indulgence, the point at which necessity accelerated its long mutation into pleasure. Futurologists in the middle of the last century foresaw a time, not far ahead, when food would be entirely de-natured and our bodies fuelled by hyper-nutritious pills and powders that would turn us into sleekly efficient machines for living, freed from the tyranny of mealtimes. Was there ever a grosser misreading of human nature? We don't want to be freed from the tyranny of food, any more than we want to be freed from the tyranny of sex; we want to be free to enjoy more of it. Asceticism is as far from our natures as a Big Mac from a bullace.

What the seers did get right was the relentless advance of mechanization and mass production, and the gradual sidelining of muscle power. What they *didn't* see was that these accelerating trends would have as profound an impact on diet as they would on transport and communication. Food is everywhere – cheap, abundant, sweet or salty, hot or cold, hard or soft, wherever and whenever we want it. In developed countries we live in an age, unique in history, when poverty is relative not absolute, and where temptation never stops. Tesco in the UK now stocks more than 40,000 product lines, most of which are food or drink and the bulk of which are bought by people who are not rich. Almost everyone eats between meals; some people eat *instead* of meals. We even eat for sport. In June 2007 a man called Joey Chestnut, from San Jose, California, set a new world record by swallowing 59.5 hot dogs in twelve minutes. Most of us find this obscene, and feel no temptation to view the performance on YouTube. Yet it's nothing more than a stretched-to-absurdity example of something we all do, most days of our lives. One way or another, like it or not, we *all* eat competitively, and always have done.

We are all proselytizers. Wherever we live or travel, we talk up our native cuisines, or those of our favourite holiday destinations, as the world's best. You won't convince a Turk that a Greek knows one end of a kebab from another, or a northern Italian that there's anything worth eating south of Naples, or a Frenchman or an Englishman that anyone else knows anything about food at all. You'll hear similar from Moroccans, Chinese, Indians, Japanese, Spaniards, Poles, Russians . . . Even Americans and Australians have a shout. As every tongue contains some rough equivalent of 'yum-yum', so it does of 'foreign muck'. We shall consider national pride in its wider context in Chapter 6. Here we are concerned only with the social and cultural significance of food, and the way it influences what we eat.

National cuisines are the most obvious examples of 'food loyalty', though not perhaps the most important. 'You are what you eat' is a cliché rolled out by every kind of dietary sectarian who would like us to share their disgust at whatever foods they happen to proscribe. The miracle of metabolism makes nonsense of their literal-mindedness. Horses are not made of grass, nor Joey Chestnut of dough and frankfurters, nor even vegans of pills and leaves – but there is another, quite different sense in which the cliché comes closer to the truth. We advertise our status just as much by what we eat as by what we wear or how we pronounce our vowels. For this to work there has to be a range of choices (so we can show our discernment) and a hierarchy of values (so we can display our wealth). We imagine this to be a modern phenomenon, and in a way it is, but, as Martin Jones explains in *Feast*, competitive dining is as old as food on a plate. Hierarchies have always been defined by where, what and how people eat. We don't know when cooking began. Some experts give it a history of 180,000 years; others cite bones in Africa apparently burnt half a million years ago, or burnt clay three times older even than that. What's certain is that the Neanderthals knew that cooked food tasted better than raw, and that cooks in the Stone Age, while not quite rivalling Tesco for variety, worked with a far wider range of ingredients than the meagre handfuls of nuts and seeds we tend to imagine. Jones counts 20 species of mammal, 16 families of bird, numerous fish and 140 taxa of fruit, nut, seed and pulse, all on the menu 23,000 years ago. Some of these will have been preferred to others, thus creating a hierarchy of taste and, hence, of diners.

In *The Naked Ape*, first published in 1967, Desmond Morris introduced us to some controversial ideas about evolution, cooking and feeding. It was meat-eating, he argued, that had given us our convention of large meals taken at intervals – this is the habit of carnivores, who eat heavily and then take time to digest. In the treetops, however, we can see our primate cousins nibbling more or less non-stop on fruity snacks. It was in our ape ancestry, therefore, that he saw the origins of the human 'sweet tooth' and the habit of snacking between meals. He is no less opinionated about cooking. The reasons we like hot food, he suggests, are threefold. First, it simulates the 'prey temperature' at which carnivores eat their still-warm kills. Second, cooked food tastes better than raw. Third, and most importantly for a species with small teeth and feeble jaws, cooking breaks down tough fibres and makes food easier to chew and digest. It is this last point that is worth dwelling upon, and which may explain more than just our preference for *poulet à l'estragon* over raw jungle fowl. Social anthropology in the mid-1990s came up with something called the 'expensive tissue hypothesis', which led to some startling conclusions about the role of cooked food in the growth of human intelligence.

The first bits of evidence are our teeth. They are much smaller than our early ancestors', and much smaller in relation to body size than other mammals'. The same is true of our barely half-size gut, or alimentary tract. And yet our brains over the same period have grown very much bigger than early hominids', and hugely bigger than other species'. So there seems to have been a trade-off. The deal was: nutcracker teeth, capacious gut and walnut brain; or rice-pudding teeth, constipation and the theory of relativity. How did this happen? The expensive tissue hypothesis says that different organs and tissues burn energy at different rates. Martin Jones lists skin and tendons as low energy users, and liver, gut and brain as incontinent big spenders. 'What a consideration of the energy economy alerts us to,' he writes, 'is the need to balance the books . . . With a brain that big and consequently using up a lot of sugar, something else has got to be small.' The liver can't be compromised, so the principal donor has been the gut which, compared with the steaming industrial complex inside a cow, is pitifully ill-equipped to deal with fibrous plant material. Neither are our downsized teeth capable of cud-chewing or any other kind of serious breakdown work – we would use more energy masticating than we would gain by swallowing the result. With jaws and gut not up to the task, the work of breaking down the fibres and making them digestible has to be done some other way, outside the body. Hence the evolutionary importance of cooking.

It is a neat theory which dovetails nicely with the material evidence. Brain expansion in the fossil record does indeed co-incide with the earliest known cooking-hearths, and teeth did shrink as food got softer. Thus it happened, as a result of our own genius, that we destruction-tested our willpower and transformed the virtue of opportunistic eating into the vice of eternal greed. Cooked food is more flavoursome than raw, and so it is more seductive. Worse: flavour enhancers and other modifying techniques now present us with a multi-coloured, sweet 'n' salty cornucopia whose attraction to eye and tongue often exceeds its nutritional value. No previous civilization, certainly no wild ancestor or other species, has faced such temptation.

What has *not* changed is the relationship between diet and status. If we assume that human nature is as old as humankind, then the idea of 'high table', where social elites get the most and best to eat, must have begun deep amid the ashes of prehistory. For thousands of years it has conditioned the way we perceive each other, and has framed our ideas of fashion and beauty. We swallow not just the foods themselves but the values that go with them. In no previous age has competitive eating reached so far down the social and economic pyramid. Advertisements even for mass-produced foods – instant coffee, industrial wine and cheese, ice cream, chocolate – project images of sophistication and exclusivity. ('This is not just food,' as one of the more irritating UK television campaigns has insisted, 'this is M&S food.') The message is hammered home by celebrity chefs and cookery writers who look for ever more inventive ways in which to deploy the Tesco 40,000. Words like 'roast' and 'grill', formerly the preserve of the rich, now give upward mobility to packeted snacks. We forget that there was once a hierarchy not just of foodstuffs but of cooking methods too. 'Peasant' meals involved boiling or stewing not just because cheap, tough scraps needed to be tenderized, but also because nothing was lost – whatever fats or juices ran from the meat or vegetables would remain in the water and be saved. Only the well-off could think of roasting, which loses so much weight through shrinkage.

Social distinctions in food have not been abolished, but – with the probable exception of the English upper classes – they have shifted their boundaries. Gentry for the most part are no more interested in what they eat than in what they read, drive or wear (ostentatious dining, like pumped-up muscles, designer labels and flaunted intelligence, is vulgar). My small experience of English country houses suggests an almost philistine aloofness – a desire not to be seen to be trying too hard that harks back to the overboiled cabbage, grey meat and mouth-puckering claret remembered from public school boarding houses. For the vast and variegated sprawl of the middle classes, however, the competition has never been hotter. It matters not just what you serve your guests at dinner (or, more likely, 'supper'), but where you shopped and whose recipe you followed. In England, for example, it's OK to say 'Nigella' (Lawson, daughter of a former chancellor of the exchequer and wife of Charles Saatchi, founder-patron of Britart) but not 'Delia' (Smith, Essex-vowelled owner of Norwich City Football Club), even though Delia's recipes are tried, tested and as near foolproof as it's possible to get. It matters which restaurants you eat in and which tables you are given, and it is as important to know the variety of olive in your extra-virgin oil as of the grape in your wine (which only in the most particular circumstances may be Chardonnay). Words like 'free-range', 'unpasteurized' and 'organic' are evidence of refinement; 'sugar' a sign of undeveloped taste. Desmond Morris's ape theory may not be widely discussed, but a 'sweet tooth' is a reliable indicator of lower-class origins, and the consumption of sweet wine, unless as an accompaniment to foie gras or 'pudding' (never 'dessert' or, horror, 'sweet'), rivals farting at table as a social signifier. There is a keen discourse, dividing the stubbornly English from the obdurately Francophile, on whether cheese should precede pudding, or vice versa. Tea must be poured before milk is added.

Such things are of little importance to those lower in the social scale, yet the 'milk-in-firsts' as I have heard them called are no less sensitive than their bank managers to the nuances of display. They are the principal targets of advertisers who use sports and film stars to inject their products with an essential dash of bling. In the basic sense of creating dishes from raw ingredients, they might not cook much – they consume most of the large 'convenience' element in the Tesco 40,000 – but it doesn't mean they are un-interested or unjudgemental. They have connoisseurship of their own, involving everything from the strength of a vindaloo to the specific gravity of a Czechoslovakian lager. Thanks to modern preservation techniques, the range of pre-cooked dishes now available to 'ordinary' people would surpass the imagination, if not the appetite, of a Bourbon.

All these sub-divisions of the British national cuisine (which I admit I have caricatured) are beloved of their tribes, and all divide again into regional, sectarian and family variants. Even dieting is competitive. In its absorption with detail and 'correctness', it is as obsessive as *cordon bleu* and every bit as concerned with image and specialness (perhaps even more so – unlike gourmets, vegans seldom justify their choice by arguing that it tastes better). Wherever and however we live, the pressure to consume is un-relenting. Regardless of 'high' or 'popular' taste, we are all in possession of substantially similar bodies, prey to the same instincts and urges.

From deli counter to microwave, the script is much the same. Our food choices overwhelmingly are based on image and flavour rather than nutritional value or dietary need. (Yes, be honest, they are – 'yum-yum' hits the brain much harder than 'good for you'.) George Orwell was appalled by miners' wives in the 1930s refusing to switch from expensive white bread to cheaper, 'better' brown, but acknowledged that people leading impoverished lives would choose what they enjoyed rather than what was healthy. (More than seventy years later a British health minister, John Reid, would say the same about smoking.) I hesitate to quarrel with Orwell, but I don't believe the 'peculiar evil' of instinctive rather than reasoned food choices is confined to the working class. Regardless of budget, or of our daily ration of professional fulfilment, we all swim together. Food has shot so far up the social agenda that its indulgence on 'feast days' has supplanted even the gods they were supposed to celebrate. Christmas in Britain is all about turkey and pudding, not the infant Jesus.

In his entertaining little book *How We Eat*, Leon Rappoport, professor emeritus of psychology at Kansas State University, credits the early 19th-century French politician-gourmet Anthelme Brillat-Savarin with inspiring new culinary standards that 'inverted conceptions of eating'. Instead of food being prepared to enhance a special occasion, the meal *itself* now became the cause for celebration. I'm not sure that any single voice – even Brillat-Savarin's – can take credit for a phenomenon that needed so much economic, social and scientific change to bring it about, but the point is well made. The fat of the land has become the fat of the supermarket; and the fat of the supermarket has settled around our waistlines. Hunger is not the spectre that stalks the lives of men and women in modern consumer societies: the enemy now is greed.

But there is a pygmy in the room. As the world gets heavier, so the counter-currents of body image and fashion become more paradoxical. If obesity is a modern phenomenon, then so is its reactive opposite, the peculiar and even more damaging idealization of fleshlessness. Sexual attraction and the greed it inspires are material for the next chapter. Here it's enough to reflect that Victoria Beckham would have held no more attraction for Peter Paul Rubens (or Botticelli, or Raphael, or the sculptors of ancient Greece) than a stick of celery for Henry VIII. Ideas of beauty change over time (though, I believe, not by as much as people imagine). What remains constant is our preoccupation with status and its all-important visual ciphers. Clothes, shoes, hair, luggage, jewellery, *maquillage* – all these are coded signals of economic firepower, and none is more powerful than body shape. The old chestnut 'You can never be too rich or too thin' is attributed to the Duchess of Windsor, who certainly looked as if she believed it. She might be appalled now by some of the more extreme acts of bone-fetishism sponsored by the fashion industry, but I doubt she would recant. In an age of calorific plenitude, it costs money to stay slim. Less is more.

In earlier centuries this would have made no more sense than low-fat yoghurt. For most of history, *more* has meant exactly what it says: bigger, fatter, creamier. One of the more amusing features of the British Museum's 2001 exhibition 'Cleopatra of Egypt: from History to Myth' was the speculation it caused about what this fabled Ptolemaic mantrap had actually looked like. We can rule out any likelihood of resemblance to the Duchess of Windsor, or even to the curvaceous amplitude of Cleopatra's own most celebrated impersonator, Elizabeth Taylor. The Ptolemies were no sylphs (Ptolemy VIII was known to his people as *Physkon*, or 'fatso') and both Cleopatra and the women who modelled themselves on her were depicted with bands of fat around their necks, which art historians call 'Venus rings'. In Ancient Egypt you couldn't be too rich, but you *could* be too thin. At a time of hunger, plumpness, like fancy shoes or the courtship of emperors, was the hallmark of wealth.

A few months before 'Cleopatra of Egypt', I went to visit a businessman at his home in southern England. Hugh was not his real name but it is what I agreed to call him. He was a man who enjoyed all the comforts of a well-planned, disciplined and profitable life. He lived in a large and beautiful house in classic English countryside. There were large cars glinting on well-raked gravel. Expensive clothes. Paintings on the walls. A big, well-furnished office lined with books. He had a fulfilling cultural life; successful children; no financial worries; plenty of friends. I found him urbane, educated, a fluent and amusing talker, instantly likeable. Such men do not usually need to guard their identities, but Hugh insisted. This was his secret:

At night he would lie awake until his wife was asleep, then creep downstairs and 'pinch' (his word) a tub of ice cream or a slab of cheese from the fridge. It was not that he hadn't tried to reform himself. A few years earlier he had kept to a low-calorie diet long enough to shed 10 stones but now, in the classic lose-and-gain pattern that so many obese people describe (doctors call it a 'chronic relapsing condition'), he was back up to a 'shameful' (his word again) 22 stones. And there was another, even worse weight to bear – 'a permanent sense of guilt'.

Having met and interviewed many other obese men and women, I had a good idea what his answer would be. But I asked it all the same. Why guilt? 'It's knowing I shouldn't be this weight. *I shouldn't look like this.* And I could do something about it if I had the willpower. And yet for some reason or other . . .' It compels you to wonder: if a strong-minded man like Hugh, so disciplined in every other way, cannot control his appetite, then who can? I spoke to a few 'fat is beautiful' proselytizers, and a few others who toughed it out with humour, but the deepest emotion, to which the conversation almost invariably turned, was misery. (It is a moot point, which I acknowledge, that misery and obesity are chicken and egg – it's not always clear which came first, and there are many cases in which psychological or psychiatric factors may be the most important. Here, however, I am restricting myself to physiology.)

Many of their problems were all too easy to predict – the impossibility of finding ready-made clothes (even extra-large tights are too small, which is why you see so many fat women with bare legs); the uselessness of cinema and aircraft seats, where fat people are not given the same right of access as wheelchair-users; the absence of meaningful help from doctors who are more inclined to be judgemental than sympathetic; the pitfalls of social eating; the stigma of seeming out of control and the assumption that 'obese' means 'stupid'. 'When you're overweight,' said one woman, 'you don't feel you're part of life. You're a spectator.'

'Without going into the details,' said Hugh, 'even going to the loo is difficult. I find that I can't use the ordinary men's urinal. I have to go into a closed cubicle and take my trousers down to have a pee.' 'The details', I deduced from what others told me, would have involved the problem of cleaning himself after defecation. To ask obese people what they most regret about their lives is to be shocked by the ordinariness of what most distresses them.

'Being unable to cross your legs in a ladylike way,' said a woman.

'Not feeling confident when I walk into a restaurant with my wife,' said a man.

Cutting your toenails, tying your shoes, scratching your back, walking downstairs, reversing the car, making love – the whole of life is an obstacle course in which every step is a pratfall. Why would anybody put themselves through this if they felt they had a choice? How could a midnight snack, or a double helping of cheesecake, be worth this much suffering? Are such people different from the rest of us in some way they cannot help? Or are they just the deserving products of their own contemptible greed, like the rest of us only more so? Is this something else for which they have to blame their mothers?

At a lunch party recently I met a university dietetics lecturer. Having registered her (evidently extravagant) appetite for roast potatoes, I asked her opinion. Why do we eat so much more than we need to stay healthy? Why does appetite vary so much from person to person? She did not think these were very interesting questions. It is, she said disappointingly, 'not rocket science'. Like sex, 'it's just a question of availability'. We eat more because there is more to eat. Simple as that. It's why there are more fat people in Florida than there are in Ethiopia, and more fat people in the 21st century than there were in the 19th. We do it because we can. It's not that our natures have changed – they are as old as sin, fixed since that earliest hominid came down from the trees, found his tongue and set off in search of god and dinner. The differences are circumstantial, but then circumstance is all. On the savannah, the grasping hand and the ready mouth were instruments of survival. Like all animals not knowing where their next mouthful would come from, we packed our bellies with all they would hold. To eat was to live another day, survive another night and pass on our genes. From cave to kitchen, from *mashamba* to the breadbaskets of the West, we've been doing it ever since. There may be a different kind of urgency in equatorial Africa, but Florida's basic instinct is just the same.

A popular British television series featured a practitioner armed with tubes and syringe whose speciality was to confront fat people with the contents of their own bowels (they were all obediently disgusted). I can't remember what the stunt was supposed to prove, but it makes a pretty good symbol for the bind we are in. On the one hand we are urged to give in to temptation; on the other, to hate ourselves for doing so. In an era that combines pitilessness with self-obsession, the result is a particular kind of double standard that has turned hypocrisy into a market force. Few motors of greed are more rapacious than the red-top newspapers and celebrity magazines that pay five-figure sums for paparazzi shots of overweight royals or film stars, then publish them with preachy, quasi-moralistic texts. This should really make us think about ourselves, and the corner into which our liberal sensitivities always seem to box us when we consider the less pleasing aspects of our species' behaviour. Everything is normal, and nothing is.

Normal. It is a big, formless blob of a concept with nothing like a handle to grasp it by. What is normal? What is *natural*? What is surely *not* natural is the fashion industry's de-sexing of young women into breastless, hipless and bottomless boylettes. (One nutritionist I spoke to, with grand disregard for political correctness, ascribed this to the indifference of gay fashion designers to the sexual paraphernalia of the female body.) What's not natural is the use of appetite suppressants, exclusion diets and meal substitutes in place of proper food. The diet trade employs more cranks, spivs, charlatans and crooks than any racket since bits of the 'true cross' were hawked around medieval abbeys. Science conclusively has stripped credibility from every kind of diet that promises rapid weight loss, spot-reduction, 'detoxification', improved metabolism or melting cellulite, or that relies on a single food (grapefruit is a favourite) or the avoidance of proteins and carbohydrates in the same meal. A diet programme that rests on one or more of these is self-defining tosh. (Any book by a qualified nutritionist or dietician will spell it out for you.)

What is especially unnatural is fear of food, obsession with body shape and believing that bananas, crackling, chocolate cake, whelks, cheese, chewing gum or anything else is intrinsically bad for you. It's a favourite truism of radical nutritionists that there is no such thing as bad food, only bad diets. Beware, too, the 'need not greed' brigade of Presbyterian killjoys who are as muddled about food as they are about sex. Food is not all about nutrition; sex is not all about procreation (which is why we have procreated so freely). As Orwell more or less conceded, pleasure is a necessary component of any life worth living, and food is one obvious way of achieving it. This is precisely why the futurologists got it wrong with their pills and powders, and it's why the word for any kind of aesthetic discrimination is 'taste'. Your tongue is every bit as entitled to titillation by strawberry or lobster as your ears are to enjoy Beethoven or your eyes Botticelli. Nothing good ever came from philistinism; and asceticism, which seeks its rewards in other spheres, is only greed at prayer.

What *is* natural is to respond to your appetite. As everyone knows more or less by instinct, food divides into five broad categories: milk and dairy; meat and fish; fruit and vegetables; fats; cereals and starches. A 'balanced' diet is one that includes all five and keeps them in proportion. As everyone also knows, this means more cereals, fruit and vegetables than meat or fat, but – ignore the charlatans – it does *not* mean cutting out all fats (the

World Health Organization recommends 30 grams a day). A no-fat diet is neither natural nor healthy, and your body's interest in fats – expressed through appetite and their high 'yum' factor – is part of your genetic make-up. Your awareness of it came literally with your mother's milk. As an infant you 'knew' when you were hungry, and knew how to let your mother know. Your brain still receives and transmits the same messages, but they are overlain by such a babble of noise that you don't hear them clearly. The inter-ference is both psychotic (advertisers selling us bad stuff and thinking it's OK) and neurotic (healthy people satisfying healthy appetites and worrying about it). But listen to your inner child and you'll find the message is pretty simple. Your body contains a highly efficient internal communications system. If your stomach is empty or your blood sugar low, it will tell you to feed. When it's full, it will tell you to stop. And it will do so with dis-crimination, registering that you've had enough of one kind of food but still need more of another. This is why you can feel fit to burst after the meat course but still find room for something sweet. It is this very appetite for variety that helps us get what we need, and that makes the 'traditional' European meal of meat (or fish) and three veg, followed by pudding – a convention to which we were led by our appetites, remember, not by scientists – such a comfort and a pleasure. We'll return to the body's auditing and restocking systems in a moment.

In the language of the restaurant critic, 'plump' is a term of approbation second in rank only to 'delicious' and 'succulent'. Snails are plump. So are oysters, quails, strawberries, chickens, garlic, prunes and rice. Plumpness is juicy, generous and good. The only thing that may *not* be plump is the human consumer of the plumptious plateful. Plumpness in people is where life goes pear-shaped. It is unhealthily, offensively *bad*. Except of course it isn't. Botticelli's Venus would never win a contract as a 21st-century fashion model but would be likely to outlive anyone who did. The subjective opinion of most men is that a curvaceous feminine shape is more enticing than a size zero, hormonally depleted girlboy. The objective conclusion of most health surveys is that plump women enjoy better health and live longer than the starvelings. They get less heart disease and are less likely to suffer from early menopause or osteoporosis. There is a misconception about heart disease in men, too. Obese men statistically are at higher risk than thin ones (though the risk factor might not be the weight itself but rather some associated morbid condition such as diabetes or hypertension). The mistake is to conclude from this that there is some kind of sliding scale on which thinner always means better. There isn't. Imagine, for example, the typical Finn – spare, angular and bony, a thin man from a sparse landscape. Now compare him with the typical Italian – well-filled, smoothly contoured, an altogether plumper type from an altogether plumper landscape. The stereotypes are not wrong – Italians on average *are* fatter than Finns – but it's the Finns who are more likely to die from bad hearts. It has also been recorded that fat men survive heart attacks better than thin ones – perhaps because their hearts have to work harder and, like any other muscle, are strengthened by exercise.

Health statistics are a quagmire in which the pathways of reason are notoriously hard to follow. Sirens of false logic sing in your ear, making you see causes where there are only associations. Clean-shaven men die younger than bearded ones? Then there must be some prophylactic value in facial hair! Many statistical associations are exactly like this (invented) example – not straightforward indicators of cause and effect, but useful evidence of a socio-economic peculiarity in bearded men's lives that makes them different from the pink-chins. Perhaps they smoke less, or take more exercise. Fat and thin are socio-economic indicators too, and just as likely to muddy the waters. Beyond the boundaries of clinical obesity there is no Orwellian mantra of Size 10 good, Size 16 bad. The one bit of solid ground is that plumpness is not just good for snails and prunes. It's good for people, too.

The advertising standards regulators for printed and broadcast media in the UK do not allow manufacturers to make unsustainable health claims. The media themselves can do this as much as they like (health and beauty editors by and large share their bathwater with the astrologers on the next page), but advertisers have a code to follow. Health claims must be backed by 'sound scientific evidence'. The result is that the benefits of weight loss are described in terms of dress size, not extra years of healthy life, and the market is driven by vanity. The health message to slimmers is hardly more audible than it is to gourmets. 'To look better' is the commonest reason women give for trying to lose weight. When *Slimming* magazine surveyed its readers, only 21 per cent said they were dieting 'for health'. Thus we may conclude that in some individuals the desire for a fashionable body shape exceeds the lust for ice cream.

We may conclude also that they give insufficient credit to their own metabolisms. Over the course of a year most of us will eat around a million calories, yet our weight fluctuates on average by less than 1 per cent. The 'internal communications system' I mentioned earlier would inspire awe if it were installed on a computer. Our personal motherboard is the hypothalamus, which continually receives and processes signals from the gut and other parts of the body. It registers whether the calories we consume are more or less than the number we use. If there is a surplus, the brain presses the metabolic accelerator to burn more of them off. If there is a deficit, it makes us feel hungry. It does this by prompting the gut and fat cells to produce hormones. For my awareness of these I have to thank the Medical Research Council, which sent me articles by Caroline Cross (published by the Wellcome Trust) and the world-leading obesity expert Professor Stephen Bloom, of Imperial College London (*Physiology News*). Both of these go deeper into detail than my non-scientific brain can follow, but Caroline Cross's summary is admirably concise: 'The gut and fat cells produce hormones such as ghrelin, which signals hunger, and leptin and peptide YY, which signals fullness. They travel via the blood to the hypothalamus, where they bind to receptors on neurons that transmit signals to other parts of the brain. And, via a complex series of feedback circuits, they influence feeding behaviour and energy expenditure.'

When energy levels fall, we are prompted to become active and wakeful so that we can hunt for food. This mechanism is then switched off when we are full (which, says Caroline Cross, 'may be why we feel sleepy after a meal'). The problem is that we have inherited an evolutionary mechanism that was of enormous value to us throughout most of our history – literally a life-saver when food was scarce, but much less efficacious in the age of surplus. Because the consequences of starvation are worse than the consequences of overfeeding, the mechanisms that control weight loss are more powerful than the ones that inhibit gain. So if 'greed' is defined as eating as much as we can, it also must be defined as obedience to nature. This genetic legacy, says Professor Bloom, 'makes us voracious overeaters', with the result that, worldwide every month, more than 150,000 people die prematurely from obesity. All of them suffered, and all now lie dead, because they ate too much.

In August 2007 the chairman of the British Medical Association, Dr Hamish Meldrum, earned a glutton's helping of column inches by declaring that fat people were 'greedy'. This provoked a number of different responses – disapproval from people who thought a doctors' leader should show more sensitivity; hero-worship from right-wing commentators who applauded his bang-to-rights honesty in giving it to the fatties straight. One columnist rose to the fly with a story about an obese woman – 'fat trout', in his words – who had got herself trapped in a deckchair. Another, whose multiple chins raise questions of their own, declared it to be 'an obvious truth of our existence' that fat people 'are usually greedy'. Under the heading 'Pork pies and fat lies', the *Sunday Telegraph*'s leader writer administered a snappy rebuke to Dr David Haslam, clinical director of the National Obesity Forum, who had observed to Meldrum that 'there is a lot of genetic predisposition to obesity'. 'No doubt there is,' said the writer. 'We all know thin people who wolf down huge meals and fat people who only eat salads. We don't, however, know very many. Isn't a predisposition turned into a certainty the more frequently one grabs for the cake tin? . . . It is a harsh but observable truth that for every fat person who eats like a sparrow, there are many more who guzzle like gannets.' This was accompanied by a footnote: 'Terry Wogan is on holiday.'

It is a harsh but observable truth that for every fat person who eats like a sparrow there is a weekend columnist who knows what he is talking about. The genetic predisposition to obesity and the tendency to 'guzzle like gannets' are not different perceptions in opposition to each other: they are one and the same. The predisposition derives from the very failure of the body's internal communications system to deliver the message: 'You are full. Stop eating.' Hope for the obese lies not in the truisms of glad-to-be-glib leader writers and the pull-yourself-together school of pre-war family doctoring, but rather in the capacity of medical science to find drugs that will mimic the hormones that suppress appetite and block faulty hunger signals from the brain. These have been promised for some time, and newspapers have had plenty of 'breakthroughs' to report. There have been some false dawns (injecting leptin, for example, did not have the desired effect), but there are enough slimmed-down laboratory rats to justify the hope that it won't be long. Professor Bloom himself is working to synthesize a hormone called pancreatic polypeptide which is released naturally after meals. Others are looking at the hunger hormone ghrelin. Another kite being flown at great height is the theory of 'nutrigenics', which holds out the hope that personal diets can be tailored to individual genomes, thus reducing (or even eliminating) the risk of all diet-related diseases and not just obesity. It is a race that drug companies will be hungry to win. The prize will be to do for the dinner table what Viagra has done for the bedroom – to release people from fear and guilt to enjoy one of the most fundamental pleasures of life on earth. I am not much given to biblical quotation, but can find no quarrel with Ecclesiastes 8:15: 'A man hath no better thing under the sun, than to eat, and to drink, and to be merry.'

Exploring this philosophy with my family over the last week I have enjoyed barbecued spare ribs, lemon chicken, slow-roast shoulder of lamb, boiled lobster, cheese soufflé, grilled sea bream, prawn curry, home-made bread and muesli, cheeses from four countries, plus many more salads, vegetables and fruit than I can remember, wines from three continents and locally brewed beer. Oh, and a pork pie.

It sounds like gluttony, and in comparison with the life of a Buddhist it probably is. I can't argue that I needed every calorie, or that my food choices and portion sizes were determined by anything more exalted than my appetite. I simply ate what I fancied – call it greed if you like. With one exception the food was fresh and good. Most of it was produced within a few miles of my home; and, though I didn't give much thought to it at the time, I find in retrospect that it closely fits the model of healthy eating – foods from all five groups taken in proportion – that nutritionists extol. I have unshakeable faith in nature's ability to create and sustain equilibrium, and faith in my own body as a natural organism with its own systems of checks and balances. I interfere with it as sparingly as I can. Greed is part of my make-up; but evolution and parental example have also given me a portion of common sense (not to mention pancreatic polypeptide, leptin, gherin and the rest of nature's diet police).

Which brings me to my lapse of judgement – the pork pie. Having grown up in a family whose local butcher baked his own, I have always loved the things. Good, peppery shoulder meat with a thick rim of jelly and crisp hot-water crust, eaten with pickled shallots and fresh white bread and butter. It beats all the gussied-up combinations of poultry and game, and the over-smooth 'rare breeds' goo in shiny pastry that delis seem to think are improvements. One of the principal excitements of financial independence in my youth was that I could have a pork pie whenever I fancied one. But that was then. 'Pork' and 'pie' were simple words with simple meanings that no one needed a Trade Descriptions Act or any other law to define. It was honesty on a plate.

Things are different now. Greed – the real, eyeballs-out, grasping McCoy – has slunk into the mixing bowl and done its dirty worst. You could choose any part of the industrial food trade and see the same – technological genius employed not to improve the quality of what we eat but rather to degrade it. Ever-poorer ingredients are chemically stabilized, artificially coloured and 'flavour-enhanced' to line stomachs with homogenized garbage and manufacturers' pockets with silver. I've picked on 'meat' because of the awful pie I was fool enough to buy; and because in no other food group does the gulf between 'natural' and 'manufactured' yawn so widely. Nothing else, quite, fills me with such disgust. This is the kind of filth that gives greed a bad name.

Buyers of cheap processed meats are possibly not the most discriminating of consumers, but most will have twigged that the 'meat' in their dinners, laid out in its raw state, would not look especially appetizing. In fact it would test the appetite of a hyena. To keep their products on the shelves, UK manufacturers have to satisfy a European definition of 'meat' introduced in 2003, which – no surprise – differs in several respects from anything your granny might have recognized at the butcher's. This has been tightened up somewhat (it now excludes, for example, brains, feet, intestines, lungs, oesophagus, rectum, spinal cord, spleen, stomach, testicles and udder), but there's still plenty of slithery stuff going on, and half the 'meat' could be fat, rind and gristle. Remember mechanically recovered meat? The official definition of MRM, quoted after the UK's devastating BSE outbreak in the mid-1980s, was unflinching: 'residual material, off bones, obtained by machines operating on . . . pressure principles in such manner that the cellular structure of the material is broken down sufficiently for it to flow as puree from the bone'. As far as the law went, it was perfectly OK for these intimate scrapings, with their cellular structure broken down into gloop, to be described on packaging as 'meat'. It was this very stuff, gleaned from places other recipes could not reach, that built the bridge between BSE and Creutzfeldt-Jakob disease. What has altered as a result? Nothing that would be noticed by any shopper not armed with a legal glossary of terms. Manufacturers now are not allowed to describe this slurry as 'meat'. It will appear on the labelling as, for example, 'recovered pork'. In practice it makes little difference. Butchers' leavings continue to be scraped up, homogenized and stuffed into pastry, and the fat barons go on piling up their fortunes.

The law's view of 'meat' has an unfortunate echo of Marie Antoinette – *Let them eat cack*. Legislators have crawled through the carcasses of every species we might eat, and ruled on every blob and nodule. There has been some fine-tuning. In the old Meat Products and Spreadable Fish Products Regulations, meat was defined as 'flesh including fat and skin, rind, gristle and sinew in amounts naturally associated with the flesh used'. The new European definition refined this to 'skeletal muscle with naturally included or adherent fat and connective tissue', which sounds marginally less off-putting but means pretty much the same.

The exact quantities of fat and connective tissue – that's skin and rind, ligaments, tendons and cartilage (aka gristle) – vary from species to species. If you've studied anatomy you might not be surprised by how big the amounts 'naturally included or adherent' actually are. If you are an ordinary shopper who visualizes 'meat' as rose-coloured lean, then you might not have understood how the 'Quantitative Ingredient Declaration' (QUID) on a meat product translates into standard English.

Pig-parts, for example, can contain 30 per cent fat and 25 per cent connective tissue and still pass as 'pork'. Birds and rabbits are allowed 15 per cent and 10 per cent respectively. Beef, lamb and 'mixed meats' get away with 25 per cent of each. But this doesn't mean that extra fat and spare parts are barred from your burger, pie or sausage. Makers are free to add more, but the excess must be listed separately and cannot count as meat. No QUID is needed, so you won't know how much.

The term 'naturally included or adherent' is another master-piece of legal double-speak. What's implied is that meat comes to the kitchen whole and is cooked with the fat and other tissues 'naturally' attached to it. But it means nothing of the sort. In practice, all this stuff – back fat, chicken skin and pork rind, for example – is stripped from 'primal joints' as waste, then brought to the mixing bowl separately. The only nod towards 'natural adherence' is the stipulation that all the flesh, fat and sweepings stirred into any named 'meat' must be from the same species.

Even so, you might suppose that all these bits and pieces would be recombined in more or less the same proportion in which they occur naturally on a carcass. Wrong again. Lean pork with a small amount of visible fat – the kind you buy from a butcher – contains 13.8 per cent fat and 7.8 per cent connective tissue. The regulations allow 30 per cent and 25 per cent respectively. Even untrimmed pork belly with the rind left on is only 23.8 per cent fat. Stewing beef may be as little as 6.2 per cent fat (against 25 per cent in the regulations), and skinless chicken breast just 2.1 per cent (15 per cent allowed). Even with the skin left on, chicken breast registers only 6.7 per cent, and the very fattest chicken joint – skin-on thigh, at 12.9 per cent – is still leaner than the chicken 'meat' in manufactured products, which is likely to be plumped up with a concoction called 'mixed chicken meat with skin' (23 per cent fat).

Bizarrely, internal organs and other spare parts – heart, tongue, liver, kidney and most head meat – don't count as 'meat' at all;

nor may they be labelled generically as 'offal'. They must be listed separately by name, but do not need a QUID so you'll have very little idea of what you're getting. Almost every useful fact has a place to hide. Uncooked meat products may not include any of the nasties – brains, lungs, rectum, spinal cord and the rest – for which we may be thankful. But this begs the question of *cooked* meats, to which no such restrictions apply. Post BSE, bovine brains and spinal cord are still banned – otherwise the pig-squeak principle pretty much holds good, and the best you can say is that you're helping to reduce waste. Neither do the limits on fat and connective tissue apply to meat described as 'cooked' (fried chicken, roast pork, etc.). The QUID will simply declare the weight of cooked meat in the recipe, so you'll have to guess its provenance.

The one concession to healthy eating is another by-product of the manufacturers' greed, seasoned with unintended irony and wholly accidental. The Meat Product Regulations allow them to include so little 'meat' in their formulae that you don't actually have to eat very much of it. To pass muster, an ordinary burger need contain no more than 62 per cent 'beef', and an economy one 47 per cent. Meat pies and puddings pass at 12.5 per cent 'meat' (or 10 per cent if the pie is small), which is more than double the minimum (just 6 per cent) for pasties and sausage rolls.

I didn't read the label on the pork pie. Whatever it said was a lie. This was 'pork' only in the sense that MDF is a tree, a 'pie' only insofar as it was wrapped in some flour-based material with a lid, 'edible' only in the purely literal sense that it might be chewed and swallowed. Obedient to the natural reflexes of my eyes, nose and gut, I put it in the black wheelie-bin with all the other non-recyclables. Greed might be the life force of the species, but – I am glad to affirm – it has its limits.

3

Your Place or Mine?

In one of his last television appearances, Sir John Betjeman was asked whether there was anything in life that he looked back upon and regretted. Rug-wrapped in a wheelchair, the frail-looking laureate didn't hesitate: 'I haven't had enough sex.' Probably no one has. The much-quoted 'statistic' that men think about sex once every seven seconds is a myth to set beside the aphrodisiac power of onions. It is the only example I can remember of someone actually managing to *exaggerate* the influence of sex, or man's appetite for it. How much is enough? Most men are dead before they know the answer.

Google fits none of the criteria necessary in a statistically valid opinion poll, but I am daring to assume that the number of hits is a reasonably reliable if rough-and-ready barometer of taste. Once you have adjusted to the sheer scale of the internet, where numbers seem to have been imported from astrophysics rather than the mundane arithmetic of daily life, it's no surprise to find that 'porn' returns 113m results, or that unadorned 'sex' outstrips it at 461m. Search engines are more discriminating than they used to be. You have actively to search for porn sites now – it's rare to hit them by accident. In the beginning, even to type 'Essex' was to be sent a catalogue of speciality sites in California, most of which believed 'slut' to be the most irresistible come-on since the sirens sang to Odysseus. There is nothing especially remarkable about this, or in the worldwide sleaze bazaar that now crawls across the net. The medium may be novel, but not the message. The sex trade is as old as biology, and it will be the last to go out of business.

Pornography and prostitution may be the most blatant ways in which greed is fanned by sex, but they are not the most important or interesting. Let us try another Google search: 'love'. Would it beat sex's 461m (or even pair-bonding's surprising 1.9m)? Yes it would. By a street.

Eight hundred and ninety million.

Which is an awful lot of interest in something so difficult to define. 'Whatever that means' was Prince Charles's notorious and perhaps prescient caveat when asked to confirm his 'love' for Lady Diana Spencer. Whatever it *does* mean, this adjustable, often combustible mix of passion and *tendresse* is the basic propellant of human life. We cleave to it like plants to sunlight. For love, or the promise of it, we surrender our freedom as individuals (and become 'love-rats' if we transgress). The great civilizers – literature, drama, art, music – are not so much soaked in it as mined from the same lode. What are comedy and tragedy if not the Janus faces of love? Every societal structure described by anthropologists, from the most primitive mud-hutted hamlet to the most sophisticated sky-scrapered capital, rests on enduring 'love'. You could call it biology; you could call it the temptation of the devil; you could call it god's gift to man. Sex is not just the bait on procreation's hook; it's the closest any rationalist will get to an idea of god, a force that not only engenders life but determines the way we live it. Its fingers are everywhere and in everything – in bathroom cabinets, wardrobes, garages, bank accounts and football scores. It's what we mostly have in mind when we talk about 'morality', and it obsesses churchmen as much as it does pornographers, film directors and stand-ups. It drives us to extravagance and to inhibition; to heroism and to treachery; and to greed not just for more orgasms but for everything that marks out alpha from beta and beta from gamma. It's why size matters.

As it happens, one of the ways men differ most strikingly from apes is in the size of their penis, which by comparison is huge. Due to our upright stance and unique frontal mating position it is also much more prominent and ready for use. Desmond Morris argues that it was modesty, not cold, that first obliged people to cover themselves. Without a fig leaf, any face-to-face encounter between the sexes would bring their mating gear rather too provocatively into alignment – a distraction, or threat, unknown to other species which, by moving on all fours, keep their private parts private, and in which receptive females are required to offer their bottoms. Even today, where primitive peoples survive without a wardrobe, the bare essential is usually a loincloth (though there are some spectacular exceptions in which the penis becomes an *objet d'art*).

But modesty doesn't have things all its own way. By adjustment of hem and neckline, the tightness or gauziness of cloth, women in western societies expertly use clothing to emphasize what lies beneath (hence the 'asking for it' defence in rape trials). For young people overdosing on hormones, every meeting is charged with the possibility of sex. Apes probably feel something similar but, compared with humans, their sexual acts are perfunctory (just a few seconds, usually), are not preceded by anything remotely like courtship, afford no obvious pleasure to the female and do not lead to a lifelong pair-bond. Female apes are also more sparing with their favours, being receptive only while they are ovulating – ie for about a week a month. Sex for them seems to be what elders of the sterner churches would like it to be for humankind – a biological chore focused on procreation. I am reminded of the rhyme, written anonymously in the 1880s, about two famous school principals and paragons of probity, Miss Dorothea Beale of Cheltenham Ladies' College and Miss Frances Mary Buss of North London Collegiate:

> Miss Buss and Miss Beale
> Cupid's darts do not feel.
> How different from us
> Are Miss Beale and Miss Buss.

Well indeed. Moralistic spinsters, ministers and imams can preach what they like – hormones have no ears. The fact is that human females are immensely sexier than their hairy relatives in the trees. Most of their sexual activity is outside the short period of ovulation and therefore has no procreative purpose. In ruing his failure to take advantage of it, John Betjeman was an entirely typical British pensioner. In 2006, 1,500 of them were polled for the television company UKTV Gold and asked what in their lives they would change if they could have their time again. Twelve per cent said they would give more time to study, 16 per cent would start their own businesses, 21 per cent marry a different spouse, 40 per cent put more into savings and 57 per cent see more of the world. There was chagrin, too, about not changing their jobs more often, and not standing up to the boss. But in the league table of regret, one failing stood out way above the rest. Seventy per cent of grandmas and granddads, granted a rerun, would have more sex. Not more children or grandchildren. Just more sex.

So there is a conundrum. On the one hand we are fired with barely controlled randiness, a species that invented the zip because it was too impatient to fiddle with buttons. On the other, we want long and happy marriages to faithful partners who forgive our smelly feet. We promise fidelity but practise deceit. How can these two seemingly irreconcilable urges be felt not just in the same species but in the same person? Sexual statistics are about as reliable as paper condoms. But never mind. Even if you can't believe the figures, they reveal habits that are at least consistent with what we suspect about our friends and neighbours (one of which, perfectly mirrored in the 'sexologists' themselves, is prurience). Desmond Morris in 1967 reported with absolute confidence, possibly relying on Kinsey, that 50 per cent of women and 84 per cent of men will have had sex before marriage, and that 26 per cent and 50 per cent respectively will have committed adultery before their fortieth birthdays. A survey in 2004 by the UK marriage guidance charity Relate cut this to 24 per cent and 32 per cent respectively, which suggests either a remarkable improvement in the quality of marriage or an enduring tendency for survey respondents to bend the truth. At the same time, a survey of married women in America claimed an extramarital strike rate of 60 per cent, which suggests . . . well, who cares what it suggests? It's enough to know that an awful lot of people claim to be sexually multi-tasking which, though it may not be an accurate record of fulfilment, certainly indicates a salty swell of desire. Or, to put it another way, *greed*. Greed, that is, for more orgasms, more partners, more admiration, more cigarettes in bed than anything remotely necessary to ensure the survival of the species. And along with it goes greed for all the other things – wealth, power, beauty, achievement – that make sexual conquest more likely. Successful men have always adorned themselves with young and beautiful women (the only thing new about 'trophy wives' is the phrase itself). Beautiful women have always equipped themselves with successful men.

It's a status thing, and – so the theory goes – it can be traced back to the caves of prehistory. Sexual decorum in the earliest hominids may have been no more refined than their table manners. The cartoon cliché, of club-wielding caveman hauling his favourite by the hair, might be on the crude side, but it's hard to imagine much in the way of etiquette or candle-lit horsemeat suppers. Living on the hoof, you ate where you could and fornicated likewise. All this would have changed as people began to gather in settled communities. Communities need rules, and they need trust between neighbours, otherwise they don't stay settled for long. Just as the dominant males and their intimates would have enjoyed the choicest cuts of meat, so they would have taken the pick of the females. And they would have wanted to keep them. Women, too, would have sought reliable partners to ensure successful child-rearing, and breeding success would have handed the evolutionary advantage to those of monogamous habit. Without divorce courts, marriage guidance counsellors or agony aunts, rough-hewn men and women would have mounted a rough-hewn defence of their relationships. The alternative would have been sexual anarchy and violent chaos in which civilization would have been impossible. In these circumstances, not coveting your neighbour's wife is not morality: it's politics.

There is another theory, too, which has nothing to do with the virility of cavemen but – alas for machismo – everything to do with little boys and their mothers. *Homo sapiens* takes much longer to nurture its young than other species do. The entire lifespans of most mammals are shorter than the mother-dependent childhoods of humans, who hang on virtually into adulthood before they let go of the dug. The result is a far deeper bond between parents and children than any ape would enjoy, and a much larger void to be filled when separation finally occurs. Into this void steps the young adult's wife or husband. I don't know about this (I mean I really don't know; not that I reject the idea), but it fits very neatly with the almost mystical value attached to marriage by world religions, and the universal veneration of mothers. The mother-worship and sexual repression of the Catholic Church are as mysterious to non-believers as the transubstantiation of the host, but in this context perhaps they are not wholly incomprehensible.

One of the most striking characteristics of early humans, graphically illustrated by reconstructions of their skulls, is that by modern standards they were far from lovely. Anyone born that ugly now might find employment in a rugby scrum but couldn't expect much in the way of pillow talk. And yet in their own epoch they would have had their own standards of beauty, and would have been as susceptible to eye-appeal as any man or woman since. This is the basis of what Darwin called 'sexual selection'. There are two elements – contests between males for ownership of females (plumage displays, stag-fights and powerful cars are all examples of masculine competition for mates); and the preference of each sex for particular characteristics in the other (bright colours, big beak, fat wallet). Though standards may slip as the pubs close, we do not choose our sexual partners, and certainly not our lifetime pair-bonds, at random. Looks may be superficial, but they are profoundly important. We are attracted or repelled by them, and discriminate as far as our own attractiveness allows us to – ie we take the best we can get. 'Sexual selection' therefore means that the prettier you are, the better your chance of becoming someone's ancestor. This is why, over the millennia, we have evolved from obvious cousins of the chimpanzee to the sculpted beauties we confront in the mirror today. It is our genes speaking in sign language. Looks and physique are valuable clues to the health and strength of potential breeding partners, and the modern coining of 'fit' to mean sexually attractive could hardly be more apt. Logically this seems to dispose of another popular theory – that we prefer partners who resemble our mothers or fathers. If that were the case we'd still have ridged brows and tiny penises, and the biggest turn-ons would be bonecrusher teeth and coconut body hair.

Psychologists also tell us that marriage partners tend to be of equivalent physical attractiveness. This seems reasonable enough. You would expect the most desirable men to get the most desirable women, and on down the scale until you reach the two ugliest people on the planet (who, being excused temptation, will enjoy the perfect marriage). One quasi-academic website even claims you can identify partners within a large mixed group by appearances alone. I tried and couldn't, but still believe the principle holds good. It is important to remember that this is a tendency and not a rule. For women in particular, the issue is more complicated. Anyone who opens a newspaper will know that rich, short, frog-faced men can jump the queue for big-breasted sexpots as easily as they can for a Mercedes. Again, though they might not have given it too much thought, the sexpots' frog-tolerance has a basis in genetics. Over the millennia, women have developed an instinct for men who can best provide for them and their children. 'Fitness' is one clue to this, but 'success', signalled most obviously by wealth, is a more than adequate substitute. This also explains why women tend to favour men slightly older than themselves (on average by three and a half years), and why the language offers no female equivalent of 'sugardaddy'. A survey of students in the United States revealed that, *as a minimum*, women wanted their marriage partners to be in the 70th percentile – ie the top 30 per cent – of salary earners. Men on the other hand would happily accept wives in the top 60 per cent only. This is precisely analogous to the values of the Stone Age – males measured by their ability to provide food and shelter, females by their ability to arouse desire.

But this, too, is a sign of evolution. In a beautiful woman the selfish gene travels by Rolls-Royce. Even if men don't understand how it works, they will always appreciate a well-designed machine. This may explain their preference for the classic hour-glass figure, and their weakness for the Monroe wiggle that goes with it. Someone apparently has proved that men's favourite waist-to-hip ratio in women is 0.7 (the average for glamour models and beauty queens). Possession of such a waist is evidence of youth and baby-making potential; lack of one suggests mid-life weight gain and declining fertility. There is evidence, too, that the distribution of body fat in this 'ideal' body form means lower risk of heart disease, stroke, diabetes and other illnesses that might curtail a woman's efficiency or longevity. There's lots of other stuff about pheromones (T-shirt-sniffing is a popular experimental procedure) and the precise geometry of facial features (symmetrical, but not precisely so) that make people attractive.

All this is interesting, but it serves only to confirm what we have known since puberty. We are genetically programmed to want sex, as much of it as we can get, with the most desirable partners we can find. When we are young, life has no higher purpose.

It is easy to see how this stimulates greed, but greed is not a sin in a vacuum. At its extreme it encourages crime, deceit, violence and duplicity – all the ancient ills that newspapers and politicians in opposition ascribe to 'modern society'. It provides also a springboard for its close relative and fellow deadly sin, jealousy. Few emotions are stronger, or more inclined towards violence, than the sexual jealousy of a cheated husband or wife. Murder in such circumstances is assigned a special category – 'crime of passion' – and (especially when the accused is a woman) courts tend to be lenient. 'There but for the grace of god,' judges might think, and they could be right. Jealousy is a tool of evolution, made expedient by its very nastiness. 'People who failed to prevent infidelity in a mate had less reproductive success,' explains David M. Buss, professor of psychology at the University of Texas, in *The Evolution of Desire*. A man whose partner strayed might waste his energy in nurturing children not his own, and thus perpetuate another man's genes. An abandoned woman risked losing support for herself and her family. Jealousy ensured mutual vigilance, hostility to trespassers and the threat of mortifying rage if the sanctity of the marital cave were breached. Liberalized attitudes, contraception and the commodification of sex have done nothing to alter this. If anything, wider opportunity brings keener suspicion and fiercer competition. Jealousy is aroused not just by frontal assaults on a partner's chastity. It pours fire on anything that could make a rival – *any* rival, real or imagined – seem more desirable. It is striking how often political, religious or educational dogma runs counter to natural instincts (especially when the instinct is sexual). Competition is anathema to politically correct egalitarians who would prefer the human psyche to exclude every sort of impulse that causes winners to win and losers to lose. This bland utopia will remain a dream until the last testicle has disappeared from the planet. Sexual beings are competitive beings. Species throughout nature, from insects upwards, will always strive to be biggest, brightest or best equipped, and each modicum of breeding advantage gives evolution a nudge. Having bigger brains, we humans are uniquely able to override our instincts and practise self-restraint. But what we more commonly practise, and use our brains for, is self-aggrandisement. There is no 'enough'. Even the wealthiest men need to be wealthier still, and will fight for their next billion, or their next yacht, as if it were the last crust in a famine. What distinguishes us from stickleback, stag or bower bird is just a matter of style and sophistication. Small nest good, big nest better. My other car is a Porsche. Your place or mine?

Quite recently I went to see an arthouse movie in a small private theatre in a remote Norfolk village and had to defend my trousers. They were old, well worn and comfortable, just as trousers should be, with exactly the right number of mud-flecks consistent with a rugged outdoor lifestyle. They were also a very pretty shade of pink. Arthouse movie-goers by and large are fear-less cruisers of the spectrum, but on this occasion they included a young military type in lovat V-neck and brown corduroys. 'Glad to see you're in touch with your feminine side,' he said.

I recalled a remark of Kenneth Tynan's – that the mark of a man secure in his sexuality was to share his wife's perfume. I'm not sure I'd go that far, but pink trousers? What's the problem? My wife wears a lot of blue, and nobody thinks she's butch. Why should pinkness be so irreversibly feminine? In my early days in journalism, toiling in the macho sweatshop of a provincial news-room, I was struck by the lip-curling contempt of the older, school-of-hard-knocks reporters for young, university-educated types who were interested in 'style', used adjectives and wore deodorant. Young women they could forgive. But blokes!

'Pink-shirts', they called them, and 'nuff said. True, this was in the 1960s when it was crime enough just to be young. Homosexuality had not long been legalized and any sign of sensitivity, 'artiness' or even a liking for suede shoes would mark a man down as 'queer'. For all kinds of reasons – the obsession with fashion, the blurring of 'high' and 'low' culture, the new journalism that the pink-shirts introduced, the prosperity that made all this possible and laid such emphasis on individuality – things are very different now. Give or take the odd dung-hued military throw-back and the enduring greyness of office dress-codes, most people read nothing more into the colour of a chap's shirt or trousers than good or bad taste. Nevertheless, for all that we have trespassed on the feminine precinct, pink is ours by adoption only. We have borrowed it, but this has not made it any less the preserve of women.

A rational explanation for this seemingly irrational phenomenon was proposed (I suspect not for the first time) in the summer of 2007, when neuroscientists at the University of Newcastle tracked its evolution. They were not surprised to find 'gender differences' in masculine and feminine colour choices, but they *were* surprised at the 'robustness' and consistency of them. The university's professor of visual neuroscience, Anya Hurlbert, saw the explanation not in the colour-coded nurseries of modern family homes but in the hunter-gathering of our earliest ancestors. The results, she said, 'appear to give biological and not simply cultural substance to the old saying: pink for a girl and blue for a boy'. Boiled down to its fundamentals, the theory is that women in prehistory were the principal gatherers of fruit and would have been sensitized to the colours of ripeness – ie deepening shades of pink. Men on the other hand would have looked for good hunting weather and sources of water – hence their liking for blue.

Squawks of derision followed. 'Load of tosh . . . mumbo-jumbo pseudo science . . . quackery . . . absolute insanity . . . a very sad day for science,' said visitors to the *Daily Mail* blog. One knows from experience that newspaper blogs and mailbags are not happy hunting grounds for admirers of rational thought, and that letters to the editor are the favourite literary form of the marginally insane. Nevertheless, in this case one does have a certain sympathy with their inchoate splutterings. 'This just demonstrates,' said one of the more thoughtful, 'that these people have been influenced by gender stereotypes as they were growing up. I am sure if all boys' toys were pink and girls were given train sets and Meccano, the stereotypes and "natural preferences" for blue or pink would be completely reversed. It's all to do with cultural expectations, not biology.'

This is a fair point, but one wonders how the writer justifies his certainty. And it begs the question: where did the 'cultural expectations' themselves come from? What made parents across the world (it's the same, for example, in China) choose blue and pink in the first place? Did some ancient tastemaker make an arbitrary choice that the rest of us simply followed and made traditional? Could it as easily have been yellow and green? No: the neuroscientists may not have hit the nail on the head, but surely they have struck it a glancing blow. A habit so deeply ingrained must have followed some kind of evolutionary pathway and cannot be explained by chance alone.

But so what? Why does it matter? Because, for whatever reason (and here we surely must all agree), feminine and masculine tastes are different; and any man who wants to attract and keep a mate will do well not to forget it. He needs to think pink – ie be fully cognizant of her desires and ready to line the nest accordingly. This is one of the most powerful engines of the retail economy. No one becomes poor by overestimating man's desire to please woman – that is the basic premiss from which the advertising industry derives its motivation. From the scanty-pants models straddling 1000cc superbikes in motorcycle magazines to the cosy ads for pensioners' holidays and 'equity release' in the weekend supplements, there is always a satisfied woman in the frame. Sex sells dog food as well as knickers. We may not approve of ourselves. We may construct feminist, socialist or anti-consumerist ideologies, but the animal within us will not lie down.

For a man, nothing is more uplifting than the company of a beautiful, intelligent woman. Let me speak personally. The woman in my life makes a better, more confident man of me than I could be without her. I am proud of her, and want her approval above all else. After six million years of evolution, I feel and behave exactly as the textbooks say I should. Ridiculously in our ultra-safe lives, I will sit or walk on her right, leaving my sword-arm free to protect her. In the street I place myself between her and the traffic. I hold doors open. I bring her cups of tea, carry the bags and attend to masculine tasks such as emptying the dustbins and calling the plumber.

Her own behaviour is not dissimilar. Though she is a strong-willed, successful professional woman who loathes stereotyping, she still performs most of the household tasks conventionally thought of as 'feminine' (childcare in the past; laundry and list-making now), monitors my alcohol intake and makes sure I don't forget my medicine. Every so often she will drag me into a clothes shop and smarten me up. Just as frequently I will take her into a dress shop and commit unpremeditated acts of ostentatious generosity which she neither needs nor asks for, but to which I feel myself driven. Even though I know she could manage very well without me (far better than I could without her), I still need to feel indispensable, or at the very least *useful*. I take my turn at the stove and the sink, help with the shopping and come over all alpha-male when it comes to roasting and carving my trophies from the butcher's shop.

So far as I can tell, our friends all work in much the same way. The men regard themselves as liberals; the women as liberated. Even so, not everyone will like the sound of this. What I have been describing is 'marriage' (or lifelong pair-bonding) and 'the family' – two institutions upon which feminists have been training their fire for more than forty years. Some of them simply want a better deal for women. Others want to smash capitalism, of which the 'patriarchal' family is the base unit (wives are the workers, husbands the capitalists), and to replace it with a kind of anarchism – either promiscuous or sexless, depending on taste. Blinded by 'testosterone poisoning', men are violent and possessive predators binding women in servitude. Women trapped in marriage are slaves, prostitutes or 'sexual spittoons', and all husband-killers are entitled to plead justification on grounds of 'battery'. In her book *Sexual Correctness: the Gender-Feminist Attack on Women*, the Canadian feminist Wendy McElroy quotes (but does not applaud) an outfit called the Women's International Terrorist Conspiracy from Hell (WITCH), which she says 'disrupted a 1969 fashion show for brides by chanting to the tune of the Wedding March: "Here come the slaves/Off to their graves"'. She recalls also Jill Johnston's *Lesbian Nation* (1973), which denounced heterosexual women as traitors. Marxist feminists, proclaiming that 'the personal is political', argue that families, like hospitals, prisons, salt mines and the army, should be under state control. If you need a marriage guidance counsellor, look no further than Engels.

Couples living in mutually supportive, chore-sharing harmony are no answer to this. They are exceptions that cannot disprove the rule. If I understand McElroy correctly, she rejects the man-hating, anti-evolutionary extremism of the 'gender feminists', and sees marriage as a three-way contract between man, woman and the state. It is the state, not the couple at the altar, that gives the transaction legal definition, and the state that decides under what circumstances it may be terminated. Given its controlling interest, she says, 'the State must bear a great deal of the blame for the current evils of marriage'.

Individualist feminists agree that a revolution is necessary . . . but one that gives power to individuals and not to institutions, like the

State. Women need liberation, not State control. In essence, marriage must be taken out of the political realm and fully back into the private one. The new slogan of feminism should be 'the personal is personal'. In marriage, as in all other peaceful pursuits of life, let individuals choose.

It's hard to disagree with this, though if marriage for women really is 'an involuntary state' in which the wife/chattel is disempowered by the physical and economic strength of her husband, I don't see how it makes life any easier. Of course men are possessive, and of course that is a restraint upon the sexual and economic freedoms of their wives. But you could transpose the sexes in that sentence without diluting its truth. For reasons I have already explained, I believe possessiveness and jealousy are evolved behaviours that contribute to the success of the species. Couples who defend their relationships have a better chance of successfully rearing their young than those who don't. Like its cousins selfishness and greed, possessiveness has an ugly ring to it. Like them too, it has its uses.

Through all the dogma and the dialectic, one fluffy little comfort-word has fallen from the lexicon. The Prince of Wales may have had trouble with it, and we may bestow it glibly upon anything from a sexual partner to a biscuit, but it is indispensable, cherishable and necessary. Possessiveness with a soppy look on its face. *Love*. Eight hundred and ninety million Google hits, against feminism's 19.7m. But what *is* this uniquely indefinable quality? Whence does it come? What is its substance? Why do art, literature and music hang so much weight upon it?

Evolutionary psychologists convincingly explain the urge to find a long-term mate, but the specifics of individual choice – why we choose one partner over another – remain harder to crystallize. Physical attraction and lust are the driving forces over the first few days and nights, but after that we're pretty much kissing the wind. There are myriad reasons why intimate acquaintance will either cement a relationship or blow it apart. Making an effort clearly helps. David M. Buss in *The Evolution of Desire* ably demonstrates the genius of scientists for re-codifying the obvious. His 'mate-keeping studies' showed the importance of 'fulfilling the initial mating desires of the partner'. For men this means dispensing honeyed words and kindnesses, and providing 'economic and material resources'. For women it's love and kindness again, followed by 'enhancing appearance'. 'Women go out of their way to make themselves attractive to their partners, making up their faces to look nice, dressing to maintain a partner's interest, and acting sexy to distract a partner's attention from other women.'

None of this gets us very much closer to what we're looking for. All that, and more, we already knew. I love my wife and frequently tell her so, but I'm flummoxed when – ever the contro-versialist – she wants to know why. A recitation of qualities and characteristics is a list of ingredients without a recipe. There's more to it than that, something that goes far beyond David M. Buss's lipstick-and-frillies theory. The first ingredient is circum-stance. Measured across time and space, our meeting 25 years ago was a colossal improbability, a random chance event like two flecks of dust colliding in a cosmic wind. Without all the millions of random chance events that preceded and created it, and the millions of others that created those, we would never have found each other. And yet it feels like destiny, something ordained: I can-not imagine myself as a viable entity without her. Like twins we finish each other's sentences, and many of 'my' thoughts begin inside her head. Love surely is a process, not a condition and still less an event – a gradual fusion of minds, a slow growing of inter-dependence, understanding and trust that turns strangeness into symbiosis. Love by this reckoning is our own creation, magical but not supernatural, a payout on investment. It's in our nature to work for what nature makes us want.

Sometimes we succeed, sometimes we don't. I've experienced it both ways. But in every corner of every land, with or without the blessing of gods or governments, in war and in peace, in countries both developing and developed, boy-meets-girl is the story of life, and boy-keeps-girl the story of the economy. Men buy diamonds for their wives, laptops for their children and cars to carry them in. They will improve their homes; trade the cottage for a villa; the villa for a mansion. They will fly between continents in search of sun and snow. In every way, they – *we* – acquire, accumulate and consume so far in excess of 'need' that the word itself has fudged its meaning. Men will always want 'the best' for themselves, their partners and their children, and measure themselves – evaluate their very manliness – by the degree of their success. I keep writing 'men' because that is the word in the textbooks. But women, too, in a more emancipated world, are no longer just passive receivers of masculine bounty but pro-active seekers of their own wealth and fortune.

Bigger, faster, louder, rarer. Family values are not the values of Bible-quoting Victorian moralists: they are the values of the copy-writer. That does not mean they are new, or distorted or deranged. They may have been amplified by modern media, but it is the amplification of an echo that grew from the caves of antiquity. Your credit card or mine?

4

Handbags to Die For

A full-page advertisement that ran in UK newspapers through December 2006 showed a blonde woman on a white horse galloping towards a forest. The advertiser was Barclays Wealth, a division of the high-street bank. The text was printed in capitals:

IT'S BEING ABLE TO TELL THE WORLD TO GET LOST.
WEALTH. WHAT'S IT TO YOU?

Well, what *is* it to you? A reality? An aspiration? A crime? In a sub-Saharan African village, wealth is a pair of shoes. In a rich English one it's a tennis court. The odd thing about wealth is that everyone dreams of it or aspires to it, and yet hardly anyone admits to having it. This is not just avoidance of the tax man or fear of begging letters. It's a polychromatic cocktail of confused and conflicting emotions – a bit of false modesty ('but it's a very *small* chateau!'); a dash of envy ('the neighbour's chateau has got a moat'); and a top-dressing of guilt ('I know nurses and firemen can't afford houses at all'). It's instructive how often the word 'porn' is appended to displays of conspicuous consumption. For our titillation now we have food porn, fashion porn and travel porn, all aping the drooling, self-tantalizing lasciviousness of the original.

Wealth precisely replicates our muddle over sex – we cannot quite get our intellects in gear with our emotions. Mother Church once again has her garters in a knot. Saints are venerated for their rejection of earthly comforts. Congregations are instructed in the virtues of modesty, abstinence and charity: priests, cardinals and popes prostrate themselves before the ultimate image of self-denial. Yet they do so in jewelled temples that invite the second coming of Mammon. Opulence and piety kneel at the same altar. In Seville, for example, the altarpiece in the cathedral's High Chapel is a floor-to-ceiling cascade of gold. Even a waterfall this big would be a crowd-puller in the Lake District. The sculpted tomb of Christopher Columbus (if indeed it is him – there is a rival in the Dominican Republic) would befit a saint, and an account of the cathedral treasures is like a court inventory – tonnages of gold and silver, circumferences of pearl, roll calls of precious stones, monstrances, tabernacles, crowns . . . If greed is virtue, then here, surely, is the nearest we will ever get to heaven on earth.

Other denominations, other faiths, compete for gods' grace in a myriad ways involving everything from Semtex to hair shirts, and embracing every sort of practitioner from the mohaired con-men of American evangelical television to self-embalming Buddhists in Tibet. Avarice and its kin – gluttony, envy, lust – are deadly sins fatal to spiritual progress. And yet in return for prayer, or even for deathbed conversions, religion offers rewards so extravagant that they transcend the boundaries of time and space. Whatever is illuminated by *lux perpetua*, it is not self-denial. Whether in the here-and-now or in the hereafter, whether pursued through conspicuous consumption, good works or self-flagellation, and whether the longed-for reward is an off-screen blow job or 72 virgins in paradise, the enticement to virtue is personal gain. It was by holding out such promises, by the elevation of the venal to the vestal, that the Christian Church became the earliest exponent of globalism (a subject to which we shall return in Chapter 8). In the Parable of the Talents, it also provides a blueprint for sound financial investment – a fable which the UK's son-of-the-manse prime minister Gordon Brown identified as his father's favourite, and which lays down the moral foundation of his own messianic faith in economic growth.

The funniest political row of 2007 erupted during the election for Brown's deputy when two of the candidates, Harriet Harman and Hazel Blears, came out swinging their handbags. Harman – the eventual winner – kicked it off by regretting that Britain was a 'divided society' in which some women struggled for a mouthful of gruel while others could spend £10,000 on a handbag. To confirm her socialist credentials, she revealed that none of her own bags had cost more than £50. Blears meanwhile was toting her lipstick in something called an 'Orla Kiely' for which she owned up to paying 'around £250' (though some fashion types reckoned it was worth nearer £400). The culture secretary Tessa Jowell – not one to do indiscretion by halves – also forced her way into the frame with a 'Chloe', priced somewhere between £500 and £750. Confronted with her misdemeanour, Blears not only fronted up but launched a feisty counterblast against sanctimony and the 1970s-style politics of envy that had kept Labour out of power for eighteen years. It was not the business of politicians, she said, 'to tell people what they should spend their money on'. A week later the outgoing prime minister's wife, Cherie Blair, lined up for the cameras at a G8 summit clutching a £995 white 'Eva' bag which the *Daily Mail* traced to 'the top London leather goods shop Tanner Krolle'. She looked happy.

The designer handbag is a perfect example of the kind of personal badging with which the 'luxury goods' industry now bids to adorn us. All that's new about this is the promotion of vulgar display from social understorey to the *soi-disant* high pedestal of Taste. For all the lemon-lipped Harmanisms of social reformers across the centuries, and with the exception of tracts and fables, virtue is seldom partnered with poverty. Heroes may start out poor, but wealth always gilds the future. The Barclays advertisement is pure Jane Austen – our blonde heroine, having hooked her Honourable Gentleman, now kicks on to her rightful destiny. Virtue in wig-and-bonnet fiction typically is rewarded by an advantageous marriage or sudden inheritance, as if moral and material values fitted the same glass slipper. When rewards fail to materialize, the result is 'tragedy'. If Mr Right ever seems poor or ugly, then it is only to test the mettle of the Chosen One (who is always demure as well as lovely). She kisses the frog and gets the prince. The difference now is that whereas Jane Austen invited readers to *identify* with her heroes and heroines, advertising copy-writers hold out the promise of *being* them.

And they make it sound so easy. 'It's your watch that says most about who you are,' says a long-running campaign for Seiko. Pause for a moment and you find yourself wondering: what kind of idiot could write a line like that? And what kind of idiot could be influenced by it? Only a self-loathing loser would want to be defined by the way he tells the time. And yet no product in any category is too humdrum to be aspirational. 'Exclusivity' is mass-produced and sold by volume. Cars, chocolate, coffee, jewellery, holidays, alcohol, ice cream, bathrooms, skin creams, 'fragrances', pasta sauces, furniture polish – these and a myriad others are shoved at us like balm for failing lives. Fashion editors write without irony of shoes or handbags 'to die for'. The *Financial Times* has a magazine unblushingly called *How to Spend It*, whose readers are flattered with advertisements for multi-million-pound yachts with creaming wakes and bikini'd deck-candy. On mainstream television channels, advertisers promote germ-killing, wind-releasing or stain-removing chemicals in a style of commercial known in the trade as 2CK ('two cunts in a kitchen'). Some of the aspirations might be low, but they are aspirations all the same.

Yet the advertising industry is not a force of nature. It did not invent avarice or insecurity; it simply noticed them and turned them to advantage. For people of power and wealth, conspicuous consumption – owning and displaying the 'right' things; keeping the richest tables – has always been the hallmark of their caste (this was why Cleopatra liked to reveal rolls of fat). For those of lower caste, the luxury of choice was a long time coming. Not until the middle of the 19th century could most Westerners aspire to own more than they needed, and even then poverty was in no hurry to let go. In England it was not until some time between the wars that everyone owned a pair of shoes. Now 'poverty' in the developed world has been reclassified as 'relative' rather than 'absolute' (in the UK, it's defined as a family income of less than 60 per cent of the national median). To find the other kind you have to travel to other continents – to Central America, Asia, and particularly to Africa, where corruption and greed vie with famine and disease to kill the most people. The rest of us are 'poor' merely because our neighbours crunch more gravel. It is desire, not need, that furnishes our lounges, stocks our fridge-freezers and fills our carports.

With cash or credit we can acquire anything we like except – as psychologists, philosophers and men of religion never tire of telling us – the elusive quality of contentment, which seems to exist only as a false crest on the flank of a cloud-topped hill. No matter how high we climb, there's always further to go. It's an early lesson of childhood, but I didn't understand it then (for what could make one happier than a new bike?) and I don't properly understand it now. Is there *nothing* exchangeable for money that could make us happy? You want to ride the trans-Siberian railway, write sonnets, fly a balloon over Everest, breed chinchillas, learn Esperanto, spend more time with your dog, serve the community, endow a children's home . . . Seek fulfilment where you will, it's easier on a billionaire's budget than it is on social security. Is there not more pleasure in wine than in water? Would the television quiz *Who Wants to Be a Millionaire?* have been any less popular if it had been *Who Wants to Be a Happy Bunny?*

Well, yes ... of course it would. Wealth is tangible and accountable, the scale against which aspiration is calibrated. Whatever we enjoy, need or fancy, money will buy more of it. That much is obvious. 'Happiness', on the other hand, seems to want something else – a worry-free detachment from material concerns that, on the lips of idealists, can sound spiritual or even ascetic. Too often, though, it looks like a self-declared, trans-cendental state beyond definition, a literally worthless consolation prize for hippies, hermits and dropouts who need to justify their failure to prosper. Outside the happy-shack, the rest of us look in and see only smugness, indolence and complacency. Contentment, we think, is the enemy of progress. It's all yoghurt and yoga, and we don't trust it. Contentment would have kept us in the cave chewing gristle. And yet every belief system in the world – religious, political, moral – holds somewhere in its philo-sophical underpinnings the conviction that greed is wrong. Only biology and economics see selfishness as material to the common good, and only biology speaks its name aloud. The barrier to happiness in our economic wind tunnel is not so much the *having* as the *wanting to have*. Materialism proposes an infinite gradient of aspiration, each step on the cloud-topped hill more elevated than the last – newer, bigger, richer. I enjoy good wine, but would prefer better. If I could afford better, then I would want the best. Then more of the best; then the vineyard, the dukedom and the chateau. No emperor or media mogul can ever have everything; no tycoon is too big to open *Forbes* and find no one to envy. Whatever rung we cling to, there will always be one above, social pinnacles left unclimbed, vistas blocked by chateaux bigger than our own. The only certainty therefore is failure, and how can failure make us happy?

Social reformers often compare materialism with religion. Facile, perhaps, but not altogether wrong. An infinite number of people cannot expect infinite benefits from the limited resources of a finite planet. Only blind faith makes us think otherwise. The language of this religion seeps so deeply into our thinking that we no longer need to think about it at all. It is lodged in our sub-conscious, a given, alongside breathing, balance and fear of snakes. It tells us we 'need' things – new cars, greener lawns, bigger breasts, fancier watches – when we only desire them. Our leaders hear the same voices in their heads (example: the British government's insistence that we 'need' more runways in the south-east). Churches, too, covet things – jewelled monstrances, gold altarpieces, painted ceilings, palaces – that have little to do with the needs of the soul. Most of us can quote more advertising slogans than we can verses from the Bible. They give us not only our *lingua franca* but an entire inverted pyramid of virtue. When called to worship, we answer with plastic.

The theology of consumer heaven attracts as many prophets as the other kind. One well-canvassed idea, called 'set-point theory', proposes that each of us has a kind of happiness default setting. Our genetic imprinting means that we can be neither more nor less happy than our natures allow us to be. Disease, divorce or a lottery win might blow us temporarily off course, but we will always return to this same 'set point'. Its parent was a theory of body weight, also called 'set-point', which said that loss through dieting is only ever temporary, and that people always grow back to the weight their metabolisms and psyches have marked down for them. It is not implausible that genes contribute something to an individual's capacity to feel emotion. Think about people you know – what else could explain such wide divergence of person-ality? But it is, surely, impossible to believe in a happiness quotient so firmly fixed that it is proof against circumstance. The loss of a limb? Bereavement? Marriage? Relief from debt? The same individual might suffer a paralysing injury or a million-pound windfall. In either case, it is beyond belief that he would rebound to the same set point, and be as sad or as happy as he would have been if nothing had happened. Standard economic theory, which says that happiness advances in parallel with personal wealth and benefit from the state, emerges from that skirmish with hardly a scratch.

But standard theory meets a more formidable obstacle in the 'Easterlin paradox', named after Richard Easterlin, professor of economics at the University of Southern California, where he is lauded as 'the father of the economics of happiness' (and where else but California would you look for one of those?). It began in 1974 with Easterlin's paper 'Does Economic Growth Improve the Human Lot? Some Empirical Evidence', in which he argued from evidence that happiness does not increase in parallel with wealth. In a subsequent paper he would report that 'most people' thought more money *would* make them happier, and typically believed that a 20 per cent salary increase would be enough to do the trick. Thus his research at first did offer some support for standard theory. Snap surveys showed that people with more money by and large were happier than those with less. But that is not the point. The question is whether individuals become happier over time as they earn more money. The Easterlin paradox says they do not. He cites a survey of Americans born in the 1940s:

> Between the years 1972 and 2000, as their average age increased from about 26 to 54 years, their average income per person . . . more than doubled, increasing by 116 per cent. Yet their reported happiness in the year 2000 was no different from that 28 years earlier. They had a lot more money and a considerably higher standard of living at the later date, but this did not make them feel any happier.

It was the same with children of other decades. 'Although the point-of-time result seemingly confirms the economists' assumption that more money makes you happier,' wrote Easterlin, 'the life cycle result contradicts it.' The reason is easily guessed. Quality of life is like poverty – comparative, not absolute. As we grow wealthier with age, so do others around us.

By comparison with our neighbours, friends and colleagues, our financial and/or social status remains broadly the same, and so does our portion of happiness.

Easterlin limits himself to the observable truth that wealth and happiness are not connected. Others go further. In his best-selling book *Affluenza*, Oliver James argued that 'selfish capitalism' in Britain and America was responsible for spiralling rates of mental illness. Our me-me, more-more materialism, with its locked-in sense of frustration and failure, quite literally was driving us mad. To prove it, he compared rates of mental illness in the UK with, among others, those of Nigeria, Shanghai and Denmark. It led him to conclude that 'citizens of English-speaking nations are twice as likely to suffer mental illness as ones from mainland western Europe'. But this begs a number of questions. Unlike, say, smallpox, 'mental illness' does not conform to a precise clinical definition which is uniformly applied and universally accepted. Different practitioners in different countries diagnose it in different ways, and countries vary widely in the quality and methodology of their medical record-keeping. For these reasons, international comparisons are notoriously unreliable. With too much money to spend, America has become a therapy-obsessed society that can't wait to throw itself on the couch and dredge up a neurosis or two. With nothing at all to spend, Africans are hard-pressed to find treatment for even malaria or AIDS, and have no words for stuff like 'anxiety syndrome' or 'stress'. This is why, if you read the statistics like a recipe, you'll conclude that the best prophylactics against mental disorder are poverty and malnutrition.

Neither is there much support for James's conclusions in Europe. A detailed report, *The State of Mental Health in the European Union*, published by the European Commission in 2004, shows Britain comparing well with other countries. Its prevalence rate for 'depressive disorders' is 2.8 per cent, against Germany's 8.3 per cent and the Netherlands' 5.8 per cent.

Differences in survey methods, study periods and sample sizes make definitive conclusions impossible, but there is nothing here to suggest that English-speakers are any more depressed than other Europeans. Indeed, suicide rates suggest the reverse is true. In a survey of EU states in 1997, the UK's 6.5 suicides per 100,000 population was bettered only by Portugal (5 per 100,000) and Greece (3). James's exemplars of mental stability, the Danes, at 14 per 100,000, killed themselves more than twice as often as the Brits. Other Scandinavians (Norway 11.5, Sweden 12.5) didn't do too well either, and Finland at 24.5 was, by a wide margin, the single most self-destructive country in Europe. The more general finding, consistent across a range of surveys, that mental disorders are more common in economically deprived areas of high unemployment, is not wholly inimical to James – the misery of poor, jobless people may well be exacerbated by envy of their wealthier neighbours. But this is not an affliction much suffered, say, in sub-Saharan Africa, where there is no affluence to envy, and it does not mark the divide between sanity and madness. The disease of 'affluenza', says its inventor, is 'a contagious, middle-class virus causing depression, anxiety, addiction and ennui'. It's a fine piece of tub-thumping, but as a clinical diagnosis it's right up there with possession by evil spirits.

We like to call 'mad' anyone who lives by a different value system. I know people with barnfuls of boats that are never sailed; others whose bare floors are lit by unshaded electric bulbs; others who talk to their pets, or collect teapots, or live on exclusion diets, or wear hats indoors, or fill their rooms with Stockhausen, Cage and Glass. I know people for whom nirvana is a Mercedes or a Rolex, or knowing the telephone number of someone famous. I know one woman whose behaviour is modulated by the knowledge that she is being watched 24 hours a day by her long-dead mother. All of these I have called mad. They in turn find madness in others. They cannot understand time wasted on golf, and doubt the stability of people who pursue chancy careers in the arts. ('*Opera?*' I heard a builders' merchant exclaim to his neighbour at dinner. 'Is there any *money* in that?') So we must be careful. 'Misguided' or 'ill-advised' is not the same as 'mad'; nor is 'not like us'. Trite but true: different does not mean worse. People behaving legally in a democracy are entitled to spend their money as they choose, and to enjoy what pleases them. Is Richard Easterlin, then, right to suggest that most of them are looking in the wrong place?

It seems that he is. We don't have to be mad to be unhappy. Since the dawn of thought, wise men have been telling us that wealth and fame are the antitheses of life's true meaning. The mountaintop sages of antiquity, literally with their heads in the clouds, did not have the benefit of research grants or professorships in psychology or social science. They just observed, pondered and pronounced. You couldn't get away with that now. People want *proof*. Easterlin himself has given us a bit, but we need more. In *The High Price of Materialism*, Tim Kasser, associate professor of psychology at Knox College, Illinois, describes a programme of work 'exploring how people's values and goals relate to their well-being'. It took him on an intellectual journey to the dark side of the American dream. By questioning students about their attitudes and aspirations, he was able not only to confirm what Easterlin and the sages had said (that money and celebrity are divorced from happiness), but also to take the idea a step further. It was not just the *possession* of wealth that did the damage. Even to *aspire* to it was a passport to misery. Aspiration meant stress, anxiety and damage to both physical and psychological health. And it worked both ways – unhappy people by their nature were more likely to be materialistic and narcissistic (ie in psychologists' terms, given to grandiose and empty bragging).

There is, however, a moralistic overtone in Kasser that will not be to everyone's taste. He argues that 'materialistic teens' are more likely than others to indulge in a whole catalogue of bad behaviours, amongst which he lists not just alcohol and drug abuse but – horror! – 'sexual intercourse'. This might cause a fluster in Illinois, but it wouldn't redden too many cheeks in rural England. You could argue that materialism and teenage sex were inextricably linked, but you might just as easily argue the opposite. Those who rejected materialism in the freewheeling 1960s – the beats, the hippies, the flower children and the communards – never thought of renouncing sex. Nor was this something which that misremembered and misunderstood decade could call peculiarly its own. Not even Philip Larkin really believed that 'sexual intercourse began in 1963'. For when were things any different? Look around you. Look in the *mirror*. Do you see any connection between anti-materialism and sexual abstinence? No, neither do I.

Nor is this the only glimpse we get of the author's singular moral perspective. A 'materialism scale', supposed to measure our tendency to possessiveness (a negative value, obviously), asks us to agree or disagree with statements such as: 'I get very upset if something is stolen from me, even if it has little monetary value.' Well, yes, actually I do. I also get upset when I lose things, and I 'tend to hang on to things I should probably throw out'. Does that make me a bad person? And if I forgive others for stealing, as Kasser seems to hope I will, does that mean I must forgive myself the same? Is ownership theft, or is there a subtler point here that I'm missing? In his distaste for the 'capitalistic consumer society', Kasser delivers a message that is more political than scientific. 'SMASH CAPITALISM' was a favourite slogan of student agitators in the 1960s, if not quite their policy of choice when they grew up and took power. (What they actually gave us was the greed-obsessed 1980s, Thatcherism and a smooth pathway for Tony Blair and George W. Bush.) 'FREEDOM' was what we wanted, but when it came to the point we could find no other system that offered more of it than we already had. Kasser I suspect would have us all in therapy.

Yet none of this materially harms his thesis. The sages were right, and Kasser's provoking and passionate little book stands in the great tradition of radical opposition to hand-me-down thinking. He would not accept, for example, the purely biological explanation for pair-bonding that I set out in Chapter 3. Women look for wealthy mates, he says, not because of genetic imprinting but rather to compensate for their own lack of economic opportunity. I am not sure how real this distinction is. Biology has always been the enemy of militant feminism (for 'dearth of opportunity' read 'desire to bear children'), but it is useful to be reminded that culture, too, is important. Nurturing mothers, Kasser says, have less materialistic children. By 'nurturing' he means rewarding them with love and stimulation, not with expensive gifts and hours of television. Connecting 'love' with 'no-expense-spared' is one of the most corrosive malfunctions that we force upon children's minds. It teaches them that love *is* materialism – an economist's wet dream eternally reinforced by programme-makers, schedulers and their commercial sponsors. Only Christmas objectifies children more ruthlessly than television.

I must confess to a clutch-in-the-guts hatred of Christmas that goes much deeper than bah-humbug. A latterday Charles Dickens would give *A Christmas Carol* a very different kind of villain – not the misery-monger Scrooge but his cynical and sociopathic inheritors in the entertainment, media and advertising industries. In Santa Claus we have created the ultimate perversion of love and good will, a patron saint of greed whose metamorphosis from 4th-century Orthodox bishop in Asia Minor to international marketing symbol is a parable in its own right. 'Santa' began life as Nicholas, born around AD 270 at Patara in what is now southern Turkey. He was a generous man whose personality was shaped by the twin forces of inherited wealth and early orphanhood. The most popular version of his story blends Dickens with the brothers Grimm.

Once upon a time, it is said, a poor man had three daughters. He could not afford dowries for them and, without husbands, they faced a future of prostitution. But then a miracle occurred. On three consecutive nights, bags of gold flew in through the poor man's window – a dowry for each of his girls! On the third night, eager to know his benefactor, he stood in wait, and in his gratitude next day did not hesitate to let the town – the whole world – know of Nicholas's generosity. In paintings, the saint traditionally is identified by these same three bags, represented as golden balls – a device later hijacked by pawnbrokers. Along with sailors, merchants, children and Russia, they also made him their patron saint.

Nicholas became bishop at nearby Myra, and died some time in the 340s after a spectacular career of miracles and good works. Shortly afterwards he was declared a saint. Ironically, this was the first step on the pathway to spiritual ruin. In May 1087, a commando of 63 mercenaries and sailors broke into the shrine at Myra and made off with his bones to Bari in southern Italy, where they still remain as a tourist attraction in the Basilica di San Nicola.

It was some French nuns in the 12th century who accelerated the process which eventually would put an out-of-work actor into every department store, pyramids of nuts and oranges into every supermarket, and a digital games console at the foot of every child's bed. Inspired by Nicholas's compassion for the impoverished girls, on 5 December, the eve of his traditional feast day, the nuns delivered stockings stuffed with fruit, nuts and oranges to the homes of the poor. The idea caught on, sped across national boundaries and quickly became a pan-European tradition. By the 16th century, the saint's soaring popularity was warping the patience of Dutch and German Protestants, for whom the only permissible objects of worship were God and Jesus.

In a crackdown against unholy present-giving, Amsterdamers were ordered not to carry sweets on the saint's day. The people first rioted, and then came together in one of history's most improbable outbreaks of civil disobedience. Gifts were exchanged in defiance of the law, and the Dutch continued to tell their children about the saint whose name in Holland translated as Sinterklaas. Finally, in a brilliant legal shimmy, the St Nicholas Day celebrations were shunted along the calendar to merge with the unbannable festival of Christmas.

Dutch settlers later carried the legend to America, where the new world rewrote it from the boots up. To complete his journey from 4th-century virgin-protector to patron of incontinent consumption, Sinterklaas would get a new outfit, a new tradition and a new name. In 1809 under the pseudonym Diedrich Knickerbocker, the writer Washington Irving described Sinterklaas riding to a feast on horseback and proclaimed him patron saint of New York. In 1822, Clement C. Moore in his poem 'A Visit from St Nicholas' (more popularly known as ' 'Twas the Night Before Christmas') added flying reindeer to the story – an idea probably borrowed from a Lapp tradition in which reindeer-borne shamans dropped in with presents through smoke-holes in roofs. In this version the saint became a 'right jolly old elf' with a sack of toys. In 1860 the illustrator Thomas Nast in a Christmas drawing for *Harper's Weekly* gave him pipe, beard, waistcoat and the evolved name Santa Claus. The process of corruption was almost complete, but not quite. A Christmas card in 1885 had suggested a red coat, but what permanently fixed the image was a series of red-suited Santas in a Christmas advertising campaign for Coca-Cola that ran from 1931 for more than thirty years – the perfect, cashed-up icon of modern commercial sainthood.

It is a pity that the fiercest opponents of 'Santa's grottoes' and other grim public displays of 'seasonal' cheer are municipal jobsworths and the boot-faced magi of political correctness who fear causing offence to other religions, as if – in the name of multiculturalism, or the multi-faith community that the Prince of Wales wants to be 'defender' of – festivity has to be portion-controlled and one idiocy balanced by another. Very often, as tinselled packaging begins to infest retail displays in late summer, I hear myself say that this year we'll give the entire Greedmass thing a miss – travel abroad, or stay at home with the letterbox sealed. We've never done it. Tradition, the expectations of others, the fear of Scroogery, have such a tight hold on us that the freedom to opt out is as frail an illusion as Santa's cotton-wool beard.

Psychologists talk endlessly about the quest for freedom. Materialism, they say, is the enemy of autonomy. To be properly free, you have to tear yourself away from enslavement to self-enrichment and status-seeking. You must do things for their own sake and not for the approval of others; for the pleasure of meeting a challenge, not in expectation of any reward beyond the sheer joy of *doing*. This is called 'intrinsic motivation', drawn from within; quite unlike the self-destructive 'extrinsic' sort that looks for external reward. I remember a schoolmaster who talked like this – a prissy idiot, so we thought, in charge of 'hobbies', who hated everything we loved (music with drums in it; light-weight racing bicycles with dropped handlebars; Coca-Cola; chewing gum; American jeans and basketball boots; sideburns), and who couldn't understand why we didn't want to build crystal sets or make piano stools. It still makes me smile, though not quite as much as Tim Kasser's suggestion that a 'great example' of an activity pursued for 'sheer joy' is 'writing books'.

Here is the fly in the psychological ointment. Put aside the fact that, regardless of how motivated or 'inspired' you might believe yourself to be, writing for a living is hard work and failure is all but inked into the contract. (Few books measure up to their authors' expectations, so the 'sheer joy' of creativity mutates into a clinging sense of inadequacy.) What is it that makes someone a writer? Or a painter, or a footballer, or a director of human resources, or anything else that it's possible to be 'good' at? The answer is that fine old extrinsic motivator, the approval of others. 'No man is an island, entire of itself,' said John Donne, whose talent was hitting nails on heads. Perhaps it's different for professors of psychology. The rest of us can call ourselves anything we like, from pastrycook to Emperor of France, but it's meaningful only if others accept our pastries, our royal decrees, our sonnets or our symphonies. We cannot simply be what we declare ourselves to be – albeit well trodden, that is the pathway to delusion. It doesn't mean that there's no release from the hamster-wheel, or that the wheel itself must be forever joyless.

Back in the 1980s when fortunes in the City of London were being amassed by young men who sounded like costermongers, a rather haughty social commentator declared that the English middle classes would have to redefine themselves. In future, he said, the qualifying standard would no longer be a top salary; it would be an interesting job. We can see how wrong he was. No kind of work holds a monopoly of interest, and where is the evidence that the middle class has lost its taste for money? Nevertheless, in his maladroit way, he was realizing the importance of balance. On its own, undiluted intrinsic motivation turns you into a fantasist, playing air guitar outside the economy. On its own, extrinsic motivation turns you into an economic stooge. To be a halfway happy, satisfactorily self-determining, unsanctimonious and involved member of society, you need a bit of both. We have the intelligence to override our genetic impulses, but we cannot delete them like unwanted software. We can modulate our greed but we can't escape its gravitational pull. Snouts were made for troughs.

It is to Marie Lloyd that we owe the philosophy-in-a-nutshell, 'A little bit of what you fancy does you good'. Lloyd's trick, the reason for her notoriety, was that she could load the most innocent lyric with coy licentiousness. Arbiters of Edwardian moral rectitude were outraged (or claimed they were) by the nudge-wink suggestiveness of the music-hall stage. Now it is a cultural period piece, exiled in all innocence to Christmas pantomimes, a cigarette card in the age of video. Mainstream audiences – for comedy, music, film, theatre, even gallery art – now enjoy a diet of such full-on literalness that anyone born before the Second World War can scarcely believe what they are seeing. Simulated sex long ago replaced the saucily arched eyebrow, and *vérité* was not far behind. Film, rock and sports stars cultivate images of petulant self-indulgence. If a little bit does you good, then a lot will do you better and too much is a great way to die. Megalomaniac rockers and pop divas travel in caravanserai that would exhaust the credulity of ancient emperors fattened on peacocks. They keep their customers waiting, and escalate their backstage demands up to and beyond the expectations of princes – dressing-room lavatories re-oriented for enhancement of Chi; cocaine and Cristal, spicy Doritos, Beluga and ketchup to be laid out ready after the second encore; ditto the blonde in Row D. The only thing they cannot bear is 'no'.

We have become so desensitized, so addicted to superlatives, that 'excess' must constantly change its meaning. In 2007 an £85 Wagyu and foie gras sandwich was received as an amusing folly, not as an offence against decency. Footballers in the English Premiership were earning a hundred times the national median wage; City traders were receiving annual bonuses bigger than the lifetime earnings of a production worker. A member of the royal family used an RAF jet for a golfing trip. The power of celebrity was – and continues to be – such that bankable names expect not just to be given designer clothes but to be paid to wear them, and their 'image rights' are traded like works of art.

But are these people not just grotesque exaggerations of a common truth – our own selves stretched to absurdity? In their position, with celebrity thrust upon us, how would our behaviour be any different to theirs? And do we not have cause to be thankful for such people as well as to envy them, or condemn? Thankful, that is, for their *greed*? Which of us is beyond enticement, or innocent of dreams? Greed is not all about material possession. We crave also image and individuality. For reasons of our own we pursue excellence and achievement, and desire to be praised for what we do. Even altruism and faith have greed on their soles, for who would waste kneeling-time on any god not offering rewards in the hereafter? Faced with a Richard Dawkins or a Christopher Hitchens, churchmen defend their faith by reminding us of Christianity's (or Islam's or Judaism's) 'good works' – bringing comfort to the poor and weak, providing the spiritual foundations for law and government. We may or may not agree that this is a fair return for holy wars, religious persecutions, obstruction of science and intolerance of dissent. But it is something to remember, and its focus on the bottom line is the model for all who feel driven to improve. We salute excellence, but excellence is seldom born of modesty, and still less of moderation.

We salute especially the self-gratification of men and women whose genius across the millennia has created a world of infinite possibility that comforts, feeds and entertains us – a process that has raised us from cave-art to YouTube, eolith to space lab, mammoth-haunch to twice-baked cheese soufflé. Think of anything you might call 'great', in whatever sphere you like. *King Lear*; Bach's Mass in B minor; *Citizen Kane*; Chartres cathedral; *tournedos Rossini*; Puligny-Montrachet; *Jude the Obscure*; the Ordnance Survey; Land-Rover; the American Declaration of Independence; the Uffizi; the recordings of Kathleen Ferrier; Venice; *Bohemian Rhapsody*; Concorde; the magnifying lens; antibiotics; the violin; cricket; the Burton brewing process; electricity; the banking system; MS-DOS; chips ... You could write down a thousand things, then cross them all out and write a thousand more; then a thousand more, on and on until your eyesight failed. For whatever we value, we have to thank its creators – people who were not always in the conventional sense 'nice' but whose determination to succeed was more powerful than all the obstacles and discouragements laid in their path. Many of them consciously sought greatness or, at the very least, acceptance and reward. Call it hunger; call it self-expression; call it ambition; call it greed. What drives the genius is what drives us all. What profits the genius is what profits us all.

The problem with ambition is that it has no brakes; no concept of 'enough'. When the founder of Tesco, Jack Cohen, opened Britain's first supermarket in a former cinema at Maldon, Essex, in 1956, he democratized the shopping basket and opened the way for a kitchen revolution that would improve all our lives. His legacy is an international monster whose power strikes fear into the hearts of governments and, by destroying local markets, now threatens the very freedoms it once championed. As an individual I use the only freedom I have: I spend my money elsewhere. Perversely, maybe, and not always advantageously, I also boycott the subjects of offensive or irritating advertisements. This is my small, impotent revenge against Seiko, Honda, credit companies and 'designer' labels.

Fashion is materialism gone mad. It drives a throwaway culture in which nothing is for the future and the past is best forgotten. It was hatred of history, along with Tony Blair's embarrassing 'Cool Britannia', that turned the Millennium Dome from *grand projet* into farce. History belongs to that peculiarly modern region of hell, *yesterday*, and it's filling up fast. The old idea of 'consumer durables' is as quaint as paying with cash. Design, not utility, determines the lifespan of what we buy. Perfectly good, workable mobile telephones become junk as soon as Nokia launches a new range. Music becomes junk the moment we've heard it. Clothes age faster than mince. We read of 'must-have' haircuts, and are told what's right or wrong to wear. Fashion has become the antithesis not only of style but also of democracy – a tyrannical, flash-card orthodoxy that parades uniformity as choice and 'the season's essential look' as exclusivity. To buy is to belong. Notice how often the word 'luxury' is slipped into advertisements. Notice how lingeringly it is pronounced – the *luckshry* of my youth (when it meant extra-long cigarettes and furniture you could sit on without bruising your backside) now is sibilantly stretched into *luck-syuree* (when it means any mass-produced item with a dab of chocolate on it).

Luxury had its heyday between the wars, and briefly again afterwards. At its height it was epitomized by the transatlantic queens of the Cunard Line that spanned the continents like floating principalities. In the staterooms of the *Queens Mary* and *Elizabeth*, fashionable women sheathed themselves in silk and diamonds, and matched exquisite manners with scandalous behaviour. After the cognac, 'Would you care for a cigarette?' quickened more pulses than Marie Lloyd's lyrics. Fashionable women were individually dressed by the small, discreet and ultra-exclusive couture houses of the once and future capital of style, Paris. They were photographed, gossiped about and envied by those ashore, but not *emulated*. Secretaries and shopgirls might as well have dreamed of marrying a crown prince. It was not their place.

On to the scary glamour of aristocrats, heiresses and plutocrats' wives was grafted the even more seductive, and even more unreachable, gloss of Hollywood. Queens of the screen smouldered in mink and pearls while their audiences made do and mended. War turned thrift into a national duty, nylon stockings into hard currency and 'housewives' (as they were then still called) into Nijinskys of needle and thread. In the years of austerity that came afterwards, every woman had a sewing basket and a tin of salvage – buttons, press studs, ribbons and tapes – with which to extend the lives of her home-made frocks. The gulf in wealth, elegance and social class was, if anything, widened in 1947 when the first emperor of post-war fashion, Christian Dior (improbably, the fifth son of a fertilizer manufacturer), launched his wasp-waisted New Look. In the old-world tradition of privilege for the privileged, his collection was presented privately to the British royal family in London (though George VI forbade the princesses Elizabeth and Margaret to wear the Look, for fear of appearing ostentatious at a time of public hardship). It was a screen queen, Rita Hayworth, who most publicly took it up and made Dior the designer of choice for the Hollywood glamocracy.

No one could have known it in 1947, but this was a turning point worthy of comparison with Henry Ford's production line in Detroit. Couture was still – as for the very wealthy it would remain – a bespoke, hand-sewn business of high craftsmanship (some would say high art), in which elegance and discretion said all that was necessary about a woman's taste and breeding. But things were about to change. Luxury was on the move, and it was Dior himself who would be the catalyst. Capitalizing on its master's fame, and with an eye fixed on the dollar, the House of Dior soon had a perfume to its name (Miss Dior) and a ready-to-wear business on Fifth Avenue. Dior became a *brand*, and 'luxury' took its first faltering step away from 'exclusivity'. Everyone knows what happened next: you can see it in every high street. Haute couture would survive, but only as a way of keeping its designers in the headlines. Companies lost money on bespoke, but coined it in the ready-to-wear empires that traded on their names. Production shifted from the *ateliers* into local factories, then from those into Chinese and Indian sweatshops where children as young as eight stand in for the craftsmen of the Belle Epoque, and where the most important task – the moment of magic that can multiply thirteenfold the value of a nondescript glued-together, kit-of-parts handbag – is the attachment of the designer label (though this sometimes is not done until it has been returned to its 'country of origin'). You could call this exploitation, but let us instead call it the democratization of fashion. When the Dior empire really got going in the 1950s, the couture industry was serving 200,000 customers worldwide. Now it is just 200. That's democracy for you – or, rather, that's business. Luxury has been globalized, commodified and placed in the hands of everywoman.

It is a cult that became a religion, and a religion into which any-one can be ordained. To bear the name of your god – Louis Vuitton, Prada, Gucci, Armani, Chanel, Hermès, Asprey – is to receive a blessing. All you need is a credit card.

It is not easy to remain aloof from fashion. You can only buy what's in the shops, and it's fashion that fills the shelves. For most of us, taste in clothes is a bit like our taste in popular music – fixed in the styles of our youth, and modified only by the diktats of age and decorum. My father died recently at the age of 88, still wearing the side parting he'd had since he was in his twenties, and leaving a rack of trousers and jackets that were styled before the invasion of Poland. He believed he was immune to fashion, and in a way I suppose he was. In truth he was resistant to every style except one (his role model might have been the mufti of King George VI). His real resistance was to change. This of course entitled me in my youth to regard him, typically of his generation, as a baggy-trousered sartorial dinosaur for whom shirts were white (or off-duty check), shoes were Cherry-Blossomed black or tan, and colour meant grey, lovat or fawn. Now I find I have done the same – you could date me as easily from my wardrobe as from my birth certificate. The canvas and the linen, the open-necked patch-pocket shirts, the unstructured jackets and jean-cut trousers, the boots and mini-alp of sockless open sandals, the absence of suits, ties and polished shoes, are lines of perspective whose vanishing point is somewhere in the sixties. And of course I, too, just as erroneously claim indifference to fashion.

My only professional involvement with the subject was a brief interlude more than twenty years ago when, by some grim mischance, I had editorial oversight of a newspaper's fashion pages. The fashion editor wept when I asked what was the point of an item about cashmere jumpers, and I failed altogether to persuade her that prices and sources should be listed only for garments that could be seen in the photographs and not for shoes or jewellery that were obscured or out of shot. Apparently this was not the way the system worked *at all*. I can see that it still isn't. For my understanding of the way it does work, I have to thank a quite brilliant book, *Deluxe: How Luxury Lost Its Lustre*, by *Newsweek*'s Paris-based style writer Dana Thomas. From her I learn that the current (2007) value of the luxury goods industry is 175 billion dollars; that 35 brands, many of them co-owned, control 60 per cent of the business; and that in 2006 40 per cent of the Japanese population owned something bearing the mark of Vuitton. I cherish her description of Vuitton as 'the McDonald's of the luxury industry', and thank her for the spot-on observation that mass production of designerware has shifted the emphasis from what the product *is* to what it *represents*.

In the language of the fashionista, it means 'buying into the dream', and the phrase could hardly be more apt. *Living* the dream would be a contradiction: the whole point of dreams is that they are not real. Rita Hayworth, when she adopted the New Look, may have had some idea of the power of her own image (if she didn't, the Dior brand managers certainly did), but she could hardly have foreseen how eagerly the developed world would swallow the cult of fame. Sixty years later, 'celebrity' is the new ubiquity, a label stuck, however briefly, to anyone who ever blinks at a camera. The salary deals of screen and sports stars make bigger headlines than the performances for which they are paid. In 2007 the British sports minister, Gerry Sutcliffe, lodged the inevitable 'obscenity' charge against the £150,000-a-week, or £7.8m-a-year, contract awarded to the Chelsea and England football captain, John Terry, a handy scapegoat for an industry whose greed exceeds any known boundary of proportionality or reason. Who can forget the reaction of Terry's Chelsea colleague Ashley Cole in 2004 when offered £55,000 a week by his former club, Arsenal? In his book, *My Defence*, he recalls a telephone call from his agent, Jonathan Barnett, which he received while driving to visit his mother:

'Ash! Are you listening?' said a virtually hyperventilating Jonathan. 'I'm here in the office and [the Arsenal vice-chairman] David Dein is saying they aren't going to give you £60K a week. They've agreed £55K and this is their best and final offer. Are you happy with that?'

When I heard Jonathan repeat the figure of £55K I nearly swerved off the road. 'He is taking the piss, Jonathan,' I yelled down the phone. I was so incensed. I was trembling with anger. I couldn't believe what I'd heard. I suppose it all started to fall apart for me from then on.

The outcry over Terry and Cole, however, was an inchoate whinge to set against the furore caused by the BBC's £6m-a-year deal with the chat-show host Jonathan Ross. In part this was a matter of taste. For those not charmed by his high smut-quotient, Ross would fail any value-for-money test. Even before he got himself suspended, along with Russell Brand, for using radio airtime to leave obscene messages on the 78-year-old actor Andrew Sachs's answerphone, he was notorious for his question to the leader of the Conservative Party, David Cameron: 'Did you or did you not have a wank thinking, Margaret Thatcher?' Most of the anger, though, stemmed from his employment by the publicly funded but forever cost-cutting BBC. We didn't like it because it was 'our' money, and we could think of better ways to spend it. Ross himself enjoys provocation, and characteristically baited his critics by claiming to be worth 'a thousand BBC journalists'. In itself this was not the most risqué of jokes (for who cares about journalists?), but people then converted 'journalists' into 'nurses', 'teachers' or even 'chancellors of the exchequer' and wondered how any one man doing any one job could be worth as much as that. He made a big, inviting target, and took some heavy flak. And yet . . .

In the various blogs across which the argument raged, as many voices were raised in Ross's support as were ready to snipe. How could this be? The answer is that we have fixed expectations of the way stars ought to behave. We *need* them to be rich, ostentatious and extravagant. That is the 'dream' we buy into; why we want to be like them. That's the whole point. It is the basic premiss of 'luxury goods' marketing. It is why fashion houses pay Hollywood's finest to wear their clothes; why the likes of Brad Pitt, George Clooney, Elizabeth Hurley, Nicole Kidman, Scarlett Johansson, Penelope Cruz *et al* so often beam out at us from the advertising pages of weekend magazines. The campaign managers might be too young to remember Rita Hayworth, but they are old enough to know about Audrey Hepburn and the effect of Givenchy's 'little black dress' in *Breakfast at Tiffany's*. It's why the latest 'face of Chanel' or 'face of Estée Lauder' is flammed up into a news event. It's why stars get to launch their own fashion or fragrance ranges. It probably even accounts for the word 'fragrance' itself. Manufacturers earn their big bucks from mass marketing, from the *illusion* of exclusivity rather than from the genuine article that survives only as a loss leader. In the process of democratization, expensive *parfum* was diluted into affordable *eau de toilette*, and *eau de toilette* became cheap cologne. The appealing but non-specific portmanteau word that lumps them all together, and binds shopgirls to the stars, is the egalitarian 'fragrance'. Selling the dream, the glamming up of humdrum lives, is the stock in trade of an industry that knows more about human nature than any psychology faculty. It explains Prada and Vuitton. It explains the Labour Party's handbag wars. It explains why colleges and universities offer degree courses in Fashion and Luxury Goods Management. It explains even the most pathetic of all advertising slogans, 'As seen on TV'.

More pertinently in a chronicle of greed, it explains the easy exploitation of the little people – the mark-up on 'designer' handbags of up to 13 times the cost of production. Luxury goods now are like chicken nuggets. Companies scour the world for the cheapest sources of supply, which are seldom in the wealthy countries where their customers live, and still less in a brand's own country of origin. The decision-makers are not the design aristocracy of the Cunard era, when 'value' meant quality and life expectancy, but hard-nut business school graduates looking for fast turnover and cheap labour. They find it in China, where production costs may be 40 per cent lower than they are in Italy. Dana Thomas, who went to see for herself, found workers being paid 120 dollars a month for daily ten-hour shifts and literally dying of fatigue. Items destined for the labels of top European brand names are knocked out in North Africa, Turkey, Egypt, Mexico, Vietnam, Cambodia ... Respect for human rights in these places is about as common as snow in the Sahel. Conditions are bad enough in the legitimate company factories. They are even worse in the sweatshops that flood the market with fakes, and into which children may be sold by their parents. Workers are the moving parts, instantly replaceable, in a vast counterfeiting machine that accounts for between 5 and 9 per cent of world trade. It has been estimated that the UK alone buys 56.5m fake items every year, including jeans, trainers, handbags, belts, pharmaceuticals, cigarettes, DVDs, CDs, cameras, watches, personal stereos, jewellery, perfume, sportswear and every kind of clothing. Whatever William Wilberforce had in mind when he put an end to the slave trade, it was not this.

Third World sweatshops of course do not figure very prominently in the chic advertisements and glossy emporia through which luxury goods come to market. That would kill the dream. And yet there is nothing new or surprising here. There have been so many exposés of the fashion industry and its satellites that it is hard to imagine anyone with regular access to news media being unaware of them. Let us be fair, though. These are not the only industries with reason to be coy about the origins of their materials, the treatment of their suppliers, their production methods or the mess they leave behind them. Think broiler fowl, salmon farms, agri-chemicals, beam-trawls, nuclear and electronic wastes, air travel, gold-mining, tropical hard-woods, biofuels, cotton, bananas, sugar . . . Think about all the decent, morally upright people who manage to ignore the true cost of what they consume; who, when challenged, will speak pragmatically of 'living in the real world'. I do it myself. No word in any language is subject to more distortions than 'reality'. Those whose values differ from our own are always divorced from it, while we ourselves remain perfectly in touch.

When my father died, I looked up the life expectancy of a male infant in his birth year, 1919, and was shocked to find that it was just 52.1 years. Now in the UK it is 76.9 (81.3 for females). But of course 'average' is a statistical artefact concealing wide regional differences. The highest life expectancies – 83.1 for males, 87.2 for females – are exactly where you would expect them to be, in the wealthy London borough of Kensington and Chelsea. Early death, too, clings to its ancestral heartland – the city of Glasgow, where males can look forward to 12.6 years less than the Kensington cohort, and females 10.2 years less. Similar trends are evident in the USA. Average life expectancy (both sexes) in the District of Columbia, for example, is 72; in Hawaii it is 80. All this is interesting – shocking, even, when you consider that the discrepancy between Glaswegian and Kensingtonian men is 17.9 per cent. But then consider Zambia.

Average life expectancy: 32.4 years.

Now consider all the different local norms – of diet, of education, of health, of income, of housing – that are parcelled in those numbers, and ask: what is reality? Our wealth is a vehicle in which we pass through the world, heated or air-conditioned according to 'need', and through whose tinted glass we catch only passing glimpses of other lives. And we, too, are only specks in the savannah when viewed from the rarefied altitudes of the super-rich. The lives of these people are so unlike our own that we need a different language, a different concept of geography and mathematics, to chart the world they live in. The *Wall Street*

Journal writer Robert Frank, in his book *Richistan*, depicts them as citizens of a parallel country. By 2000, he says, the number of millionaires in America had reached 8m – more than the entire population of Sweden. By 2004, the richest 1 per cent of Americans were pulling in 1.35 trillion dollars a year, thus exceeding the total national incomes not just of busted African republics but of Italy, France and Canada. In Richistan, their idea of a crushing put-down is 'affluent'. Theirs is 'new' money, earned in new ways and driving straight to the heart of the American paradox. Everyone has an equal chance to become unequal.

But, as I have said, greed is not just about *things*. It is about intangibles too – about art, experience, emotional gratification, education, image . . . All these are chased with the same voracity as Rolex, Sunseeker and Ferrari. The jailed media tycoon Conrad Black did not want to be seen as just rich and powerful – he wanted to be *clever*. Nothing in Britain is more socially divisive than the school you went to. In 2006 a survey of the Conservative parliamentary front bench revealed a total of 15 Old Etonians. Where else in the world would this be seen as a failing of the party rather than as an achievement of the school? Where else, too, would grown-up directors of merchant banks, with millions at their fingertips, still want to know where their colleagues learned their Latin? The tribalism of 'school', and the jealousies and reprisals of those beyond the scholastic divide, will be discussed in Chapter 5. For the moment we need only to reflect that here once again, in educational privilege, we see the genetic imperative in full flood – a Severn Bore of selfishness, though excused by 'higher purpose'.

But what higher purpose? For reasons we don't need to be clever to understand, cleverness confers evolutionary advantage. It's what gives *Homo sapiens* its self-aggrandizing name and power over bigger, nimbler and swifter species. It crucially enhances the likelihood of one person becoming richer, living longer or having more and healthier children than another. It is essential to our development as individuals, and as a species. We want cleverness for ourselves and, more importantly, we want it – lots and lots of it – for those in whom we have planted our genes. Is there any creature on the planet more boastful than the parent of a talented child?

As with material wealth, we tend to exaggerate our intellectual gifts and like to show them off. As with material wealth, too, it's not just the have-nots who puff themselves up. See, for example, the high-minded 'books of the year' round-ups that dominate the review pages at Christmas. What distinguished contributor ever admits to sharing the taste of the common reader? Best-sellerdom is intellectual bling, a gold medallion nestling in the chest-hair of the mind. Credibility rests instead on drily-written literary or political biography (with bonus points for obscurity), academic history, philosophy, global economics and anything attacking Richard Dawkins. Others in the wider world must content themselves with merely looking the part. At a performance of Benjamin Britten's *Albert Herring*, my wife observed that all the men in the audience had 'intelligent hair' – by which she meant vaguely Byronic, not recently cut and implicitly neglected by people with better things to think about. Bookishness is a 'look' too. It's not by accident that so many women at literary festivals come dressed as late-period Iris Murdoch. Look at us, they say. We may not be sexy, and we may not be rich, but look at the size of our *brains*. Men do it too. One I know, an author of literary repute, will not wear a shirt in public until it has started to fray (he has a vast collection, which he rotates). Another handed his barber a portrait of Samuel Beckett: 'Make me look like that.' Another with perfect eyesight wears plain-glass spectacles in the style of T. S. Eliot. Elsewhere, people falsify their degrees or flaunt phoney qualifications bought on the internet. Only Tim Kasser's intrinsically motivated paragon of self-gratification knows no desire for the admiration of others. But then the Kasser paragon is a theoretical construct untroubled by the realities of actual existence.

Greed makes of us what we are, and what we are not. It turns us into predators and victims, criminals and fools. It exposes us to scams, hopeless investments and the lacerating follies of betting shop, casino and credit card. Before the credit crunch, consumer debt in the UK was going up by £1m every four minutes. Families owe the lending industry an average of £47,000 each, of which £8,800 is unsecured. If you want a definition of institutional madness, then this is it. *By the summer of 2007, consumer debt in the UK stood at £1,345bn – £15bn more than the gross national product.* Various words may be used to describe this. 'Sustainable' is not one of them; nor is 'fun'. Eighty per cent of the population confesses to overspending and debt-related stress. The collapse of the American sub-prime mortgage market in 2007 (the not altogether surprising outcome of banks lending money to people who couldn't afford to pay it back) threw the world financial juggernaut into a speed-wobble, with the occupants of the driving seat not knowing whether to brake, accelerate or yank the wheel. In scenes reminiscent of the Depression, investors in British cities jostled to take their money out of a cash-strapped bank, Northern Rock. Yet Christmas came, and economists emerged from the madhouse to warn us that the ensuing crunch would hurt the economy, and that banks were losing a chance to 'drive up customer lifetime values'. (By which of course they meant the lifetime value of the customer to the *bank* – how much they could milk him for before his executors inherited the debt, not how they could enhance his own security and happiness.) As one of them helpfully explained: less credit means less consumer spending, and less consumer spending means economic downturn. We have a patriotic duty to live beyond our means.

The 'slippery-slope' argument, popularized by Victorian moralists and echoed by prohibitionists ever since, has little connection with reality. A sip of sherry does not an alcoholic make. A puff of cannabis does not mean heroin addiction; smacking a child does not lead to murder; admiring a pin-up is not the inevitable precursor of rape. But never mind. These are matters of degree, hedged with common sense, and we understand the dangers. No one tells us that too much drink or drugs is good for our health, or that non-consensual sex is our right and duty. Financial incontinence, however, navigates by a different compass. Mortgage companies before they caught a cold were routinely lending *five times* a borrower's salary, and up to 110 per cent of the value of a property. The pressure to borrow – for cars, holidays, sofas, new bathrooms and kitchens, even to pay off existing debts – was remorseless. Banks I'd never heard of wrote to offer me credit. Call centres on the Indian sub-continent telephoned unbidden to offer some unspecified service connected to some unsecured loan they were convinced I must have. 'Debt consolidation' companies stalked those who had exhausted their credit, and the Blair government convinced itself that the best medicine for a depressed local economy was a casino. Well, hey, you want to bet?

In the pay-whenever, shit-or-bust desperation of a debt-powered economy, gambling seems less a perversion of the consumer ethic than one of its essential organs. Nottingham Trent University has a 'Betting Research Unit', which in 2006 declared that a deregulated and expanded gambling industry could 'only be good news for the economy'. A parliamentary committee already had been told that greater freedom for gaming would 'increase net output by up to £8bn pa, create more than 100,000 new jobs and generate an additional £3bn pa in tax revenue to the Exchequer'. The predictable howl went up from the primitives in the backwoods. The Salvation Army foresaw 'huge social costs' and a likely rise in the number of 'problem gamblers' (of which it said there were already 370,000); the Mothers' Union declared that 'the social good should not be compromised for the economic benefits'; the Royal College of Psychiatrists warned that allowing casinos to advertise would 'inevitably lead to more gambling' (well of course – what else is advertising for?) and that 'health warnings' on gambling would be no more effective than those on tobacco and alcohol. All such risk-averse wusses were swept aside. The Betting Research Unit's director, Professor Leighton Vaughan Williams, put it winningly: 'I'm not a sociologist, I'm not a psychologist, I'm not a moralist, I don't come from that moral philosophy background. I'm an economist . . .' Well, who'd have thought it?

One of the benefits claimed for the Gambling Act (which came into force in September 2007) was that a new permissive climate would help to wrest the betting and gaming industries away from their long-term dancing partners in the criminal underworld. We don't yet have the benefit of an economist's justification for crime, but no doubt one could be found. Stolen property is sold on; money laundered and fed back into the regular economy; stuff replaced by the insurance industry; premiums raised and insurance companies' investment portfolios fattened to the wider benefit of the stock market. Bring on the swag! In 2004, the UK criminal economy (not including Scotland) was valued at £18bn, or 2 per cent of GDP, which is no one's idea of chicken feed. A survey in the same year revealed that one in seven people (one in five in the North and Scotland) knew of at least one person who made their living from crime. I can find no equivalent figure for the USA, but would be surprised if it were very much different. Most of these publicly visible crooks are small-fry – manual labourers of the crime trade, engaged in petty acts of theft and violence, often to finance a drug habit. They do not supply many candidates for *Mastermind*, and count as bloody nuisances rather than threats to the global economy. But criminals, too, have hier-archies. There are street traders, retailers, middle-men, wholesalers and (if you stretch the definition a bit) primary pro-ducers. There are also, in the worlds of law, finance, information technology and politics, individuals of high intelligence with both the means and the inclination to exploit their position.

Fraud worldwide is a growth industry whose practitioners – the executive officers of crime – blend into their professional backgrounds, invisible to the naked eye. In October 2007, the multinational financial services conglomerate Pricewaterhouse-Coopers published research showing that half of all companies worldwide had been victims of economic crime in the previous two years, that the average annual loss to each one was 2.4m dollars, and that 80 per cent of them had suffered 'collateral damage' – reduced share price, loss of public confidence and staff morale. And this is just the stuff we know about. Criminals don't advertise themselves, or register their results at Companies House. Only the failures who get caught reveal the full extent of their activities. The clever ones flit like vampires in the dark. We don't even know how much blood we've lost, still less how to get it back.

In truth it has always been like that. Most gangland profit – not just the sophisticated portion tucked up in offshore bank accounts – has been as hard for the authorities to lay their hands on as a greased pig in a bath of lard. Buying 'legitimate' goods with the proceeds of crime was the easiest kind of money-laundering – a simple scam which allowed millionaire fraudsters, robbers, drug-dealers, counterfeiters and pimps to leave prison by Rolls Royce. The sight of them rolling in caviar, bling and blondes, two fingers to the world, grated on the British police and government like grit under an eyelid. The result in 2002 was the Proceeds of Crime Act (POCA), which gave law enforcement agencies (Customs and Excise, local authorities, trading standards officers and others, as well as the police) the right to freeze offenders' assets and pursue them for the value of what policemen still cannot resist calling their 'ill-gotten gains'. Under POCA, crime *would* pay, but the beneficiary would be the public purse, not the underworld's Mr Bigs in their sunny hideaways. In future the game would be played on a tilted pitch with Crime City playing uphill and defending a much bigger goal. Suspicion alone would be enough to freeze an offender's property and bank accounts, and the civil courts' 'balance of probability' (rather than the more stringent 'beyond reasonable doubt' required by the criminal justice system) would be the test for confiscating them.

On the face of it, law officers in the UK now have the power of medieval royal commissioners. If police or customs find £1,000 or more in cash, cheques or bonds, and believe it is either the wages of crime or likely to be invested in criminal activity, then they can simply seize it. They don't have to prove an offence has been committed – it is up to the 'owner' to prove the legitimacy of his money – though they do have to get approval from magistrates within 48 hours. Crown courts can also restrain suspects from selling or gifting their property before they are brought to trial, and after conviction they can confiscate a sum equivalent to the criminals' profit. This often means the enforced sale of houses, cars, jewellery, racehorses and other 'ill-gotten gains' bought with dirty money. It sounds like a runaway winner – a vast brantub of billionaires' baubles for the state to run its fingers through, and 'free' money to reinvest in the fight against crime. Yet POCA got off to a slow start. Even the police seemed unaware of, or reluctant to use, their new powers, and in 2007 the Assets Recovery Agency (the body initially set up to lead the hunt, subsequently merged with the Serious Organised Crime Agency) was criticized by the National Audit Office for spending £65m to recover £23m. In 2006–7, the total amount secured under POCA was just £125.04m, which, as a proportion of an £18bn criminal economy, was not going to leave many gang bosses wondering where their next Spanish villa was coming from.

Neither was there much joy in the crime figures. The overall numbers of vehicle-related thefts and burglaries were almost exactly what they'd been 25 years earlier. The inescapable conclusion was that, for all the brave talk and high-noon appointments with vengeance, POCA had about as much effect on criminal behaviour as global warming and the price of cocoa. The fact is, you can threaten offenders with anything you like –

stoning, flaying, thumbscrews, exile to Iowa – but it won't be worth the price of a prison breakfast unless you can catch them. It's not the threat of punishment that deters them, any more than appeals to their better nature; it's the risk of discovery. If arrest were inevitable, then there would be no crime at all. For those in full possession of their wits – ie the Messrs Big – criminality is a business calculation like any other, potential gain weighed against chance of loss. The criminal investor works out the odds and concludes that, yup, all things considered, the timeshare scam or bale of fake Mickey Mouse pyjamas is a risk worth taking. At street level, of course, the drug-fuddled impulse criminals, desperate for a fix and with nothing to lose, are beyond any kind of reasoning whatsoever. Show them a crime and they'll commit it.

Fans of POCA nevertheless insist that the criminal economy is like a poisoned rat, trapped by its own greed and condemned slowly to bleed to death. I spoke to an English chief constable who likened POCA to DNA testing – a novel technique that took time to catch on but was now central to every criminal investigation. Policemen were learning to use their eyes, he said – to notice any mismatch between lifestyle and income, and to understand the power that POCA gave them to be nosey. The result, he said, was that criminals no longer dared to live so flamboyantly – 'They are driving around in five-year-old cars and taking their children out of private school' – which on its own was a powerful corrective. 'If you can't benefit from your criminal assets,' he said, 'then what's the point of acquiring them in the first place?'

Oddly, he begins to sound like Tim Kasser. Rephrase the question only slightly – 'If your possessions give you no pleasure, then what's the point of having them?' – and we're right back to the conundrum with which we began. People have different opinions about what is legal, decent and honest. As we shall see, the stock defence of exploitative behaviour by governments and corporations is that they contravene no law, though the basic

impulse – to separate other people from their cash or property –
is not easy to distinguish from Mr Big's. In the credit economy we
are like riders on the Wall of Death, held above the void by speed
alone. If we slow down, we crash. There is no safety net. This is
not an image that would have meant anything to Charles
Dickens, but he still would recognize all too clearly the brutality
of money. The state takes away criminals' homes. The banks do
exactly the same to families they have lured into unaffordable
mortgages. We don't have debtors' prisons any more, but the
stigma – of the criminal and the economically dispossessed –
remains much as it was when Dickens's father was imprisoned for
debt in the Marshalsea, and Dickens himself wrote *Little Dorrit*.

For ourselves, the only justification necessary for owning something seems to be that we can afford it, and we are condemned to
want what we cannot have. Within myself, I can see no remedy.
Like you, I am intrinsically selfish and define my portion by how
much I can pile on my plate. There is something deeper in our
natures than our brains can tear us away from. Kasser advocates
advertising bans, and community ownership of property whose
benefits might be shared – tools, for example, and books. Who
can say he is wrong? How can we answer anyone who tells us we
are consuming more than the planet can bear? How can we
silence the voice that whispers 'More!', or restrain the worm of
avarice we carry in our brains from infecting the workings
of every institution on the planet, from flower girl to global
corporation?

It is the week before Christmas. The postman calls, and I sign
for yet another parcel containing yet another gift which, despite
my loathing of the season, I hope I shall enjoy – a gift for which
I must show gratitude but which I know I do not need. I try to
feel guilty, but the worm will have its way. There is a bottle of
Montrachet in there, and I'm only human.

Part Two

Kinsfolk

5

Blood Brothers

A few years ago I was asked to make up the numbers in a cricket match. It was played on a village green between teams raised by two local businessmen who had known each other since they were boys. Team selections were prioritized as follows: first the two captains chose themselves (opening batsmen both); then came their oldest friends; then their sons; then their friends' sons; then as many of their neighbours as they needed to make up the 22, plus two umpires and a scorer. When the day came, the locals trawled their wardrobes for items of pale clothing – white shirt and chinos in my case – which from a distance wouldn't look too unlike cricket gear. The captains, their friends and sons came dressed for Fenner's: immaculate whites, proper cricket sweaters with banded trim, blancoed boots and hooped caps. They knew the names of all the field positions, and of all the strokes of the bat. Though they had travelled from different parts of the country, they also seemed to know each other. The caps, the colours, the similarity in the older men's ages, the chiselled vowels – all marked them down for what they were. Old schoolfriends. This was a tribal reunion marked by the tribal rituals of spin and swing, 'Well played, sir,' and tea.

The word 'school' in England, when spoken with a particular intonation – hard to describe but impossible to mistake when you hear it – does not just mean any old place of learning. It means 'public school' – a term which, to the eternal confusion of Americans, actually means 'private school', currently available only to parents who can afford uphill of £20,000 per pupil-year. Free education for the bulk of the population is provided in 'state schools'. Public schools tend to occupy grand old buildings in sumptuous grounds. They have their own chapels, theatres, swimming pools, shooting ranges, all-weather sports pitches, art and music blocks, combined cadet forces, libraries, dormitories and every kind of technical and electronic teaching aid that wealth can buy. Pupils are taught in small groups – 15 is typical – by well-rewarded staff who generally have had the benefit of private education themselves. Sons in particular often enter not just the same schools as their fathers, but even the same boarding houses.

State schools are not like this. Their shortcomings, in terms of teaching quality, class sizes (30-plus), educational output, extra-curricular activities, buildings, facilities and discipline, are a regular source of lurid headlines in British newspapers. The problems are often exaggerated. There are good state schools as well as bad, and bad public schools as well as good. But what cannot be exaggerated is the width of the gulf between the two systems, and the tensions it creates. Our afternoon's cricket concluded amicably. The Old Boys were kind to the villagers, and appreciative of their efforts with bat and ball, but there was no concealing the picket fence between Them and Us.

Not all confrontations are as pleasant. I have heard public schoolboys deride as 'chavs' all those not similarly privileged. More often, I have heard state-schoolers conflate 'privilege' with gormlessness, as if intelligence and money could only ever have existed on opposing gradients. This effort, posted on his weblog by the Labour MP Austin Mitchell, is typical: 'People don't want paternalism but involvement, and for all, not just the pushy middle classes. They don't look up to public school twits any longer. Imperialism is dead and they want a more equal society, not one characterized by class and privilege.'

The words 'public school' or 'upper class' seldom appear in effusions of this kind unaccompanied by 'twit'. Mitchell breaks tradition only by failing to precede it with 'chinless'. All it takes to satirize such people is a funny hyphenated name – the Harry Enfield character Tim Nice-But-Dim, for example, or Oliver St John-Mollusc in *Monty Python*'s 'Upper Class Twit of the Year' sketch. The plebs get their share, too. In the US, think Homer Simpson; in the UK, Vicky Pollard. But it's a bit like the Jewish joke – all very well when told by Jews against themselves, but offensive when it comes from others. Hence the sphincter-lipped moo of outrage in the summer of 2007 when pupils at one of Scotland's most expensive boarding schools, Glenalmond College (£23,000 a year), posted on YouTube a spoof video showing 'chavs' being hunted like foxes. Somehow that wasn't amusing. But, then, how funny was this effort from the *Guardian*, in its preview of a television documentary called *Who Killed the Playboy Earl?*

> Had Anthony Ashley-Cooper been born on a different kind of estate – council rather than stately home – the last years of his life, during which he squandered his money on drugs and prostitutes, would likely be viewed as feckless. As he was the 10th Earl of Shaftesbury, his squalid descent, which ended with his murder, is imbued with a tragic air that it doesn't warrant. That said, posh people are more interesting when they're dead, so it's not a complete waste of time.

The loyalties and enmities that churn in the guts of the English class system are a prime example of the 'herd instinct' – the tendency of people with shared interests or common backgrounds to look out for each other and turn against a common enemy. It's another of those things we have always known but which only recently have been given a scientific label. Understanding the herd instincts of other species helped our early ancestors first to hunt, and then to farm. Understanding those of their own species has informed the oratory of prophets, politicians and dictators in every age since grunts first turned into syllables. The term was popularized, if not actually invented, by the royal surgeon of King George V, Wilfred Trotter, who combined surgery with social psychology and in 1914 published an influential book, *The Instincts of the Herd in Peace and War*, in which he argued that men and beasts were instinctively gregarious and could function effectively only through interaction with their fellows. In this he was following a path trodden more or less unconsciously by everyone who had ever lived (for that is the nature of 'instinct'), and more knowingly by the French social psychologist Gustave Le Bon (1841–1931), who made a particular study of crowd behaviour. I offer the following quotation, from his masterwork *The Crowd, a Study of the Popular Mind* (1896), for amusement only:

> It will be remarked that among the special characteristics of crowds there are several – such as impulsiveness, irritability, incapacity to reason, the absence of judgement and of the critical spirit, the exaggeration of the sentiments, and others besides – which are almost always observed in beings belonging to inferior forms of evolution – in women, savages and children . . . Crowds are everywhere distinguished by feminine characteristics, but Latin crowds are the most feminine of all.

One wonders how that would go down with the Oxford Union. What we know from examples in every culture across the world is that crowds collectively *can* behave very differently from the way their members do individually. We see extremes of cruelty, extremes of emotion and extremes of expectation. Le Bon thought (and for a long time he was believed) that members of crowds surrendered their individuality, abandoned responsibility and became homogeneous units in irrational, primitive and violent mobs. His theory was a favourite of what used to be called the 'ruling classes', for whom any kind of popular gathering was a threat. There are places in the world today where the instinct of those in power is to break up crowds with teargas, high-pressure hoses and baton charges. Yet we have all been in crowds, and we know that Le Bon was wrong: not all crowds are alike. We see in them also extremes of good humour and fellowship. Even hostile crowds retain their diversity – militant radicals, for example, can be found marching alongside pacifists – which those with an intelligent interest in 'crowd control' now understand and exploit. (The trick for police is to isolate troublemakers without inflaming the peaceful majority.) Crowds do behave differently, yes. At their worst they can be manipulated, inflamed and led into trouble. But that is true of individuals too. It is not the norm, and it does not mean, *pace* Le Bon, that by joining a crowd we unplug our brains. Associating with others – not just in mass gatherings but in societies, trade unions, clubs, political parties, professional bodies, sports teams, campaign groups, pubs, schools, churches, extended families – is human nature. We may be less or more gregarious but we all need *something* to belong to. Like animals we seek protection, and find comfort, in groups. But unlike animals, members of human herds keep their identity even when they are dispersed.

In its innocent and mildly bucolic way, the cricket match was a perfect example of the way group loyalties work. Ourselves and/or families come first; then our friends; then our friends' families; then widening circles of acquaintance, common interest and territory. The tightest circle is parent and child. The widest, should it ever come to intergalactic warfare, would be the human race. From each band, proportionate to its distance from the centre, we expect co-operation and reward. Up close and personal, this might be the intimate benefits of sexual partnership. At a distance it might be the social support of the state to which we have paid our taxes. There are relationships for which we would sacrifice our lives; others for which we might sign a petition, write a cheque, vote, or just argue in the pub. In Chapter 1 we traced the genetic roots of altruism. 'The unconscious question an organism puts to itself before helping another is: what's in it for my genes?' Which of course translates in the conscious mind as 'What's in it for me?'

Another way to describe this kind of altruism might be 'reciprocity'. My animal behaviour primer (*Essentials of Animal Behaviour*, by P. J. B. Slater) offers the example of two jackals killing a gazelle – a feat which neither could perform alone, but from which both benefit. The advantage of altruistic behaviour in this case is obvious and immediate. Both help the other get a feed, and both get a feed themselves. Slater then offers the more interesting example of the vampire bat. As everyone knows, these uncuddlesome creatures live on mammalian blood, which they extract from their victims in the dark, often spreading rabies as they go. But there is honour among bats. If an individual fails to find a blood-victim in the night, then another will regurgitate part of its own meal to tide it over. The recipient may then be expected to repay the favour in future. As it is improbable that vampire bats have highly developed powers of reasoning, it must be assumed that this altruistic behaviour is innate and that it has arisen through natural selection. Bats with a 'co-operation gene' live longer, and produce more young, than uncooperative loners. Both are driven by self-interest, but it's the reciprocator that rides the gravy train. There are many other examples of co-operative behaviour in nature – ants, wolves, lions, bees, migrating wilde-beest – but they need not be dwelled upon. We get the point, and see the parallels in our own lives.

Almost everything we do relies upon reciprocity, the grand-motherly virtue of do-as-you-would-be-done-by. Reciprocal altruism, says Slater, 'is obviously a very important phenomenon in humans, for many of our relationships are based upon kindnesses which, while they may run in one direction in the short term, balance out in the long run'. I'd say it goes beyond that. What are industry and commerce if not networks of reciprocity? What is a redistributive tax system if not a vampire-style blood-sharing arrangement? What we invest in the common weal, we hope to recoup as individuals – education for our children; an ambulance, doctor or policeman whenever we need one; a pension; roads to drive on; protection from enemies; a constant supply of fresh water; drains and sewerage; waste collection. This is why politicians in their manifestos play their policy cards both ways up. They advertise their social commitment and sense of corporate responsibility, but emphasize the benefit to the individual. 'You're better off under the Reciprocity Party' is the model election slogan. 'You've never had it so good,' the Conservative prime minister Harold Macmillan famously told the nation in 1957. Ten years later, when his government had to devalue the pound, Labour's Harold Wilson knew exactly where voters' interests lay. Though sterling was worth 14 per cent less against other currencies abroad, he insisted that 'the pound in your pocket' had lost none of its purchasing power at home. Cunning is the basic propellant of political careers. They flatter us by appealing to our better natures, then buy our votes with tax cuts.

As a result, our lives are complicated networks of interlocking but occasionally conflicting allegiances – to people, causes, ideologies, employers, localities and many, many more – from which, one way or another, we expect to receive benefit. It makes sectarians of us all. We welcome anything that will enrich or improve the lives of a group to which we belong, or with which we identify, and resist anything that threatens them. This of course aligns us in opposition to other groups who may lose what we gain. Clever children sent to independent schools deny vital talent (and the influence of those pushy middle-class parents) to the state. Promotions for men are glass ceilings for women. Homes for the poor are eyesores for the rich. 'Privilege' when enjoyed by others is a festering eruption of inequity and greed. When claimed by ourselves it is a 'right'.

The cricket finished with a big-house supper that everyone enjoyed. English rural communities have lived with social divisions ever since tribal chieftains first carved out their hierarchies with axe and sword. Mostly they find nothing in them to take exception to, and the fault lines are between 'old' and 'new' villagers rather than rich and poor. This is why the Conservative Party, traditionally the landowner's champion, does so well in rural constituencies. Twenty-first-century *realpolitik* obliges its leaders to sound progressive. 'In a world where our economy is richer but our society is poorer,' they say, 'we must recognize that we're all in this together and not allow anyone to be left behind.' In deep countryside, however, you don't hear that kind of talk from the people who rattle the tins. They pledge rather to 'keep out undesirables'. When I spoke at a conference for the Campaign to Protect Rural England (CPRE), I was astonished by the delegates' obsession with immigration, an issue which seemed to worry them far more than rural unemployment, loss of village post offices or urban creep.

The Labour Party, with its roots in towns and cities, is very different. Handbag wars notwithstanding, it is hot to trot on freedom and choice, including the right for people to spend their money as they choose – a right explicitly proclaimed by Hazel Blears in support of her Orla Kiely. Spending it as they choose, however, is not the same as spending it with the party's blessing. For all the sharp suits and silver tongues of the Blair era, the old class divisions still gape like unstitched wounds. Austin Mitchell's populist squib, quoted earlier, contained a lot more of the party's bone and sinew than Gordon Brown's Orwellesque 'choice agenda'. In May 2000, as the parties measured their run-up to the 2001 election, Brown, then chancellor of the exchequer, hurled himself like a dyspeptic bear against what he saw as the principal avatar of educational privilege, Oxford University. A northern state-school girl with an unsurpassable exam record had applied for a place to study medicine at Magdalen College, which had interviewed and then rejected her. In a phrase popular at the time, Brown 'went ballistic'.

The girl, he said, 'had the best A-level qualifications you can have', and she had been spat out by 'an interview system more reminiscent of an old-boy network and the old school tie than genuine justice for society . . . It is about time we had an end to the old Britain, where all that matters is the privileges you were born with, rather than the potential you actually have . . . It is about time that these old universities opened their doors to women and people from all backgrounds.' As Brown remained one of the few members of the Blair government capable of uttering the word 'socialism' without irony, it was no surprise to see him pawing the turf for a bit of old-fashioned class warfare. It had all the right ingredients – plucky working-class heroine, a cruel aristocracy united against the peasantry, and a redoubtable champion ready to fight for justice. Cinderella, the Ugly Sisters and Prince Charming were all in place. The plot was written. It just remained for an admiring public to enjoy the *dénouement*.

Alas, the one thing the story lacked was accuracy. The girl did not possess 'the best A-level qualifications you can have'. She had not even taken her A-levels. What she did have was ten top (A*) grades at GCSE, but so did all the other 22 candidates for the five places that were available. Neither was it true that she had been blocked by a toff-heavy interview system. In fact it was in the interview section of the admissions process that she had performed best. It was in the written test, the test of observational skills and 'structured discussion', that she had fallen short. Only one charge remained unanswered – that Oxford had closed its doors against 'women and people from all backgrounds'.

'Yet,' said the college president, 'of the five successful candidates, three are women, three are from ethnic minorities and two are from comprehensives.' All this Brown must have known but ignored. He ignored also the fact that independent schools are not the preserve of chinless blue-bloods surfing on inherited wealth. Many parents are working people who have had to mortgage or sell their homes to raise the fees, and who value their children's education ahead of big houses, new cars or Caribbean holidays. I confess to having made this choice myself – not willingly (for who would pay for what they can have free?), but rather because, in the London district where I then lived, the state school system was in the hands of social engineers more interested in political indoctrination than in reading and writing. When I questioned the low standard of literacy and numeracy in my sons' primary school, I was accused of 'white middle-class prejudice'. In industry it would have been called constructive dismissal.

Not all middle-class parents send their children to fee-paying schools. Some prefer to move house and settle within the catchments of the better state schools. This inflates property prices, which makes the areas too expensive for poorer families to live in and effectively keeps their children out of the best classrooms. Middle-class parents are more able to help their children in other ways, too, being more likely to involve themselves in a school's affairs and thus to influence its policies. This, too, the government is determined to stop. Where schools are over-subscribed, it will end the practice of favouring those who live closest. Instead there will be lotteries, allocating places by chance. This is one of many filters being put in place to slow the tide of 'privilege'. Head teachers, for example, may no longer ask parents why they have chosen a particular school (it would place non-English speakers at a disadvantage). Neither may they see children's birth certificates (which might reveal the parents' professions) or ask parents if they support the school's ethos (it could be 'patronizing' to the poorly educated). Members of the Conservative Party meanwhile were infuriated when their leader withdrew his support for selective grammar schools.

Such are the reverberations of the British class structure, like aftershocks from a baronial past, within which 'belonging' to one group means 'not belonging' to another, and in which school-children and students are roped to the barricades. It could be argued that, with the middle classes now having expanded to include everyone with a credit card to their name, the social pyramid in the early 21st century is a lot flatter than it was at the beginning of the 20th. This may be so, but it still shrinks like a cheap Christmas tree to an etiolated stem, at the tip of which, in the fairy position, is the 'House of Windsor', formerly the Saxe-Coburg-Gothas, with their iron-clad sense of self-worth. I noted in Chapter 1 the peculiar, involuntary grovelling this family inspires in its 'subjects'. But we must notice also the complicity of the grovellees. What kind of people allow themselves to be called 'Majesty', or 'Highness'? Where on the scale of greed does acceptance of worship lie? Who with a grain of modesty or self-awareness could bear to be *bowed* to, and feel no need to return the courtesy? In a supposed meritocracy – a secular state in which war has been declared on privilege – reverence for 'high birth' makes no more sense than faith in witch-doctors, or Scientology. We cannot have it both ways. Cannot simultaneously abhor privilege and celebrate it with fanfares and hosannas. If the Queen is the crowned head, then the old-fashioned, land-based class system is the body, and the landless multitude are the knees and elbows. Here is the first paragraph of an article on 'precedence' by the editor of *Burke's Peerage and Baronetage*:

Precedence concerns itself with such matters as the order in which people go in to dinner, leave the dinner table, march in procession (though here people usually move in reverse order of precedence, the least to the fore, the most important to the rear), are announced at gatherings or are listed in an official description of some ceremonial function. But there are various tables of precedence: social, official, political, local, ecclesiastical, legal, military.

In other words it's all about knowing your place and sticking to it. The five ranks of the English peerage are duke, marquess, earl, viscount and baron. Behind them come the 'county' families, owners of lands and hyphens, with their connections in the City, the armed forces, politics and the law (the list once would have included the church but the priesthood now is for other ranks). Then come the rest of us, our standing delineated in myriad ways from vowel sounds to the ferocity of our dogs. The sheer illogic of it – meritocracy and privilege saluting the same flag, and God Save the Queen – seems peculiarly and exclusively English. But America is not so different. It might not have five ranks of peerage, but it's still pretty clear about who walks into dinner first. The eight private universities that make up the Ivy League – Brown, Cornell, Columbia, Harvard, Yale, Princeton, Pennsylvania and Dartmouth – are in the high social latitudes of the north-east and need no lessons in exclusivity from Oxbridge (though Harvard did award a scholarship to Gordon Brown's Oxford reject). Cornell's motto, 'I would found an institution where any person can find instruction in any study' (the words of its founder, the eponymous Ezra), looks like the punchline of a joke.

In a despatch to the BBC World Service the Pulitzer-winning *New York Times* reporter Tim Egan described his daughter's attempt to win a place at the Ivies' west-coast rival, Stanford. It's hard to imagine American politics throwing up anyone like Gordon Brown, or any holder of high office railing at the education system that created them. If they did, they would have plenty to aim at. For many of those heading towards the upper strata of US business and politics, the *where* of their university degree is more important than the *what*, and you can no more eliminate elitism than you can stamp out the cockroach. As the number of high-earning manual jobs is reduced, so the white-collar market becomes the only avenue of self-improvement and a university degree the essential ticket of entry. With a dash of

Blairite glibness (the former prime minister famously wanted 50 per cent of British young people to be university-educated), this can be made to sound like blue-sky liberalism – degrees and opportunities for all.

In reality, because Ivy League and Oxbridge places do not increase with demand, it creates an ever more rarefied pinnacle of exclusivity. 'A generation ago,' said Tim Egan, 'Harvard University accepted 20 per cent of its applicants. That figure has been cut in half, so now about 90 per cent of students who apply to Harvard do not get in. And these rejected kids are not slouches. These rejected kids would have been the valedictorians, the class presidents, of 25 years ago.' And this is not just the cutting edge of a tough but fair meritocracy.

> Virtually every elite college [said Egan] has a legacy system. This is the tradition by which people with average grades, but crucially with money and family ties to the school, are accepted ahead of the smart kids with no connections. George Bush, the famous C student, was a legacy at Yale, though he says now that he opposes the legacy system. Usually up to 15 per cent of all admissions in the medallion [elite] schools are legacies. And who said America doesn't have an encrusted aristocracy?

Even more than their Oxbridge cousins, the Ivy Leaguers are the top layer of a social *millefeuille*. On average, degree-holders in America now earn 45 per cent more than non-graduates, a margin that has doubled in 25 years. Sixty per cent of those without degrees end up as burger-flippers or in other dead-end jobs in the service industries. Many of them are blacks and Hispanics, but nearly half the American poor are white – a fact which, in the land of infinite possibility, counts almost as an insult to the flag and which attracts even more derogatory epithets than the racial minority groups. Such men and women are traitors to their pigmentation – *white trash, trailer-trash, hicks, clay-eaters, rednecks . . .*

The US might not share the UK's medieval overhang of dukes and princes, but its class divisions are no less rigid (if you wanted to give snobbery an enema, then the Augusta National Golf Club surely is where you would insert the tube). A rape charge in North Carolina, involving people no one had heard of, would not normally cross the Atlantic as hot news. The exception was the 'lacrosse case' of 2006, when three students from Duke University, in the racially mixed city of Durham, were accused of offences against an 'exotic dancer' who had been hired to entertain them at a party. What catapulted it into the headlines was not the particular horror of the alleged offences (worse happens every day), but the spicy aromas of race and class. Duke is a 40,000-dollars-a-year elite college, named by *The Times Higher Educational Supplement* as the '13th overall best university in the world'. The three accused were wealthy white males, whose sport alone – lacrosse! – was enough to set them apart, and whose team had a reputation for the sort of boorish behaviour which, in England, would have labelled them 'hooray Henrys'. Their accuser was a poor, black, single mother of two. She said the three players had dragged her into a bathroom where they had kicked, strangled and raped her. The story was like the agenda from a Hollywood script conference. Rich versus poor, white versus black, north versus south (the men were from the rich north-east), privileged college athletes versus common decency, and all with the reek of sex and violence. News teams swarmed into Durham like flies to a corpse. Attitudes formed and hardened; the world was united in loathing not just of the rapists but of the entire system that had spawned them. The man at the centre of it all was the Durham district attorney, Michael Nifong. 'I would like to think,' he said, 'that somebody who was not in the bathroom has the human decency to call up and say, "What am I doing covering up for a bunch of hooligans?" I'd like to be able to think that there were some people in that house that were not involved in this and were as horrified by it as the rest of us are.'

The American media caught his tone precisely. 'Lax Environment; Duke lacrosse scandal reinforces a growing sense that college sports are out of control, fueled by pampered athletes with a sense of entitlement', said a headline in the *Los Angeles Times*. 'The racially charged lacrosse team sexual assault scandal that is roiling Duke University,' said *USA Today*, 'has also exposed deep divisions between the elite private school and the more humble Tobacco Road community that surrounds it.' Across the Atlantic, the UK's *Sunday Telegraph* took the same line. 'University rape highlights racial divisions in the South', said its headline.

This was truer even than it looked. Social divides in the USA are so deep and wide that there was little sympathy for the Duke Three even when the charges against them were dropped (photographic, telephonic and DNA evidence showed that the accuser's many different versions of her story were all false), and the district attorney was dismissed for 'intentional prosecutorial misconduct'. 'Three members of the Duke lacrosse team may have been louts,' said the *Boston Globe*, 'but all the evidence suggests they were not rapists.' Even this was generous when compared with the *Washington Post* sports writer John Feinstein, who told the *Jim Rome Show* (a widely syndicated sports talk programme on American radio): 'I think they're guilty of everything but rape'; and the *Chicago Tribune* columnist Philip Hersh: 'The idea that the Duke lacrosse team's success is a feel-good story makes me ill . . . it would be a bigger mistake to believe [the acquittal] means Duke's lacrosse team was innocent of assault against common decency.' They had, after all, hired strippers. They had a history of under-age drinking, and one of them (not one of the accused) before the party had sent his team-mates an anticipatory email of shockingly violent obscenity. 'Innocent until proven guilty' is the cornerstone of American jurisprudence, the hallmark of its decency. Yet here, in the teeth of all they were supposed to uphold, people seemed to feel no pride in a system that had delivered justice. Rather, they felt cheated of victory over a tribal enemy.

Tribalism in its literal sense remains the curse of Africa, where it inspires murderous rivalries – Hutu against Tutsi in Rwanda, for example; or more recently Kikuyu against Luo in Kenya. Tribal and political loyalties often are indivisible. In the developed world most of us have little idea of our tribal origins. On a map of Romano-Britain, for example, we can see how the Celtic tribes once divided the turf – from the Dumnonii in the far south-west of England to the Brigantes in the far north-east – but it contributes nothing to our conscious self-image. What difference does it make that I was born in the territory of the Catuvellauni, moved to the Cantiaci and now live among the Iceni? Neither do I identify specifically with any of the subsequent influxes – Anglo-Saxons, Danes, Normans – whose genes I carry and have passed to my children. In developed countries tribal loyalty now is the culture of the dispossessed – 'native' Americans or Australian Aborigines – who mourn a lost identity. There are relics of it in the UK, where the Welsh fight for their language and Cornish romantics dream of independence for 'Kernow'. Most people, however, are content to describe themselves simply as 'British', and some ultra-sophisticates now even declare themselves to be 'European'.

Yet we still carry within us the primal, ineradicable urge to *belong*, to enjoy the communal benefits and protection of a group. Membership requires loyalty and reciprocity – backs are scratched, allies helped, all for one and one for all. This 'co-operation gene', combined with intelligence, was crucial to the development of human society and accounts for the pre-eminence of our species. If it is more blessed to give than to receive, as Acts 20 in the King James version of the Bible insists, then this is because giving significantly improves our chance of getting something in return. It is how reciprocal altruism works, and some organizations – the Freemasons, for example – exist for no other reason.

But alliances of course arouse the enmity of those not included. 'Either you are with us, or you are with the terrorists,' George W. Bush famously told a joint session of Congress in September 2001. Consciously or otherwise, his speechwriter was recalling Jesus: 'He who is not with me is against me' (Luke 11:23). This is what philosophers call a 'false dilemma' – a rhetorical device popular with preachers and politicians who want us to think that only two options are possible. They get away with it because it plays upon our loyalties. We want our side to win, and the other side to lose.

In categorizing ourselves – by age, income, race, nationality, religion, sexual orientation, politics, intelligence, talent, taste – we necessarily categorize others as non-belongers. The nation state, whose expectation of loyalty is nothing less than a blood debt, is a subject for the next chapter. On a local scale, the new tribalism has more than a few echoes of the old. In the US, the historic enmity between North and South is still smouldering nicely.

> Have you seen how liberals portray the South? It's sickening. They think the entire South is inhabited by KKK buck-toothed idiots who hate everything and kill black people on a regular basis. I live in Georgia, and I know for a fact this portrayal is the most twisted thing I've ever seen. And how would a liberal know? The only thing they've seen outside their home is maybe the bathroom of a gay bar.

This entry from a Republican-leaning blog is a pretty neat summary of the circulating currents of bipolar invective. Southerners are mocked as Bible-bashing rednecks, unsophisticated in everything save the art of seducing their sisters. Northerners are derided as soft-skinned hypocrites who sneer at everything the real America stands for. They rage like divorcing spouses – over which side invented rock and roll, which was the first to abolish slavery, which takes most from the other's taxes, which has the most respect for the Bill of Rights, the biggest banks, the most bigoted comedians, the stupidest accents, the best football teams. All this sounds wearyingly familiar to the English, though their polarities are the other way about. The stereotypical northerner in England is a jobless pigeon-fancier fortified by fags, chips and frothy beer, known to his family as 'Our Stan'. He reads the *Sun* and may sometimes go to the pictures. The southerner is an effete tailor's dummy, girlishly addicted to white wine and known to his family as 'Nigel'. He reads novels and enjoys film.

On both sides of the Atlantic tribal loyalties are most vehemently expressed through sport. All-seater stadiums and operatic seat prices have taken some of the violence out of English soccer, but match days are still not for those of fragile temperament or for champions of Corinthian virtue. *Those who are not with us are against us.* In the 2007–8 season, the best player in the Premier League – some would say the best player anywhere – was a Portuguese winger, Cristiano Ronaldo, of Manchester United. His due reward was to be abused by opposing fans whenever he touched the ball. Modern football crowds need no lessons in brutality from the mobs of the Roman arena. In a televised match repeatedly shown in slow motion, a home-team player sprints at full speed, ignores the ball and drives his studs with maximum force into the shinbone of an opponent. The crowd in the stadium cheers the aggressor as he is sent from the field and jeers the victim when he is helped to his feet. It is commonplace for sportswriters to salute the on-field 'warriors', and for psychologists to identify sport as a substitute for war and a safety valve for aggression. Opponents are not just beaten. They are crushed, murdered, annihilated. Shots on goal are 'fired', not just kicked; cricket and tennis balls are sent down 'like bullets'; team captains 'marshal their troops'. The hyperbole has a long pedigree. It was as practice for hunting, not just for fun, that sport began, and as practice for war that it continued. Hitler's dismay at 'Aryan' defeats in the Berlin Olympics; the win-at-all-costs determination of cold-war Eastern bloc governments to demonstrate their superiority on the running track; the effusions of grief or pride that follow the fortunes of national teams – all these testify to the potency of sportsmen as gladiators in the cause of tribal supremacy.

Once upon a time, back in the cloth-cap era of the 20th century when the UK still depended on its manufacturing industries, football tribes were local. Like the *contrada*s of Siena supporting their riders in the Palio, communities of boys and men were born to the colours – the claret-and-blues, the reds, the Canaries, the Magpies. The players themselves were authentic working-class heroes from the same families that sent their sons to the foundry, factory or pit, and who earned the same kind of wages as the fans who cheered them. When they were too old to play, they opened pubs or cleaned windows. It's different now. As geographical boundaries melt into the global *agora* of screen and keypad, and as populations become both more mobile and more aspirational, so loyalties change. People no longer want a local team; they want a *winning* one. The leading football clubs now are huge businesses, bought and sold internationally and represented on the field by multi-millionaires shipped in from other continents. A locally born player – even an English one – is as much of a novelty as an African might once have been. The only things still local are the name and the postcode.

In January 2007 Manchester United announced post-tax profits of £42m on gross revenue of £245m, making it the richest footballing business in the world. Its shirt sponsorship deal with the insurance corporation AIG (American International Group – according to *Forbes* the sixth largest company in the world) is worth £56.5m over four years from 2006, and in 2007–8 it was charging £836 for season tickets in the upper tiers of the north and south stands. Its marketing operation includes an online 'megastore' selling replica shirts (different kits for home, away and Champions' League matches), leisurewear, watches, jewellery, sports equipment, bedlinen, pyjamas, DVDs, bags and wallets, books and much else besides. It has a thriving hospitality business including a 1,200-seater conference suite, and an online betting service. Through MU Finance it offers mortgages, savings accounts, personal loans and insurance. It has its own sub-scription television channel, MUTV, which shows all its matches throughout the world. You can as easily be a Manchester United fan in Japan as you can in Salford. Like any other kind of busi-ness – cola, insurance, hamburgers – football is becoming polarized. More and more money is being sucked up by a smaller and smaller number of international super-brands, with less and less left for the rest, who are increasingly unable to compete. Manchester United's elite playing corps are the power on the pitch, but the economic feedstock – the *source* of the power – is the economic clout of the club's American owners and the trans-continental army of fans. In February 2008, the committee men of the Premier League caused outrage by suggesting that an extra round of matches between the English clubs should be arranged and played in Asia. The idea failed, but it was no more than a logical extension of a process already under way. Supporters now are like players, a commodity to be traded on the open market. What these new fans are buying into is the kudos of their chosen teams, to be 'us' against 'them' and to crow at the moment of glory. The 'actuality', of having some geographical or other bind-ing connection with one team or another, has nothing to do with it. All that matters is taking sides; having a champion.

Politics is going the same way. The balloons and trumpets of the American primaries, never mind the presidential election itself, have all the dignity of a pre-match warm-up in the NFL. The cheerleaders may not have pompoms to twirl, but they are cheerleaders just the same and ask no more of their supporters than to be whipped up by rousing music and amplified slogans; to boo the other side's fouls and applaud their own. We British, whose smaller budgets and longer history give us a too-easy sense of moral superiority, are apt to look at the American example as something to be avoided. At Sheffield in 1992, the then Labour leader Neil Kinnock's US-style triumphalist rally effectively lost his party the election. In many ways, though, our current example would be even harder than America's for a Martian visitor to understand. At least with Republicans and Democrats you can identify some genuine points of difference – on taxes, the environment, climate change, welfare and war. In England, where Labour and the Conservatives have both slid down the mattress to the same groove in the middle, it looks increasingly like a beauty contest in which expediency replaces conviction and the nicest smile wins. Blair won in 1997 because he looked like a winner and his opponent, John Major, looked like a loser. His party went on winning because it understood the power of fashion and of populism, the importance of playing to the gallery. The trick with this kind of politics is to look to the electoral balance sheet, to ensure that you please more people than you offend. Thus Labour signalled its concern for animal welfare by banning the minority sport of hunting with dogs while ignoring the immeasurably greater scandal of the chicken broiler and battery sheds that produce cheap meat and eggs for the majority. There was a lot of talk about 'the big tent', and of 'the many, not the few'. This is the appeal of a redistributive tax system. Fewer people in the economy earn above the average income than those who earn less, so the flow of wealth from top to bottom always benefits the majority (or, in hard times, disbenefits them least). If finance ministers understand nothing else, they understand this.

Historically, the clearest divide in the electorate was between those who owned the country (in the UK, the Conservatives) and those who worked for it (Labour). You could divide it another way, between those who owned or mortgaged their homes and those who rented them, and you would arrive at pretty much the same two factions. It was Margaret Thatcher who saw a way of breaking down the barrier. By encouraging the tenants of publicly owned council houses to buy their homes on favourable terms, she turned Labour-voting renters into a new generation of property owners who would have every incentive to vote Conservative. Many of them did so, and the result was (a) 18 years of Tory rule and (b) a shortage of affordable housing for which the sons and daughters of Thatcher's new middle class are now paying the price. George W. Bush encouraged the sub-prime mortgage market for much the same reason and has had much the same effect, though this time it is the mortgagors themselves who are the dispossessed, and the entire world economy that is pulsing with shock. Thus do the herdsmen of politics manipulate our instincts to bring us bleating to the fold. We are all 'stakeholders' now.

Yet the redrawing of boundaries does not mean we are any less polarized by accidents of birth or interest. Indeed, I suspect we are more polarized, and divided along more axes, than at any other time in our history. The same herds – racial, religious, socio-economic – exist as they always have done, but they are intercut by so many others that neutrality is impossible. Someone, somewhere, be it in the next street or in another continent, will hate us simply for being what we are, or for what we have become. (I once heard myself described as a 'class traitor' for having, in the speaker's view, migrated to a different part of the social veldt from the one into which I was born.) In the UK we now have a separate category of offence known as 'hate crimes'. According to the Home Office: 'Hatred is a strong term that goes beyond simply causing offence or hostility. Hate crime is any criminal offence committed against a person or property that is motivated by an offender's hatred of someone because of their: race, colour, ethnic origin, nationality or national origins; religion; gender or gender identity; sexual orientation; disability.'

Such crimes may take many different forms – assaults, threats, bullying, damage to property, abusive behaviour, printed matter, graffiti or gestures. They occur when 'any incident, which constitutes a criminal offence . . . is perceived by the victim or any other person as being motivated by prejudice or hate'. In 2006–7, police in England and Wales recorded 5,619 such crimes in which someone was injured, 4,350 crimes without injury, 28,485 cases of harassment and 3,565 of criminal damage. Most of the offenders were white, male and under 30.

Some of the issues are sufficiently clear-cut to be declared absolute. In western societies during peacetime, it is not possible to construct any moral justification for wounding or killing people for their nationality, race or religion. But then there are very few moral justifications for wounding or killing people at all. What is more problematical is the tendency of religious communities to believe that anything spoken against them is an expression of hatred and should be illegal. In the UK, Christian extremists tried to halt performances of the opera *Jerry Springer*, in which Christ appeared wearing a nappy; Sikhs attacked theatres promoting the drama *Behzti* ('Dishonour'), which depicted rape and murder in a temple; Muslims in London made violent threats following the publication in other countries of cartoons which mocked the prophet. 'Europe you will pay – 9/11 is on its way' was one popular slogan. 'Massacre those who insult Islam' was another. Moderate Muslims, of whom 10,000 marched peacefully from Trafalgar Square to Hyde Park, disowned the violence of the (mostly) young extremists, but their demand was the same. They wanted curbs on the rights of others to 'disrespect' Islam. Defenders of 'free speech' on the other hand protested their right to do just that.

Into this minefield two years later stepped the Archbishop of Canterbury, Rowan Williams, apparently arguing in a lecture to lawyers that some aspects of sharia (Muslim) law should be incorporated into the British legal system. I say 'apparently' because, as an 'intellectual', Williams seems to have transcended anything so unsophisticated as clarity of expression. His thoughts take scenic rambles through forests of subordinate clauses, this way and that, uphill and down through such a bog of caveats and syntactical S-bends that you need a diagram to follow him. He is like John Prescott translated by H. W. Fowler. Whatever he meant, it provoked a merry interlude of irreligious knockabout in which he was characterized as everything from 'idiot' to 'one of the finest minds in the country'. Among those who confronted him was Michael Nazir-Ali, the Pakistan-born Bishop of Rochester, who a few weeks earlier had complained that parts of Britain had become 'no-go' areas for non-Muslims, and who argued that sharia law 'would be in tension with the English legal tradition on questions like monogamy, provisions for divorce, the rights of women, custody of children, laws of inheritance and of evidence . . . not to mention the relation of freedom of belief and of expression to provisions for blasphemy and apostasy'.

The previous occupant of Lambeth Palace, George Carey, said Williams's proposal would be 'disastrous for the nation'. Concessions to Muslims, he said, would only embolden them to ask for more:

> This is absolutely inevitable, since questions to do with the separation of church and state are largely new to Islam. While Christianity and Judaism recognize the truth in 'rendering unto Caesar', it is resisted by mainstream Muslim countries. Sharia law trumps civil law every time. So, significantly, this would open up the problem of competition between British and sharia law . . . Many Muslim interpreters of sharia believe that it supersedes secular law and assume that its 'god-given' status would lead to its replacing civil law.

Cardinal Cormac Murphy-O'Connor, leader of England's Roman Catholics, also weighed in. 'When people come into this country they have to obey the laws of the land,' he said. (To be fair to Williams this hardly counts as a contradiction of anything he said – the debate was about what the law of the land might be, not whether or not it should be obeyed.) More forthright critics invoked the spectre of Saudi Arabia and other fortresses of Islam where rape victims can be flogged and thieves forfeit their hands. Williams's intellectual journey was supposed to lead to something called 'social cohesion', but he ended up in another place entirely. He protested afterwards that he hadn't meant what people had taken him to mean; he had intended something altogether more subtle, though he never quite made clear what this actually was. So far as one could tell, it had something to do with 'resolving disputes and regulating transactions' rather than with limb-loppings and stonings – ie cherry-picking those bits of sharia law that might fit with Christianity, and excluding the nasty bits. Idealism and naivety, always a snug fit, have seldom seemed more perfectly conjoined. It may or may not have been significant, but it was certainly remarked upon, that all this came as a furious inter-faith row was erupting in Oxford, where local Muslims wanted to amplify the muezzin's thrice-daily call to prayer.

You may agree with a friend of mine, an admired writer and normally the most courteous of men, whose patience cracked when he was cornered by a Presbyterian ideologue who thought climate change was an issue best left to the discretion of the Almighty. 'My solution to the world's problems,' he snapped back, 'is to abolish all religions.' Unfortunately, utopian solutions come no more easily to the ungodly than they do to men of faith. We all have to contend with nature. But nature, no less than god, moves in mysterious ways. Some psychologists and natural scientists now believe that we carry a 'god gene' that predisposes us to religiosity. The point was most famously argued by Dean H. Hamer, a geneticist at the US National Cancer Institute, in his 2004 book *The God Gene: How Faith Is Hardwired into Our Genes*. What he said was this (and I apologize for crushing a complex argument into a matchbox):

A number of brain chemicals are associated with deep meditative states (for example, in prayer) and with feelings of spirituality or 'transcendence'. It is likely that a large number of genes are involved in controlling the flow of these chemicals to the brain, of which Hamer identified a single example. (One would have loved it to have been called Isaiah, but it is actually known as VMAT2.) These genes convey a propensity for spirituality – in unscientific language, an impulse to which we are bound to respond. Historically, and for many people still, this response has taken the form of religious belief, though the precise nature of that belief – Christian, Buddhist, Jewish, Hindu, Islamic, ancestor-worship or whatever – depends on birth and upbringing. Others find their outlets in different forms of spiritual expression, most obviously through the experience of music, art and poetry, but also through other meditative forms such as yoga. (I would add, *pace* Dawkins, sheer awe at the beauty of the physical world. Go to any 'beauty spot' and you will see people transfixed. I would suggest also that the need to give and receive love, a transcending experience if there ever was one, comes off the same shelf. Viewed from this perspective, the line from *Les Misérables* – 'To love another person is to see the face of God' – takes on a whole new depth of meaning.) Hamer compares spirituality to the capacity for language: we are genetically pre-disposed to speak, but the exact form of expression – the language we use – is determined by learning and experience. Both these instincts or abilities (call them what you will) are products of natural selection.

The advantages of communication are obvious. A capacity for religious faith, too, would confer evolutionary advantage by uniting people in communities and spreading the benefits of reciprocal altruism. And as *Homo sapiens*, as far as we know, is the only species with the intelligence to foresee its own death, the promise of an afterlife provides powerful motivation for our earthly endeavours. This leads us to what those of faith reject as scientific reductionism – the suggestion that the *need* for god created the *idea* of god.

In 2005, a study of twins by scientists at the University of Minnesota provided further evidence that 'religious inclination' was affected by genetics. The resulting argument embraced all the usual ironies – theologians dismissing science for lack of proof, or for 'telling us nothing about God'. Well, it tells us nothing about Father Christmas either, and Hamer himself acknowledges this. The question he addressed was not 'Does God exist?', but 'Why do we believe in God?' 'Our genes can predispose us to believe,' he says, 'but they don't tell us what to believe in.'

His theory may be no easier to prove than the virgin birth or the literal truth of Genesis, but I do find myself drawn to it. It could explain why intelligent men – 'intellectuals', even – might believe in fantasy, or build philosophical towers on a foundation of myth. The distinction between 'spirituality' and its historically most important subdivision, 'religion', may explain also why some people can find fulfilment in other ways. And it explains why some people are more 'spiritual' than others. No other genetic impulse is felt uniformly by every man and woman (think of sex), and there is no reason why spirituality should be different.

What fascinates is the blurred interface between physiology and intellect, and the way it models our behaviour. Biology creates 'needs', and gives us appetites to fulfil them. It drives imperatives which are inherently greedy but which disguise themselves as morals. We claim privilege – for our faith, for our professional calling, for our own lives and our dependants' – as of right, and we have little difficulty in believing that our rights outweigh those of others. Thus the simple virtue of religious faith can shade into a frenzy of unappeasable desire, driving spiritual carnivores to hunt power in this world and paradise in the next. Faith of any kind – faith in the inherent superiority of any idea, interest or cause – can sing for virtue and dance for the devil. History is one long example. Think of the Crusaders, Conquistadors, Jihadis. Think of the godless faiths of Nazism and Marxism. All have claimed for themselves what they would deny to others. It is these huge tectonic plates of faith and dogma that have created the basic outlines of the human landscape; but in its plains and mountains the geography is constantly in flux. The whole of society is a rubble of colliding faiths and factions: it is our base motives, implanted by our genes, that make it so.

Our capacity for factionalism is extraordinary. Consider the number of organizations that have been set up specifically to champion the interests of one group against another – white against black, male against female, poor against rich, secular against religious, vegetarians against meat-eaters – and the vastly greater number of informal but no less real distinctions by which we categorize friend and foe. Our allegiances are bizarre. When I was young I owned a Volkswagen Beetle and found myself part of a nationwide fellowship which flashed its lights and saluted whenever we passed each other on the road. I don't know whether anyone does that now. Drivers more often seem united in hatred of other sub-groups – SUVs and 4×4s – than they do by any sense of fraternity in their own. Men who wear shorts, sandals or beards are singled out for weird opprobrium. Artistic and practical types mock each other's coarseness or pretensions. Ditto the young and old, faddies and foodies, tie-wearers and the open-necked. Cyclists hate van drivers, especially if the van is white. Sappy, sing-from-the-heart performers battle with desiccated academics for ownership of classical music, and ragged-arsed rockers vie with smooth synth merchants for possession of pop. Straight and gay swap insults and bring the churches of England and Rome to their knees. Smokers are deemed unworthy of civil society and banished to the doorstep. People who inhabit the most beautiful parts of the country are contemptuous of those – 'grockles', 'emmets' – who visit them on holiday (in the part of Norfolk where I live, some locals find it possible even to hate birdwatchers). Those who buy private education or healthcare are despised by those who don't.

Conservationists are locked in mutual antipathy with economists and farmers. Climate sceptics loathe those who tell them to go easy on the carbon. Country folk hate townies, and vice versa.

Wherever you look, there is entrenchment. Radio and television news programmes are constructed around the principle of confrontation: for every assertion there must be a denial, and every opinion must be paired with its opposite. From the concrete vaults of fixed opinion we hear assertions of rights god-given or otherwise, counter-demands, aspirations and points of principle. We may see in this a glorious assertion of faith. We may see bigotry, prejudice or stupidity. We may see conclusive evidence of the innate and irreversible greed that consumes all before it and will turn our once-glorious planet into a burning hell. Or we might see something quite different. In this unfettered babble of contradictory calls we may be hearing the sound of human genius. Our species is endlessly inventive; endlessly contradictory; endlessly co-operative and contrary. For this is our specialism. We know, because science tells us so, that our genes are blind to any purpose save the survival of their own. Evolution has no destination. We know, because we *know*, that we have the intelligence to emancipate ourselves from nature in the raw. This *is* civilization. Zoologists from another universe would marvel at the multiplicity of our talents, the fury of our passions, the infinite capacity to create and accept change. Tensions are inevitable, but out of them comes everything we most value – great civilizations, great art, great science, great law – as well as the petty hatreds and the cruel and costly wars with which we scourge ourselves.

We will always fight our corners and protect our own: that is what our genes require of us. In a warming, overcrowded planet of dwindling resources, the arguments can only get bigger. Fault lines have opened up between the developed countries (which caused global warming and possess the resources to defend themselves) and the developing ones (which are innocent victims but will bear the worst and earliest consequences). Living like there's no tomorrow may be a self-fulfilling prophecy. No matter where or how we live – East or West, urban or rural, rich or poor – the tremors eventually will reach into every corner of our lives, touching where and how we travel, what we eat, what we wear, how and where we build our homes, perhaps even how many sons and daughters we have. Where will fairness lie? Should the heaviest polluters with the greediest lifestyles gradually cut their carbon emissions, and the lightest polluters with the most deprived lifestyles be allowed to increase theirs until they meet at some mutually agreeable point in the middle? Should targets be set for individual market sectors or industries? Should emissions targets be calculated per unit of economic growth (a proposal unlikely to have much effect environmentally, but likely to be favoured by the Americans)? How can multinational polluters like air transport and shipping be accounted for? Biggest question of all: in a schismatic and jealous world, how can such agreements ever be reached? It is our genes that got us into this, and it is our genes that will have to get us out again. Of all the drives they impose upon us, the most powerful is the instinct to survive. We are not, yet, sufficiently frightened of what lies ahead. When we are, we will see ourselves at our best.

Part Three

The State

6

Lines on the Map

Attached to the deeds of my house is a sheet copied from a large-scale Ordnance Survey map. Drawn in red ink on this is a series of linked geometrical shapes – a couple of trapezoids and a long thin rectangle, a bit like the cross-section of a throne. The lines do not follow any discernible geological features and, though they connect at a variety of angles, they are unnaturally straight. One of the planes in the diagram follows the line of a highway. All the others are determined by field boundaries whose origins lie somewhere on the far side of the Norman Conquest. This is the outline of my 'property', the two acres of the planet's surface that my wife and I can call our own. This is our 'right', for which we have paid with cash and can prove with documentation, and anyone who infringed it would break the law. Scanning across the country on Google Earth, I see more of the same, a vast quilt of brown, green and yellow lozenges locked into place by lanes and hedgerows. Scanning the towns, I see the same in microcosm – row upon row of rectangular back gardens, all hemmed in with fences and walls. *Territory*.

From time to time I like to take stock of mine. Beating the bounds would be too grand a term for it, but I like to roam the boundary, wine in hand, and take pleasure in what is mine – the double-planted, stock-proof hawthorn hedge, the oaks and maples, the holly and the blackthorn, the bullace and the gean. It sounds grander than it is – just a couple of low-value field corners with grass and trees – but I doubt that Louis XIV got more pleasure from Versailles, or had a securer feeling of private space. It is *ours*; exactly as we want it; inviolable. And yet there lurks within me a child who will not desist from silly questions. What gives me, what gives *anyone*, the right to presume ownership of the earth? The adult's answer is not especially interesting. By popular consent, and for the sake of peace, we have adopted a system of law that allows us to 'own' pretty much anything save another person. It does not spare us from envy or avarice but it does save us from the kinds of territorial dispute to which other species have to give their lives. As I write, I can see outside my office a male chaffinch who has taken possession of a bay tree, from which very occasionally he finds time to sing for a mate. Only 'very occasionally' because he spends most of his time, and almost all of his energy, defending his perch against a most stubborn and persistent aggressor – his own reflection in the house window, against which he flings himself for hour upon hour until dusk or exhaustion defeats him. As far as possible we try not to compete with our wild cohabitees. Hedges are left uncut during the nesting season. Moles are allowed to do their worst; bats left undisturbed; hares and owls given free passage. Only rats get zapped, and mice when they invade the kitchen. Against other humans, however, the gates and doors are check-points, admission by invitation only.

Smaller-scale maps look much the same. As you pull further and further back, you see the UK divided into administrative counties, the globe divided by land mass into continents, and the continents carved into countries. Further still, and we see labels pinned to galaxies and constellations at distances beyond the reach of the naked eye and far beyond the scope of our imaginations. Wherever there are dimensions to be calibrated, the human instinct is to divide them into packages and give them names. Sometimes the result has clear and obvious integrity – an island, a peninsula or a plain – where the boundaries are defined by geography. More often they are physically arbitrary, the result of military conquest, marriages and political settlements between numberless generations of emperors, kings, presidents and prime ministers. Often, too, you can tell the age of a boundary simply from the volume of ink needed to draw it. The English counties, for example, look as if they might have been dropped on to the map in liquid form, leaving cartographers to trace around the splashes. They are puddles of antiquity, stamped out by men on horseback. Look now at the United States, Australia, parts of Africa, the Indian sub-continent and the Middle East, and you see the work of men with set-squares. Some of the lines are accorded equal respect by the people living on either side of them. Some of them are not. Some 'nation states' have developed organically around a common core of language, culture, race and religion; others are constructs drawn up by treaty, often in the aftermath of war, in which expediency, or *force majeure*, has required some nations to be divided, others to be united in unholy alliance with ancient enemies, some to disappear altogether.

Political scientists argue deep into the night about the nature, integrity and future of the nation state. It has been argued that they are 'imagined communities' composed of people who cannot know each other, and who may even feel themselves to be divided in more ways than they are united. Historically they are a new idea. For most of its time on earth, the human race organized itself into either very much smaller units – tribal villages, city states – or very much larger kingdoms and empires. It was through the crumbling of the latter, and the rise of nationalism, that the modern nation state emerged in the 19th century. Looking for a definition, I find: 'A political unit consisting of an autonomous state inhabited predominantly by a people sharing a common culture, history, and language.' But then I find also: 'A group of people united in a common misconception about their own past and a common dislike of their neighbours', which may be just as valid.

It is an idea that reached a peak of awfulness in the obsessive nationalism of the fascist governments of the 1930s, and which now is being challenged internally by multiculturalism and externally by the global economy and other supranational forces. On 29 February 1872, the German émigré and Republican senator Carl Schurz rose in the US Senate and said the one thing he is remembered for: 'My country, right or wrong; if right, to be kept right; and if wrong, to be set right.' I'd guess that no day passes without someone, somewhere, repeating those first five words. But I cannot remember anyone, ever, adding the other thirteen. Not even Samuel Johnson's famous barb – 'last refuge of a scoundrel' – could break patriotism's grip on the psyche. A hundred and sixty years after he said it, the First World War made patriotic duty a moral absolute. Those who stood back from it were handed white feathers. Those who stepped forward were emboldened even to relish their own deaths. 'I could not wish for a finer death,' wrote one young officer before the Somme in 1916. 'I died doing my duty to my God, my Country, my King.' Of those three abstract concepts – god, country, king – the second is not much easier to define rationally than the other two. Nationality, too, is an accident of birth, and how else, other than by blind faith, can an accident be *moral*? Nevertheless, no matter how we define it, nationality remains one of the most important ways in which we identify ourselves, and a principal focus of our loyalty. It is an emotion which national leaders tap into like vampires into a vein. 'Your country needs you,' said Lord Kitchener's famous recruiting poster. 'Ask not what your country can do for you,' said John F. Kennedy nearly fifty years later. 'Ask what you can do for your country.' *My fellow Americans . . . this great country of ours . . . Deutschland über Alles . . . Allons, enfants de la Patrie . . . Advance Australia Fair! . . . Land of Hope and Glory . . . Flower of Scotland . . . Viva España . . . O Canada, we stand on guard for thee* ... We are never far from a patriotic appeal. Look at the way hardened sportsmen are emotionally racked by their anthems, and how winners rush to the flag. Look at how political mobs burn the flags of their enemies – it is the worst insult they can think of, like cursing someone's mother.

And yet the state is a creature like no other. Where lies its brain? Where its soul, its beating heart? Does it respond to the will of its people, or – as the quotations above all seem to insist – are the people just instruments of its own superior purpose? Is it like a selfish gene, having no aim beyond its own survival in perpetuity? England and Germany in 1914–18 consumed the lives of their young with a voracity unparalleled in the whole of nature. The planned economies of the Soviet era similarly counted lives as units of stock to be invested – or, as it turned out, wasted – in the name of the state, rather than having any intrinsic value of their own. To plead the sanctity of life, as conscientious objectors did, is to be accused of sentimentality, weakness, moral and physical cowardice. Even when public opinion is resolute – as it was in the UK against the second Iraq war – the state will not step aside. Whether hunting alone or in packs, whether pursuing territory, commodities or trade, nation states are the most determined predators since *Tyrannosaurus rex*.

Stick a pin anywhere in history – anywhere in time, indeed, since humans displaced the Neanderthals. The story of the world is the story of imperial greed, from Ancient Egypt to 21st-century America, in which more is never enough. One of the greatest feasts in history was hosted by the German Chancellor Bismarck at the Berlin Conference in 1884/5. On the menu: Africa. Seated around the table were Germany and its 13 invited guests: Great Britain, France, Portugal, Belgium, Austria-Hungary, Denmark, Spain, USA, Italy, Russia, Sweden-Norway, Turkey and the Netherlands. Absent from the table, because they *were* the feast, were the countries of Africa. The conference itself did not rule on portion size, but it did set the parameters within which the 'scramble for Africa' would be concluded. In place of slavery, which had robbed the continent of its people, would come a land-grab which would rob the people of their continent. In 1880, scarcely 10 per cent of the continental land mass had been colonized by the European powers. By 1900 they had taken the lot. I came across this unattributed quotation in an essay credited to the late Heinrich VII Prinz Reuss: 'One took because it was believed to be necessary in order to protect earlier conquests; later one took because everything was within reach; later still one took in order to beat one's neighbour to it; finally one took in order to take.'

Germany got Namibia, Tanzania, Togo and parts of Cameroon and Benin. Britain got Egypt, parts of the Sudan, Uganda and Kenya, South Africa, Zambia, Zimbabwe, Botswana, Nigeria and Ghana. Belgium clung on to the Congo. France got most of central and western Africa, plus parts of the north. Portugal took Mozambique and Angola. Italy got Somalia and part of Ethiopia, and Spain got Equatorial Guinea. As Prinz Heinrich observed: 'This was carried out with no regard for historically and culturally evolved identities. The way colonial borders were drawn split up many African peoples. Others, enemies from time immemorial, were thrown together in unity.'

The consequences haunt us still. Local trading systems were broken up, populations displaced, subsistence economies destroyed. In place of traditional staples such as millet, maize and manioc, the European masters imposed monocultures for the world commodity markets: tea, cocoa, coffee, groundnuts, cotton and hemp. Africa has never properly recovered. It continues to pay for European avarice with blood, debt, famine and environmental degradation. Independence has brought little relief. The empires may have retreated, but the former colonies have imperial fingers at their throats and many are poorly served by governments for whom politics is one step away from tribal warfare, and power is for the benefit of those who wield it. If there is one thing

African leaders have learned from their former masters, it is that dissent is not to be countenanced.

'Globalization' was not in the vocabulary of the 19th century, but it was a word waiting to happen. The principle was already well established, with poor countries functioning as vast allotments for the rich who would turn their raw materials into wealth and power. As we shall see later (Chapters 9 and 10), the pressure has not abated. US and European companies continue to mine Africa's fragile economies for commodities, oil, minerals and the tourist dollar. Next it will be biofuels. The rich countries sooner or later will run out of oil. Gradually, like penitents on the rack, they are admitting the reality of climate change and accepting that they need to emit less greenhouse gas. Given that 20 per cent of emissions come from transport, the solution looks obvious. Instead of fossil energy we will use energy trapped in growing plants. From oil-rich crops such as rape, soy and palm we will make biodiesel. From starchy ones such as sugar cane, beet, maize and wheat we will make bioethanol (a form of alcohol) to replace petrol. Biofuels return to the atmosphere the same amount of carbon contained by the plants they were made from, so they are 'carbon neutral'. But no one can be unaware that there are profound misgivings about the efficacy of biofuels. Briefly stated, the case against biodiesel is that virgin rainforest in, for example, Indonesia and Malaysia is being cut down to make way for soy and palm, so that more carbon is being released into the atmosphere by deforestation than is being saved by cuts in fossil fuel consumption. Worse: according to Victoria Tauli-Corpuz, chair of the UN Permanent Forum on Indigenous Issues, 60m Malaysian and Indonesian forest dwellers face a future in urban slums.

The case against bioethanol is that it is made from food crops and so threatens to make hungry people even hungrier. Population growth means that the world will need 40 per cent more food by 2020, and climate change will mean less and less land to grow it on. With India and China switching to western-style grain- and meat-based diets, grain consumption could double in 40 years. In such circumstances, it is argued, growing crops to feed cars rather than people is a bit like running a transport system on human blood. And yet, time and again from within the industry, we hear Africa (and/or South America) described as 'the Middle East of biofuels'. My own view, which I argued in an article for the *Sunday Times Magazine* in March 2008, is that, by strict application of an internationally agreed certification system, it should be possible to ensure that people are not driven off their lands or starved; that forests and peatlands are not sacrificed either to biofuels or to food crops displaced by them; and that greenhouse emissions and the other environmental costs of cultivating, fertilizing, irrigating, delivering and processing biofuels are fully accounted for. Believing all this to be possible, however, does not mean that it will happen, and I can't claim much ground for optimism.

Another fear, expressed by the Royal Society, is that although rural communities might benefit from rises in world commodity prices, it would be at the expense of their urban neighbours who would have to pay more for their food. Again the biofuel lobby has an answer. It says the revived economies would halt the migration of villagers into the slums and keep traditional communities intact. The same might be true in Europe. Farming the plains in the east, reviving what was once the breadbasket of Europe and stimulating local economies, might even staunch the politically troublesome flow of migrants from east to west. *Might, would, could?* Who knows? The fact is that the bio-prospectors will not wait for international agreements. With EU emissions and biofuel targets to be met, the appetite for raw material is growing forever more acute. In July 2007, a review by the African Biodiversity Network included an anguished report from Tanzania, where European and US biofuel companies were already working. 'Huge changes in land use and land ownership are scheduled,' it said, 'meaning that fuel will be grown instead of food, and small-scale farmers will be pushed off their lands . . .' The writer, Abdallah Mkindee, reminded us that Tanzania repeatedly suffers from drought and has to rely on food aid: 'NGOs . . . ask themselves why, then, the government is not focusing on increasing agricultural production in the most irrigated and fertile areas of land, but instead looking to displace food production and precious water resources for production of agrofuels for export.'

This was exactly what the Royal Society had feared. 'Significantly,' it said, 'if market conditions are right, biofuel crops will always start to be cultivated on the most productive land . . .'; and it warned Europe not to export environmental problems to the developing countries that grow the fuels. Sterner critics say this is not so much risk as fact, and that it's brute force, not market force, that makes it happen. 'In Colombia,' says Oxfam, 'paramilitary groups are forcing people from their land at gunpoint, torturing and murdering those that resist . . .' So: meet the new colonialism, just like the old colonialism – a system of economic repression, enforced by first-world protectionism (of which more later), which keeps power in the hands of the powerful and drip-feeds the poor with false hope.

Berlin in 1884 was not the first time world leaders had made a meal of other people's countries, and it would not be the last. In January 1919 the leaders of 32 states representing 75 per cent of the world's population met in Paris to settle the future of Germany and its allies. The agenda was dominated by the 'big three' – David Lloyd George of Britain, Georges Clemenceau of France and the ailing Woodrow Wilson of the USA, all of whom wanted the Central Powers punished but had differing priorities. Clemenceau wanted Germany on its knees, stripped of all military and economic power, while Lloyd George wanted it to remain strong enough to block the spread of communism. Wilson, grown weary, simply wanted Europe to sort out its mess and get out of America's hair. The terms set out in the Treaty of Versailles imposed military, financial and territorial forfeits. Germany had to confess to warmongering and surrender its lands. Alsace-Lorraine went to France; Eupen and Malmédy to Belgium; Northern Schleswig to Denmark; Hultschin to Czechoslovakia; West Prussia, Posen and Upper Silesia to Poland. The League of Nations took over the German colonies, and Germany had to hand back what it had taken from Russia in 1918, including the future states of Estonia, Lithuania and Latvia. The collapsed Austro-Hungarian Empire also suffered. Under the Treaty of Trianon it had to surrender what would become Czechoslovakia and Yugoslavia (known initially as the Kingdom of the Serbs, Croats and Slovenes), and cede other tracts of land to Romania, Poland and Italy. A further treaty (Neuilly) transferred land from Bulgaria to Yugoslavia, and the Turkish Ottoman Empire was disbanded by the Treaty of Sèvres. Among other things, this gave control of Iraq, Transjordan and Palestine to Britain; Syria and Lebanon to France.

'Peace' is almost always like this, with settlement terms forced by the victors upon the reluctant vanquished. Old empires die, new countries are born, land and peoples taken as trophies. New boundaries bind enemies together and tear friends apart. The process rarely stops for long, and the results are always with us. The Second World War, the Iron Curtain, partition and reunification of Germany, partition of India, Korea, Hungary, Czechoslovakia, Vietnam, Cambodia, Palestine, Cyprus, Lebanon, Ireland, Kosovo, Mozambique, Rwanda, Afghanistan, Iraq, Darfur, Madrid, New York, London, Georgia . . . Flags are saluted; flags burned; anthems sung and martyrs carried to their graves. Lines on maps, bombs in trains. The 20th century began with jingoism and ended with *ethnic cleansing* – an all-time low in the history of euphemism.

On 17 February 2008 I emerged from a restaurant in Piccadilly to a discordant symphony of horns. Surging jerkily between traffic lights, a cavalcade of flag-bedecked vans and cars was saluting the declaration of independence by ethnic Albanians in Kosovo. The previous night Serbs in Belgrade, unchecked by police, had responded to the same event by setting fire to the American embassy. And so it will go on. Conservative opinion cracks its knuckles and wants tighter border controls. Liberal opinion wrings its hands and thinks again about multiculturalism. Political scientists begin to look beyond the nation state, where the terror now comes not just from narrow-eyed men in tank turrets. It comes from cold-hearted pragmatists armed with spreadsheets, the shock troops of the new world order whose weapons are debt, market economics and free trade.

In a way nationalism is easy to understand. Selfish gene, selfish individual, selfish society, selfish state – a logical progression of outwardly rippling greed towards the outer skin of our identity. But what exactly *is* this identity? What *is* this organism we give our allegiance to? Addressing the Fabian Society in 2006, the then chancellor of the exchequer Gordon Brown – prime minister in waiting but already the leader on domestic policy – called upon Labour to 'embrace the union flag' and reclaim it from the boot-boys of the far right. 'Instead of the BNP [British National Party] using it as a symbol of racial division, the flag should be a symbol of unity, and part of a modern expression of patriotism too. All the United Kingdom should honour it, not ignore it. We should assert that the Union flag by definition is a flag for tolerance and inclusion.'

Brown thought that Britain should have some kind of national day, like 4 July in the US or Bastille Day in France, on which we could celebrate its 'national identity'. There was a chorus of agreement. A Labour MP spoke of a need to 'focus on the things that bring us together . . .' The former Conservative prime minister John Major said it was 'absolutely right' to celebrate 'the concept of Britishness'. The Commission for Racial Equality agreed that it was 'important to talk about and identify our shared common values and discuss ideas and find ways to celebrate being British'. The singer-proselytizer Billy Bragg welcomed a national debate on 'what it means to be British'. 'What actually binds us together?' he wondered. 'Well, interestingly, the thing that binds us together is our civic identity which is Britishness.'

Perhaps we should mark the date and call it Platitudinous Waffle Day. What *was* interesting was the idea that we needed a 'national debate' to define ourselves as people. In the years after the Second World War, such a question would have seemed absurd, like wanting to define 'Wednesday', or light and dark. We just *were*. We were bound, as we always had been, by the things that made us different from Johnny Foreigner (Shakespeare, kindness to animals, fair play, tea); by our opposition to outsiders who threatened us; and in particular by the unifying experience of war. Most nation states – the older, settled ones – were made to a similar recipe. With a very few exceptions (Belgium, Switzerland, Canada) they had a single, 'official' language imposed by the dominant social or ethnic group. They kept to inherited traditions in how they cooked and ate. They had their own artistic and literary traditions; their own concepts of 'family'; their own social etiquette; their own sports and religions; their own educational priorities and institutions. All these had a moral significance and commanded an emotional commitment that was not unlike religious faith. Our god was the one true god; our society gave the world its template. Some time in the early 1950s I was taught by my village schoolteacher, the utterly wonderful Miss Harris, that I should buy nothing in a shop without first checking that it bore the essential mark of superiority – *Made in England*. She would have understood Gordon Brown's wanting people to plant Union flags in their gardens but would have been puzzled by his call for a day of national celebration. We already had one –

Empire Day, 24 May, when we had a half-day holiday. That 'old nationalism' – the England that was fought for in two world wars, and which generations of young brides lay back and thought of – has disappeared with those who wore its medals. It exists only in its vestiges: 'Sunday special' roasts in pubs, bitter beer, Elgar, a xenophobic press, 'olde worlde' fakery, the changing of the guard, Eton. It survives in distrust of 'Europe', and in the outbreak of flag-waving – St George, not Union – that accompanies cricket, rugby and football world cups, and in some vague notion that our systems of law and government are in some not quite definable way better than everyone else's. But it is not the same.

Two things have changed it – the emergence of supranational power blocs such as the European Union, and immigration. These have reversed the thrust of nationalism from positive endorsement of an ideal – what sociologists call a 'nationalism of inclusion', seeking to enrol as much of the population as possible – to an overwhelmingly hostile nationalism of rejection and exclusion. The supranational union is rejected because it dilutes our emotional involvement – the skin of our identity just doesn't stretch that far. The result is a culture of resistance in which the nationalists' enemy is their own government. The extreme right political groupings that emerged in Europe during the second half of the 20th century directed their fire not at other nations perceived to be in competition with their own, but at immigrants. Gerard Delanty, now professor of sociology and social and political thought at the University of Sussex, put it this way in an essay in 1996: 'Nationalism today is more likely to be a product of the breakdown in social communication than a functional product of nation-building.' Old-style nationalism has been under assault in other ways too – from ideas of political correctness, liberals' fear of 'racism' (an inevitable cry whenever there is resistance to immigration), feminism, globalism, religious fundamentalism and the internet. All the conflicting and interconnecting tribes discussed in the previous chapter have cut across the old ideas of nationhood.

This is why now we hear so much more about 'citizenship' than we do about 'nationality'. It explains the call for a 'national debate'; explains the fury that met poor Rowan Williams's excursion into sharia law; explains why the Conservative politician Norman (now Lord) Tebbit once defined the acid test of Englishness as support for the national cricket team. It is why our pens hover over the 'nationality' box on application forms. What now are we? *English? British?* It is why the debate on multi-culturalism generates so much heat, and why multiculturalism and nationalism are fighting out of opposite corners. It is why Gordon Brown wanted to get it sorted.

The most fundamental right that nations claim for themselves is to decide who belongs and who does not. In democratic societies, governed by will of the majority, this is often bad news for ethnic minorities. Indeed, the very word 'ethnic' in this context, though not exactly a pejorative, implies inferiority and alienation. It is not a label we apply to ourselves. 'Immigrant', too, is seldom meant to flatter, and the thoroughly modern 'asylum-seeker' lacks the charity implicit in 'refugee'. Populations are never static. Few of us are born and die on the same soil as our ancestors. Most of us are where we are only because various of our forebears marched, fought or bought their passages here. We are not geology. Some of us may have sprung from conquerors; some from the migrant poor; some even from ancient adventurers pricked by curiosity, or from chancers on the make. Such movements will never cease. Indeed, it is important that they don't. For some, it is a question of making a good life even better – the rich are always in the market for a life in the sun or a bigger salary. For others it is a matter of escaping persecution or poverty. It is like a climatic flow. People will always be sucked from areas of surplus population to areas of surplus wealth. It is a global manifestation of the injunction to the unemployed attributed to Norman Tebbit in the 1980s – 'On yer bike!'

At the 2001 census, the UK population included 4,896,581 people, 8.3 per cent of the total, who were born in other countries. Unsurprisingly, the two largest contributors were southern Asia (principally Pakistan, India and Bangladesh), with 1,032,376, and the Irish Republic with 533,205. There were also significant totals from eastern Europe (247,976, including 60,714 from Poland), the USA (158,434), South Africa (141,405), Australia (107,871), Italy (107,244) and France (95,059).

Between 1951 and 2005, the foreign-born percentage of the UK population rose from 4.2 per cent to 9.7 per cent. Given the fuss about border controls and 'open floodgates', this may seem less than astonishing. What may surprise people is the fact that during the 1960s and 70s more people *left* the UK than arrived here. More recently, the balance has tilted the other way. Between 2001 and 2005, net migration (the difference between arrivals and departures) accounted for 66 per cent of the total population growth – an average annual gain of 182,000 (against just 92,000 achieved by the procreative efforts of the residents). But this does not mean the outflow has ceased. In 2005 the UK was still the biggest single source of immigrants to Australia – 18,220 made the one-way trip. In the same year 19,800 crossed the Atlantic, though this was of small significance in the USA's total influx of 1,122,373. As always, the top supplier of new Americans was Mexico with 161,445, followed by India, China, the Philippines, Cuba, Vietnam, the Dominican Republic, Korea, Colombia and the Ukraine. But let's not sink too deeply into statistics. The point is that large numbers are still moving from country to country, and are doing so for a variety of reasons. For a variety of reasons, too, they can expect varying degrees of welcome. What is generally not well understood is the importance of immigration in the economies of the hosts. If it's land that makes a country, it's *people* that make a nation. If we are to educate our children, heal our sick, pension our elderly and maintain all the services and supply lines that societies need in order to call themselves civilized, then we need a working population sufficient to get the job done.

Looking at the world we live in, you might suppose we were obsessed with sex. We use it to sell everything from toothpaste to Kylie Minogue, and yet it is the greatest irony of the age. Never in its entire history has mankind been more obsessed with its reproductive organs; never in its entire history has it been less inclined to put them to creative use. In many countries, including the UK, women are not producing enough babies to replace themselves and their husbands when they die. Thus, according to the demographers, unless we get our women pregnant both earlier and more often, we face the worst social and economic catastrophe since the plague years. The elderly will outnumber the young, placing an impossible burden on the workers who must support them. Productivity will plummet. Unemployment will soar. Education will become unaffordable. Optimism will leach from the national psyche and we will become constitutionally depressed. To survive economically, the EU will have to suck in large numbers of predominantly Muslim immigrants from the Middle East and North Africa.

This all dances on the pinhead of a single, simple statistic. To maintain a stable population, women on average need to produce approximately 2.1 children each. In demographer's jargon, this is 'replacement fertility'. Where the average is higher, the population in the long term will grow. Where it is lower, the population will shrink. According to the United Nations population division, which has been making some hurried reappraisals of its long-term forecasts, 49 countries, representing 44 per cent of the world's population, were already below replacement level by 1995, and the trend was downward. In the developing world – hitherto regarded as the trigger in the timebomb – only 17 countries, representing less than 4 per cent of the world's population, had suffered no reduction in fertility. In 10 countries the rate had dropped to less than 1.5 children per woman. The UN's World Population Prospects report for 2005–10 predicts that 71 out of the 195 listed countries, including every single member of the EU, will fall below replacement rate. If you look at the 10 countries predicted to top the world fertility table – Nigeria (7.19 births per woman), Guinea Bissau (7.07), Afghanistan (7.07), Burundi (6.80), Liberia (6.77), Congo (6.70), East Timor (6.53), Mali (6.52), Sierra Leone (6.47), Uganda (6.46) – you see a pattern emerging. Poor Third World countries are producing more babies than they are able to keep alive.

Eight of these 10 are in the top 20 for mortality in children under five. At 278.1 deaths per 1,000 births (that is more than a quarter), Sierra Leone is the world's worst. Afghanistan comes next at 235.4, Liberia third at 205.2. For comparison, the US and UK, ranked 163rd and 174th respectively, score 7.8 and 6.0. Iceland in 195th place is at 3.9. No single statistic can tell the whole story, but you get the picture. Specifically you begin to understand not only what 'economic migrants' have to gain from switching continents but also what their hosts might have to gain from receiving them. In 2001 the fertility rate in the UK fell to a historic low, 1.63, but by 2007 (the most recent year for which statistics are available), it had crept back to 1.9. We are by no means Europe's worst. The Netherlands currently manages 1.73, Germany 1.35, Spain and Italy 1.29 (the same as Japan). Like most international statistics, the figures vary slightly according to source. Not enough, however, to affect the conclusion: much of the developed world, including the US, is not breeding enough babies to replace their parents. As a result, demographers, statisticians and economic forecasters are turning their eyes to the future with the anxious gaze of men fearing the worst. How could such a thing have happened?

Fertility rates have been falling since the end of the 19th century, and with each step in the emancipation of women they have fallen a little further. Early in the 20th century, university education and careers for women – like homosexuality, vegetarianism or conscientious objection – were abominations, affronts to god and nature. Without effective contraception, and with unmarried pregnancy offering a choice between disgrace and suicide, most men could get free access to a woman's body only by way of the altar. Marriage was the price they paid for sex; multiple pregnancies the price their wives paid for the security of wedlock. Educating a young woman in these circumstances was as pointless as teaching a dog to walk on its hind legs. As recently as the 1980s, the more conservative Oxford and Cambridge colleges – tail-gunners in the sex war – still barred their doors to women. With the so-called 'glass ceilings' in professional careers, and male-dominated headcounts in City boardrooms, it could be argued that full equivalence has yet to be achieved. Even to engage in the debate, however, is to acknowledge that change is happening. Industry is still short of female CEOs but we have had a female prime minister, female newspaper editors, female channel bosses in television. My editor is female; so is her publishing director.

Girls now outperform boys in the classroom and have equal expectations of higher education and employment. An unmarried professional woman is not so much 'left on the shelf' as living her own life. I do not retract what I wrote in Chapter 3 – traditional sex roles remain a potent force and are not going to vanish any time soon. But the order of priority is changing. In 1994 more than half British women aged between 21 and 23 said they wanted a child within five years. A decade later, less than 40 per cent said the same. A third of women in their mid-thirties have yet to have their first baby, and the mean age at first childbirth in the UK in 2000 was the highest in Europe, at 29.1. This has forced demographers to ditch their long-held belief that women are genetically programmed to bear at least two children. Even where a mother does want more than one, the postponement of childbearing into the fourth decade of her life, when natural fertility declines, often means she runs out of time. Twenty per cent of British women aged 36–38 remain childless, though a quarter of these still say they want a baby.

There have been other changes too. The UK's marriage rate has been falling by 3–4 per cent annually since the early 1970s, and brides have been growing older. In 1960 the mean age at first marriage was 23.3; by 2000 it was 27.3. In Sweden it is already over 30. The most obvious reason is the increasing popularity of cohabitation – what an earlier generation would have called 'living in sin' – and you could argue, as many do, that it makes no material difference. As one academic put it to me, the decline of marriage could mean nothing more than 'a shift from one kind of adult union to another'. The shift is certainly dramatic. The British Household Panel Survey suggests that 70 per cent of all new live-in relationships at the turn of the century were cohabitations. Across Europe, 10 per cent of couples living together are unmarried, and during the peak childbearing years of 16–29 the rate is even higher. By 1994 the UK had already reached 38 per cent, with France, the Netherlands and Denmark forging ahead at 46 per cent, 54 per cent and 72 per cent respectively.

It does seem to make a difference. Though 'illegitimacy' is not the taboo it used to be, and 'bastard' is almost a term of endearment, cohabitation still does not match wedlock as an engine of procreation. Even now, 'living together' is regarded as a temporary state always vulnerable to breakdown. Though the average duration of cohabitation increased steeply in the 1980s and '90s, by 1994 it was still less than three years, with the victims of failed relationships often returning to their parents. This helped to accelerate another damaging trend – the increasing tendency of young people to delay their departures from the family home. The great majority of European countries are seeing striking increases in the numbers of twenty-somethings still living with their parents (among Italian 18–24-year-olds, it has reached 95 per cent). Even where young people do leave home, many of them remain financially dependent on their parents and in no position to contribute to the birth rate.

The reasons vary. Italy, for example, has low employment for both women and young people, so that extended families are bound together by dependence on the *paterfamilias*. In the UK, the principal deterrents to early nest-building are the high price of property (the average age of the British first-time buyer is now 32) and, ironically, the hunger for self-improvement. When Britain had relatively few students in higher education, young people became wage-earners and started families much earlier than the Europeans. Now that, too, has changed. The government's aspiration to send more and more people to university, while simultaneously loading them with debt, is – for better or worse – helping delay the transition to independence. Even when they do get a bit of money in their pockets, it is more likely to ring the tills at bars, clubs and airports than it is at Mothercare. There is no more powerful a contraceptive than living at home with your mother and father.

Perversely, we carry on as if none of this were happening. We live in one of the oldest societies that ever tottered the earth, yet we remain absurdly in thrall to youth. Looking at advertisements, newspapers, magazines and television schedules, you might think we lived in a society struggling to escape its teens. But the fact is that a declining fertility rate brings with it an unavoidable corollary – an ageing population.

And this is why it matters. The UK now has more people aged over 60 than under 16. By 2014 the under-16s will be overtaken by the over-65s, more than a third of the population will be over 50 and grey will be the new blonde. The over-80s, already the fastest growing age group, will treble in 25 years and Buckingham Palace will need an exponentially larger postal allowance. Whereas in 1951 there were only 270 centenarians in Britain, there are now over 6,000. By 2030, unless we start culling, there will be 45,000. Already the average age in Europe is 39 – four years older than the US. In the UK by 2031 this will have risen to around 43.6. The result will be a colossal shift in power from young to old. Even now, says the Economic and Social Research Council, 'those over 65 have four times the voting power of those under 25' – the aggregate sum of 'twice as many people who are twice as likely to vote'.

Problem is: with a shrinking workforce and a rabbit-like explosion in the number of retirees, how are we going to pay the bills? In 2002 there were 3.35 people of working age for every one of pensionable age. By 2011 this will be down to 3.1. By 2031 it will be a little over 2.5, and by the 2050s it will have levelled off at somewhere near 2.2. Yet even this may be too optimistic. Given predicted increases in life expectancy, some believe it may fall to as low as 1.9 – a drop of 43 per cent. To restore the balance, pension age would have to increase to 73, pensioners would have to accept 43 per cent less income, or pension contributions would have to rise by 76 per cent.

We have heard warnings like this before. More than fifty years ago a national advisory committee warned that 'in 25 years' time the dependency ratio of pensioners to workers would become unsustainable'. The difference now is that it's less a matter of prediction than of recognizing what is already happening. Not only will taxpayers in the future face a heavier responsibility but there will be fewer of them to share the cost. 'By 2025,' says the Employers Forum on Age, 'for every two people employed there is likely to be one person over 50 who is retired or inactive.' The inactivity may be due to voluntary early retirement, enforced redundancy or, increasingly, the need to care for an elderly relative.

It has been calculated that some 2.8m carers in the UK have retired prematurely, at least a million of whom would rather work, and that a quarter of British women aged between 55 and

63 still have a living parent. The US yields an even more startling statistic. The average American woman now spends more time as the daughter of a parent over 65 than she does as the parent of a child under 18. Given the crisis in the UK pensions industry, it is a problem that can only worsen. As the post-war baby-boomers hit retiring age, so the downward slope gets ever steeper. In the blink of a fund manager's eye, they will transform themselves from savers into pensioners, and the flow of money to financial institutions will reverse from inward to out. Up will go interest rates to encourage the rest of the country to save enough to cover the cost. Down will come property prices as boomers trying to finance their retirement flood the market. All this was looming even before America's mortgage cowboys yahoo'd us into the credit squeeze.

There are some stark conflicts of interest. Borrowers (the young) need low interest rates and high inflation to minimize their debts. Investors (the old) want high interest rates and low inflation to maximize their savings. One of the bleakest scenarios was sketched out ten years ago (1998) by Cardinal Alfonso Lopez Trujillo, president of the Pontifical Council for the Family (to whom we shall return). Like other commentators he warned of the economic burdens likely to be faced by young people having to support a larger population of older, less active people in increasing need of care. But he went further. Providing for the elderly, he said, would leave less money to be invested in education, and the public psyche would take a terrible hit. The decline in intellectual, economic, scientific and social dynamism in an ageing population would create a mood of 'moroseness'. Which led him to the most chilling prediction of all: 'Under these conditions, in order to secure the healthy functioning of various social insurance programmes (pensions, life insurance, health insurance, welfare system), the temptation becomes great to resort to euthanasia.'

Few other commentators imagine youth taking such drastic

revenge on its elders, but neither do they quarrel with the general thrust of the cardinal's argument. Youthful societies are more productive than ageing ones. A young and growing population will borrow more and consume more, thus stimulating demand and creating profit. An ageing population will spend less and save more, thereby reducing demand and draining resources. As it happens, the UK is better off than some of its neighbours. If the UN has got its arithmetic right (and we should remember that predicting bedroom activity is not an exact science), Italy could lose 20 per cent of its population by 2050, and Spain 10 per cent. Despite its below-replacement fertility, the UK over the same period is likely to gain another 6m people. Immigration and increased life expectancy will more than balance the baby famine. Nevertheless, the age pyramid will be inverted and a rock-and-roll generation of funky oldsters, swinging their hip replacements to the back catalogue of Sir Michael Jagger, will soon be looking for a good time. They are used to gratification and greedy for more. Who is going to give it to them?

There are four possible answers. One: make better use of the oldsters themselves. Two: make more babies. Three: persuade ourselves to believe, in defiance of Keynesian economics, that a small population is better than a big one. Four: attract more immigrants. Keeping older people in work already is on the political agenda. Socially, economically and culturally, the ageist policies of employers have contributed to one of the most costly wastages ever perpetrated upon a modern society. Life expectancy has risen on average by three months every year since 1840, and rose by a full 25 years in the 20th century. How did we celebrate this achievement? *By turning success on its head and treating it as failure.* To take the strain off final-salary pension schemes, middle-aged workers were pressed into early retirement and converted overnight from asset to liability. By the close of the 20th century only 59.8 per cent of men aged 55–64 had a job, and only 30 per cent saw it all the way through to retiring age. Alan

Walker, director of the Economic and Social Research Council's Growing Older programme, complained of 'a demography of despair, which portrays population ageing not as a triumph for civilization but something closer to an apocalypse'.

Raising the retiring age is not just a matter of keeping Grandad off the street. For as long as people are in work, they create tax income for the economy rather than draining it of retirement benefits. For the government, the first objective is obvious. Some time between 2010 and 2020, the state pension age (currently 65 for men and 60 for women) will be equalized at 65 for both sexes. The EU, too, is rushing to bolt stable doors. It wants to raise the average employment rate of 55–64-year-olds from 39 per cent to 50 per cent, and has outlawed age discrimination in the workplace.

This will help, but it won't be enough to keep the workforce fully topped up. The stock remedy for worker shortages (*pace* the NHS) is recruitment abroad. If you want to see what immigration can do for a national economy, you have only to look at the United States. But there is a snag. Low fertility is a worldwide problem and migrants, too, are in short supply. The EU's member states have no surplus for export, and every defecting Polish plumber is a blow to his homeland's economy. Europe therefore will need to look elsewhere, and it will find in the Middle East and North Africa a number of much more youthful countries with higher fertility. This has emboldened some commentators to predict that by the end of the 21st century southern and eastern Europe will be Muslim-dominated. 'A demographic shift of this nature,' said the Conservative MP David Willetts, then shadow secretary for work and pensions, in a pamphlet for the Centre for European Reform in 2003, 'could mean Europe's religious and cultural map more closely resembles that of the early medieval period. Europe is going to have to think much more carefully about relations with an Islamic population that is growing, while birth rates in southern Europe collapse.' Even so, Europe's hunger for workers will not be satisfied. Migrants do bring short-term reinforcement, but it takes only 15 years of integration for their birth rate to fall to the local norm. According to UN projections, in order for the EU to maintain the current ratio of workers to pensioners it would need 700m new migrants by 2050 – seven times the predicted total population of Turkey.

Things are different in America. Rates of birth and immigration are higher there, so its workforce will grow as Europe's shrinks. According to the US Census Bureau, the population will increase by 130m between 2000 and 2050. If this is right, the implications are profound. The European population currently is 100m higher than America's but, on this projection, by 2050 it will be 40m adrift. Because growth and productivity are linked to the size of the workforce, headcounts matter. The European Commission has forecast that the American economy will grow twice as fast as Europe's – 2.5 per cent a year against less than 1.5 per cent. What this means is a colossal realignment of power. In 2000, America's share of global GDP was 23 per cent and Europe's 18 per cent. By 2050 according to the seers the US will have 26 per cent and the EU just 10 per cent. All this is stated with the confidence of experts who won't be here to account for themselves if they are wrong. They may or may not be right. Their predictions were made before the (unpredicted) credit crunch sent the world economy into spasm, and economists as a species would make most racing tipsters look like Isaiah. These are tough times for prophets. What will be the precise angle of tilt in the new economic order? Who knows? Different juries on the same evidence will return different verdicts. The only certainty is that China and India will have a big say in whatever happens.

Some people actually welcome the idea of a dwindling population. The Optimum Population Trust (OPT), a Manchester-based research and campaign group, is dedicated to the principle of reducing the number of people in the world. 'No population can expand perpetually,' it says.

It is a mathematical and environmental impossibility. Except in very unusual circumstances, all populations will age as they begin to stabilize and reduce to more sustainable levels. The ageing 'problem' therefore needs to be tackled without incurring further population growth. The best way to tackle it is to improve health, improve productivity and skills, and ensure the best use of the national workforce.

Its recommendations are startling. Bearing in mind our needs (food, housing, energy, water) and our damaging impacts on the environment (traffic congestion, pollution, waste, urban development), it reckons that the maximum population the UK can sustain over the long term may be as little as 30m – approximately what it was in the 1880s. Currently it stands at 60.6m. Even with below-replacement fertility it is expected to hit 65m by 2016. The OPT's prescription therefore looks like a pivotal moment in the history of loopiness. Cut the population by more than 50 per cent? The OPT insists there is nothing sinister in its proposal – no culling of the Zimmer-framed hordes; no compulsory sterilization; no legal limit to the size of families. All that's needed, it says, is for us to accept the low fertility rate and equalize the inward and outward flow of migrants. Wait until 2121, and – hey presto! – there's your 30m.

Well, yes, you can do a Busby Berkeley and make the figures dance any way you like, but compulsory veganism and speaking pidgin have more chance of becoming government policy than halving the population. Greed will go on creating its internal conflicts – greed for more economically active people versus greed for bigger personal shares. But people will go on shuffling around the globe, and the process is likelier to accelerate than it is to slow down. Climate change in time will produce environmental as well as economic refugees as people displaced by flood, fire or famine edge northwards in search of survivable climates. In some places as the pressure mounts they will meet resistance from selfish populations disinclined to share. Some commentators have looked into their crystal balls and seen the ultimate collision between nationalism and humanity – the rebirth of fascism. In the meantime, in the contrary but flesh-and-blood world of sub-replacement fertility and national greed, human bodies are like beads on an abacus, to be slid wherever they count the most.

We hear a lot now about 'identity'. People reared in the age of psychoanalysis talk of 'finding out who they are'. Perhaps this is admirable. Who would argue against self-discovery? But it is by definition self-regarding, an internal inventory of spiritual belongings as selfish as any miser shuffling his pennies. *Mine!* Who does not know of some relationship damaged or destroyed by a partner's neurotic self-absorption? Even so, it's in our natures to be self-seeking and maybe there is some purpose to it. Perhaps we have an angst gene that contributes in some way to our survival. Maybe God exists and looks like Woody Allen. Societies are much the same. How do we define ourselves? What is our purpose? *Ours!* In a shrinking and increasingly globalized world, it is no wonder that so much fluff is being picked from so many navels, and so much angst focused on issues of national identity. At a time when corporations are richer than governments, and when the world cries out for concerted effort, on what basis do we mark out our turf?

For its opponents, nationalism is as broad a target as gods and queens. None of the modern world's sovereign states existed at the time of Christ, or is blessed by anything holier than circumstance. There is no objective reality to our nationality. It's simply a convenient way of summarizing a history of accidents and subjective choices. You can understand E. M. Forster: 'If I had to choose between betraying my country and betraying my friend, I hope I would have the guts to betray my country.' The tragedy of nationalism so often is that 'national identity' means punishing those who don't conform, or who fail to fit the blueprint. (Think of the Spanish or any other civil war.) As such identity is likely to involve race, culture, language and religion, the dangers are all too clear. Most nation states include minority groups whose loyalties are divided between the land of their ancestors and their adoptive home. Hence Norman Tebbit's 'cricket test'. Hence the corrosive effects of established societies on 'subordinate' ethnic groups, and hence all the hand-wringing about 'old' and 'new' nationalism. 'This land,' said Woody Guthrie in the title of his most famous song, 'is your land'. Now we just need to discuss the terms.

Migrant communities may be treated in one of four different ways. If the parties of the extreme political right were to have their way – Jean-Marie Le Pen's Front National in France, for example – then the borders would be closed and they would simply be kept out. This is objectionable but it cannot be laughed off. Simple policies have direct appeal to the simple-minded, and this one raises echoes in neo-fascist groups right across Europe – the Swiss People's Party (SVP), Italy's neo-fascists, Austria's Freedom Party (FPO), Belgium's Vlaams Blok, the Danish People's Party (DPP), various right-wing groups in Germany, the Hellenic Front in Greece, Pim Fortuyn's List (LPF) in the Netherlands, Norway's Progress Party, Portugal's Popular Party and England's very own British National Party (BNP). Some of these rightly have failed to achieve political respectability, but others have enjoyed a measure of electoral success, particularly among inner-city poor whites. No one should be complacent. Le Pen in France was well beaten in the final round of the 2002 presidential election, but 6m still voted for him and France is furiously protective of its native culture. Its policy for immigrants is *assimilation*. In return for their acceptance as citizens, ethnic minorities are expected to abandon their cultures, eschew ethnic politics and adopt the ways of the French. Education is secular and admits no minority cultures (the wearing of religious symbols, most importantly the Muslim hijab, is banned in schools). Not everyone likes the look of this. Here is the French journalist Naima Bouteldja, writing in the *Guardian*:

> As the French philosopher Pierre Tévanian has argued, what is most interesting about this debate around the 'veil' is not what it has veiled (social issues), but what it has unveiled. 'There exists in France a cultural racism, which targets the descendants of the colonized, and primarily picks upon their Muslim identity.' This post-colonial anxiety helps us to understand the ubiquity of appeals to 'reaffirm' the secular principles of the republic, even as it reinvents and distorts those very traditions.

The third option – *subordination* – if anything is even more offensive to liberal opinion. This is pure calculation, economics untrammelled by sentiment. Governments may accept foreign workers to plug gaps in their labour markets, but these 'guest workers' – *Gastarbeiter*, as Germany knows them – are denied full rights and are legally second-class citizens, even though many of them stay for the rest of their lives and raise children. The system has a number of variants. One of these, popular in America and across Europe, is the turning of blind eyes towards illegal immigrants (for who else but Chicanos, Latinos, Mexicans and Hispanics would swab America's lavatories?). That way you get the dirty jobs done, but not at the expense of social rights or education for the children. Another wheeze, closer to old-fashioned slavery, is the short-term importation of seasonal labour. A couple of summers ago, a friend called me and said he had been talking to a strawberry-picker at a local fruit farm. This highly intelligent young man was working for a few pounds an hour, but was still earning substantially more than he could make in his native Poland, where he held a master's degree in micro-biology. Our plan (successfully accomplished, though I never heard the outcome) was to put him in touch with an English university. It made me look more carefully at the other field-workers – from Portugal, Poland, Lithuania, Latvia, Romania,

Bulgaria – who pour into East Anglia for the various harvests. From many of the locals they receive no more respect than did the 'gyppos' of old, and they suffer the same distrust. These are not so much second-class citizens as not citizens at all. Exploitation is too kind a word for what they suffer. Their labour is taken from them by thieves. This is greed in the raw: gangmasters trading in poverty, selling others' misery for profit, calculatedly rejecting every last remnant of decency. They are not the worst – not quite. That distinction belongs to the traffickers who smuggle 'illegals' through the ports and, having collected their fees, care little for whether their cargoes live or die (unless they can wring more profit from them as prostitutes). But the gangmasters conduct their business openly in the fields, not covertly in the backs of lorries. They are part of the national economy: not just condoned, but necessary fillers of low-paid manual jobs at farms, factories and food packing stations. Some of the workers are illegals, and so have no enforceable rights at all, but most are from the EU and so theoretically have the same protection under law as the native English. But then so does any other victim of kidnap.

They are recruited through advertisements placed by agencies in their home countries. Usually these promise flights, accommodation and all the normal benefits of working in Britain. People do not need much persuading. Unemployment in parts of Poland nudges 30 per cent (45 per cent for 15–24-year-olds). By contrast, in 2005 the lowest regional unemployment rate in the whole of the EU was 2.6 per cent in Herefordshire, Worcestershire and Warwickshire. These are like areas of low and high pressure on a weather map. You don't need to think too hard about which way the wind will blow; nor do you need much imagination to understand why people starved of opportunity will grab whatever is offered to them. What is offered very often is a 'contract' whose effectiveness is limited to the first three letters of the word. In 60 per cent of cases there is no formal contract at all, and the victims are skinned alive. Rates of pay hover around the UK national minimum (£4.60 an hour for 18–21-year-olds; £5.52 for 22 and above) and, with long hours in prospect, the sums seem to stack up nicely. But then come the deductions. Workers are told before they leave home that transport to and from work will be provided – well so it is, but the implication that it will be provided free is either an outright lie or a deception. The cost is deducted from wages. So is rent for the six-to-a-room accommodation where a 'bed' is often just a sleeping bag on the floor, occupied serially by people on different shifts; so are other 'advances' and 'arrangement fees' which the agency's gangmasters don't even bother to explain. Often the flight is charged for too, at a multiple of the actual cost; so is the 'hire' of hard hats or protective clothing. The result is that men and women can find themselves with not much more than £30 in their pockets after a long week of 4am starts and the kind of workload that would have finished off Orwell's Boxer.

The comparison with a horse is apposite: you simply would not treat one like this. Unlike Boxer, spent humans won't be sold to a glue factory if they become too ill or unfit to work; but they will be turfed out of their accommodation with insufficient money to look after themselves or to buy tickets home. For much of the time, they are stripped even of their legal identities. David de Verny, the Church of England's former chaplain for the 70,000 migrant workers in Lincolnshire and a vocal critic of the 'guest-worker' system, explains:

Gangmasters take the workers' passports on arrival at the airport for the officially required registration with the Home Office. It takes the Home Office three months and more to process New Arrivals who register. During that time foreign workers cannot prove who they are because the passport is the only legal document they have. Often, the passports are not returned to their owners when they come back from the Home Office but are sold on or used in fraud for vast profits. Taking the passport away ensures total dependency of the worker on the gangmaster – without a passport, one is nobody. Not only can the workers not prove who they are, they cannot apply for a bank account or get a National Insurance Number. If workers insist on the return of their passport they are often physically assaulted, lose their job and the roof over their head. The police are normally too overstretched to do more than issue a crime number.

If the foreign workers had their passports and were able to provide a bank with utility bills they could apply for a bank account. The farmer or packing firm could then pay the worker's salary directly into this account without the gangmaster taking his or her illegal cut. However, more than half of all workers live in the property of their gangmaster and therefore do not have utility bills of their own with their name and address on. It is a vicious circle.

On top of this they often have to endure the racist abuse of people whose understanding of economics is owed to right-wing agitators and newspapers who complain of foreigners 'coming over here and taking our jobs'. 'Name calling and spitting happen regularly,' says David de Verny. 'Even stone-throwing has been known. Migrant workers' cars are more frequently damaged than others. A Portuguese pub in Boston has its windows smashed regularly.' Sprout-picking or turkey-packing were probably not what Gordon Brown had in mind when he told the Labour Party's annual conference in September 2007 that the government would be 'drawing on the talents of all to create British jobs for British workers'. *British jobs for British workers* . . . It's a sentiment that comes dangerously close to the nationalist slogans of the far right, and a policy of questionable legality under European law. But we mustn't judge an idea just by the company it keeps. Perhaps it would be no bad thing for patriotism and the national flag (with which Labour's conference hall was bedecked) to be wrested back from the loonies and reclaimed for the political mainstream. It brings us back to the government's idea of 'citizenship' as a kind of cross-cultural badge of belonging. No one could imagine that Brown was using 'British' to mean 'white Anglo-Saxon' – he may be sectarian, but he is not a racist. Until now, the UK government's policy on ethnic minorities has been *multiculturalism*. Ethnic groups have been encouraged to retain their cultural identity while enjoying the same social and political rights as the indigenous majority. In a sense it's hardly a policy at all – just a question of good manners, tolerance and a few public notices in funny scripts. In matters of dress, diet, custom and worship, immigrants are as free as the rest of us to make their choices. Provided they stay within the law, who are we to tell them how to behave? A society is enriched, not impoverished, by diversity. This is a difficult idea to let go of, but its shortcomings, too, are hard to deny. John Rex, former president of the International Sociological Association's Research Committee on racial and ethnic minorities, former member of a UNESCO committee on race relations and now Professor Emeritus in the Centre for Research in Ethnic Relations at the University of Warwick, had this to say in a paper of 1996:

In principle all of these multicultural states would claim that they seek to foster cultural diversity at the same time as promoting equality at least in the social sphere. Very often, however, the rhetoric of an egalitarian multiculturalism conceals the existence of a multiculturalism based upon inequality. Thus French critics of British multiculturalism in practice claim that it conceals a policy of ghettoizing the immigrants . . .

This might or might not be 'policy', but it is certainly the reality. As Rex himself pointed out, multiculturalists like to argue that mainstream society is transformed by its new citizens and that 'there will be, and should be, a society whose culture is a new kind of amalgam which will supersede national culture'. It is not just the multiculturalists themselves who say this. The dilution of national culture is precisely the ground on which the opposition has built its redoubt. It is why the French, notoriously protective of their culture, are so insistent upon assimilation, and why they are so jumpy about the viral infection of their language – *le football*, *le camping*, *le parking*, *le crumble*, etc. – by English. It is why they turn up their noses at any combination of food ingredients not traceable to a region of their own country. This is a more serious point than it sounds (I write with curry on my breath), for the adoption of an immigrant cuisine is the most visible evidence of majority acceptance. Nevertheless, curry and kebabs do not threaten the structures of law, government and the established religion, which are unlikely to be altered. 'They cannot be,' said Rex, 'without the modernizing nation state ceasing to exist.'

In preparing this chapter I sampled a fistful of learned papers on the identity of the nation state, and more on the principles of nationalism. These led me on a broad sweep all the way from Garibaldi through Hitler to literati who argue nationalistically that Shakespeare, Goethe or Proust was the greatest exponent of the greatest language ever spoken. In the end, dizzy with *isms*, I felt I had tuned in to something very like a student debate – engrossing over a late-night bottle of Bull's Blood, perhaps even the stuff of PhDs, but not obviously relevant to the people of Southall, Sydney or Cincinnati. Labelling a problem is not the same as solving it. There is no future for a world whose peoples do not recognize their common interests and resolve to pursue them co-operatively. Reciprocal altruism needs to go global, but how can it happen internationally unless we get it right locally first? Looking for a definition of 'nation state', I can find none better than the one I quoted earlier: 'A political unit consisting of an autonomous state inhabited predominantly by a people sharing a common culture, history, and language.' But this is a wish-list, not a reality. All that commonality takes time. *History!* And it needs to grow organically. It cannot be done by treaty, or rocket power, or a 'road-map'. Perfect solutions exist only on paper. The reality is flesh and blood, and all the imperfections of a species for which the seven deadly sins are more like a specification of ordinariness than a catalogue of malfunctions. Imperfection is the status quo. Nation states in many instances are cursed with arbitrariness – the constructs of further-lands, not fatherlands – and no one alive will see an end to the greed, anger, envy and pride that carve the rifts. Imperfect solutions may be the best we have.

I am shocked to learn that the first year in which there was no recorded lynching of a black American occurred within my own lifetime, in 1952. Fifty-six years later, and 170 years after the abolition of slavery, people are still being trafficked or economically suppressed by 'superior' powers. Sixty years – *sixty years!* – after the *Empire Windrush* docked at Tilbury with its first cargo of immigrants from the Caribbean, we have yet to achieve racial harmony. We have instead a nervy, weasel-mouthed substitute – political correctness – and a body of law that criminalizes 'hate'. The second most senior figure in the English church is the black, Ugandan-born Archbishop of York, Dr John Sentamu. In early March 2008 he complained that the British government had failed to build a cohesive society. This came barely a month after the Archbishop of Canterbury had made his remarks about sharia law, and not long after the Bishop of Rochester, Michael Nazir-Ali, had described parts of the country as 'no-go' areas for non-Muslims. It came on the very same day that Gordon Brown, dumbing down for the Labour Party's spring conference in Birmingham, delivered some wet and slithery stuff about 'building the Britain of our dreams'. Sentamu said: 'When I came here in 1974, we were treated with dignity, with love, and in the rest of the nation there was this sense of magnanimity, the will to meet another person. Over these 34 years, we've had a rant about immigration and haven't met major questions of race. Britain is a very, very uncomfortable place.'

The rant goes on. Our attitudes to immigration (and hence to race and nationality) have been severely examined by the expansion of the European Union and the freeing of national borders. There is a wider choice of scapegoat now, and a more complex human trading system than we have ever had before. The trade may no longer be coercive – migrants move voluntarily, not chained to galleys – but it is still a trade, and it's the market that sets the terms. We have seen what this means to the eastern Europeans who pick and pack Britain's greengrocery. For others without automatic right of entry – *aliens*, we call them – it works like the market for any other tradeable commodity. The country is short of toolmakers? OK, we'll get some in. Australia, for example, has a well-established points system for aspirant migrants. Scores are awarded for age (they want them young), education, qualifications, experience and skill. During 2008 they have been advertising for automotive electricians, fitters, upholsterers, boilermakers, metal mechanists, motor mechanics, panel beaters, pastrycooks, sheet metal workers, toolmakers, vehicle painters and welders. Individual states have lists of their own. South Australia wants electricians, roofers, plasterers, stonemasons, butchers, cabinet-makers and cooks ... Victoria needs bricklayers, aircraft engineers, plumbers, hairdressers and chefs. Queensland wants carpenters, dental technicians, bakers and boat-builders. The UK government has long admired the Australian model. On 29 February 2008, it applied the sincerest form of flattery and introduced a lookalike system of its own. The borders and immigration minister, Liam Byrne, was in Delhi at the time, explaining how the 'points-based immigration system'(PBS) would apply to Indians: 'The points system means only those migrants Britain needs can come to the UK. We know that migrants contributed to our economy to the tune of £6 billion to GDP in 2006. A strong system for highly skilled migrants is vital to Britain winning these benefits because these migrants are well educated and pay lots of tax.'

At least this had the merit of frankness. As imperfect solutions go, it is probably less imperfect than most. The nation state is not an earthmother. It is more like a blind ogre or a selfish gene in the DNA of Gaia – amoral, avaricious and determined upon self-perpetuation. For its human feedstock life is a game of chance. Though governments and corporations may set the odds, they can't control the dice. Even when immigrants take jobs no one else wants, they may not be welcomed. Here is how one commentator perceived the issue in the *Daily Telegraph*:

> My late and much lamented friend Lord Harris of High Cross used to make the unanswerable point that you will have unemployment so long as you pay people to be unemployed. You will also have it so long as you let in masses of keen immigrants who prevent the natives from getting off their bottoms. If we really do have fewer immigrants, the excuses for the workshy will be that much harder to find.

What's implicit here is that community relations get trickier as we descend the socio-economic scale. Highly paid white professionals have little difficulty in their relationships with middle-class immigrant colleagues, or with the working-class immigrants who live in different postcodes. Race is a class issue too, and class itself is a deepening fault line as rich and poor grow further apart. For many middle-class people in the shires and the leafier parts of cities, the poor are another country. Their run-down, self-vandalized estates are no-go areas. The poor have the worst education, the worst employment prospects, the worst health, the worst crime, the most unruly young. The right-wing, neo-fascist groups draw their following almost entirely from this poor white urban working class, which they encourage to feel threatened. In a BBC survey in March 2008, 52 per cent of white working-class people (against 33 per cent middle class) said they thought immigration was a bad thing. The state primary school which my children briefly attended in South London thought it necessary to festoon the corridors with notices banning racial abuse and threatening punishments for those who transgressed. No such strictures were thought necessary in the racially mixed independent schools to which we moved them. Racism was not expected, and it did not happen.

The need for foreign workers, and their contribution to the economy, is generally not well understood by those who elect the government. *British jobs for British workers* might secure a few votes, but no party has ever marched to victory by promising to increase immigration. It remains a risky subject to speak or write about. Racists cloak their prejudice by talking in numbers. Non-racists risk charges of racism whenever they raise the issue of control or step outside the boundaries of political correctness. The perils were well illustrated in the early days of David Cameron's leadership of the Conservative Party. In an interview with *Times Online*, his homeland security spokesman Patrick Mercer, a former army colonel, said this:

I had the good fortune to command a battalion that was racially very mixed. Towards the end, I had five company sergeant-majors who were all black. They were without exception UK-born, Nottingham-born men who were English – as English as you and me. They prospered inside my regiment, but if you'd said to them: 'Have you ever been called a nigger,' they would have said: 'Yes.' But equally, a chap with red hair, for example, would also get a hard time – a far harder time than a black man, in fact. But that's the way it is in the army. If someone is slow on the assault course, you'd get people shouting: 'Come on you fat bastard, come on you ginger bastard, come on you black bastard.'

He said also that soldiers sometimes used racism as a cover for their own poor performance. 'I came across a lot of ethnic minority soldiers who were idle and useless, but who used racism as cover for their misdemeanours.' Then he continued: 'In my experience, when you put on the uniform then all differences disappear. If you are a good soldier, you will do well. If you are a bad soldier, you will leave prematurely. There is a degree of colour-blindness among the vast majority of soldiers. I never came across a piece of nastiness inside the battalion that was based exclusively on racism.'

The result was a hotly contested race to see who could be first and fiercest in their condemnation. Cameron himself declared the remarks 'completely unacceptable' and ordered Mercer to resign – ie, in plain language, sacked him – from the front bench. Labour's armed forces minister, Adam Ingram, charged up with flag and bugle. 'Our troops and our officers,' he said, 'are 21st-century people who recognize that there is no place for prejudice in the modern world ... Patrick Mercer may have a military background but he no longer speaks for the Armed Forces.' Jack Straw, leader of the Commons, who had defied the better judgement of most of the electorate by championing the deployment of 'our troops and our officers' in Iraq, and who had outraged Muslims in his Blackburn constituency by asking women at his surgeries to lift their veils, found Mercer's comments 'breathtaking and dreadful'. The Commission for Racial Equality applauded Cameron's swift action: 'This sends a clear signal that racist attitudes and comments are not acceptable. Grown-up modern politics has no place for bigots.'

Grown-up modern politics? I have never met Patrick Mercer. I dare say I wouldn't care much for his politics, nor he for mine. His attitude to military aggression, I suspect, would put him closer to Jack Straw and the redneck violence of George W. Bush. Nor did he show much in the way of political astuteness. Robust views are all very well, but front-bench spokesmen are expected to mind their language and not raise words like 'nigger' above the parapet. The snipers won't miss a target as big as that. But as to the actual *meaning* of what he said – that the badinage between mates at work may include references to skin as well as hair colour, and that black people may counter legitimate complaints about their performance with accusations of racism – most people could report similar experiences in civilian life. I certainly could, but is it 'racist' to say so? Does it make Mercer a *bigot*? Here is what Leroy Hutchinson, a former corporal in his regiment, had to say: 'I am a black man, who served with Patrick for twelve years. I was promoted to corporal under his command. He never tolerated racism in the battalion and not a single one of his men would consider him to be racist.'

This doesn't necessarily excuse what was said, and people will have their own views on whether or not it was allowable. But I am reminded of one of those innumerable (and, yes, *racist*) Irish jokes that circulated in the 1960s. Perhaps they circulate still – I don't know. In this one the two protagonists are, as ever, Paddy and Mick. Their troubles begin when each one buys a horse but the animals are so alike that they can't tell them apart. 'Tell you what,' says Paddy. 'I'll take the tall one.' But they are both the same height. 'Then I'll take the shaggy one,' says Mick. But they've both got shaggy manes. 'I'll take the one with the long tail,' says Paddy. But they've both got long tails. Then (to cut a very long story short) Mick has a brainwave.

'I know,' he says. 'Why don't I just take the white one and you take the black?'

I am reminded, too, of the television coverage of the (I think) 1976 Olympic Games, when commentators identified a shot-putter as 'the one with the afro hairdo' and a boxer as 'the one in the green shorts'. Both competitors were black, and their opponents white. A number of different conclusions might be drawn from this, as they might from the Mercer case, but you'd be hard pressed to see evidence of a mature attitude to race. In Britain, the issue is complicated by feelings of guilt over our colonial past. In February 2006 the Church of England Synod voted 'overwhelmingly' to apologize to descendants of slaves. The Archbishop of Canterbury seemed to believe that, even though the abolition of slavery in British territories was nearing its 200th anniversary (in 2007), we had not yet expiated our guilt: 'The body of Christ is not just a body that exists at any one time, it exists across history and we therefore share the shame and the sinfulness of our predecessors and part of what we can do, with them and for them in the body of Christ, is pray for acknowledgement of the failure that is part of us, not just of some distant "them".'

In November of the same year, prime minister Blair offered his 'deep sorrow' – though not actually an apology – for Britain's historic involvement in the slave trade. All the usual balloons went up. According to Charles Moore in the *Daily Telegraph*, there was no reason for Blair to say sorry at all. 'He is not responsible for the slave trade in any way, and by half-suggesting that he is, he surrenders to unreason and creates difficulties for his successors.' Others argued that by stopping short of a full apology, and by saying nothing about 'reparation', Blair had not done enough to expunge the stain. Esther Stanford, secretary of the Rendezvous of Victory Campaign, put it like this: 'What is now required is a dialogue about how we repair the legacies of enslavement, and we're talking about educational repairs, we're talking about economic repairs, family repairs, cultural repairs, repairs of every kind that we need to recreate and sustain ourselves – it will cost.'

More pressingly, we are talking about the character of a modern nation state at a time when the flow of people around the globe is more likely to increase than it is to lessen. If the events of 200 years ago are still such a dilemma, how are we going to handle the future? Are newcomers to be subordinated, assimilated or ghettoized? Blair's successor Gordon Brown launched a high-profile campaign to redefine 'Britishness'. A stronger sense of 'patriotic purpose', he said, 'would help resolve some of our most important national challenges, make us more confident about Britain's role in Europe and the world, and would help us better integrate our ethnic communities, respond to migration and show people the responsibilities as well as rights that must be at the heart of modern citizenship'. The old way, multiculturalism, would be the earliest casualty. He complained of an 'opportunist coalition of minority Nationalists and from what used to be the Conservative and Unionist Party', who were pursuing a 'perilous orthodoxy emphasizing what divides us rather than what unites'.

> It is an irony that this is happening just as we are waking from a once-fashionable view of multiculturalism, which, by emphasizing the separate and the exclusive, simply pushed communities apart. What was wrong about multiculturalism was not the recognition of diversity but that it over-emphasized separateness at the cost of unity. Continually failing to emphasize what bound us together as a country, multiculturalism became an excuse for justifying separateness, and then separateness became a tolerance of – and all too often a defence of – even greater exclusivity.

While the left is shuffling away from multiculturalism, the right is rushing to kick it in the head. Writing to the *Spectator*, the Thatcher-era warhorse Lord Tebbit took a long hard swing at members of the Conservative shadow cabinet who 'admired' Tony Blair. 'It was Blair,' he reminded them, 'who introduced uncontrolled, unmeasured immigration of people determined not to integrate, but to establish, first ghettoes, and now demands for separate legal jurisdiction. In biblical terms, Blairism is the poisonous tree which can give forth only poisonous fruit and must be rooted out.' Political sophisticates will find nuances to separate the anti-Blairite dogmas of Brown and Tebbit, and the Blairy new Toryism of David Cameron, but to multiculturalists they are like a three-headed dog barking in unison. In a debate hosted by the Equality and Human Rights Commission, Cameron flicked an obligatory back-hander at 'state multiculturalism' but his voice soon merged with the others. For a long time, he said, 'we've been handing a victory to our enemies – to those who want to divide and those who oppose liberal values – through the doctrine we have applied to community relations'. He complained of financial aid going to arts projects 'purely on account of ethnic background'; of public information being translated into other languages for the benefit of 'people who can then continue to go about their daily lives without ever having to learn English'; of treating ethnic populations as 'monolithic blocks rather than individual citizens'. He went on:

> By concentrating on defining the various cultures that have come to call Britain home, we have forgotten to define the most important one: our own. So we now have a situation where the children of first-generation immigrants – children, let us remember, who have been born and raised here – feel more divorced from life in Britain than their parents. In America, 47 per cent of Muslims think of themselves as Muslim first, American second. In Britain, it's nearly twice that – with 81 per cent of Muslims thinking of themselves as Muslim first and British second.

Alongside Cameron sat Trevor Phillips, chairman of the Equality and Human Rights Commission, a man who in 2005 had warned that multiculturalism was allowing Britain to 'sleep-walk into segregation'. This had triggered what might now be called the Mercer effect. The then mayor of London, Ken Livingstone, possibly Europe's most unrepentant multiculturalist as well as leader of its most racially diverse city (more than 300 languages are spoken there), predicted that Phillips – a London-born black man he had once wanted as his deputy – would 'soon be joining the BNP'. Preposterous though this was, it showed the extent to which even men of good intent may be divided. The 2001 UK census was conducted in 24 languages:

Albanian/Kosovan, Arabic, Bengali, Cantonese, Croatian, Farsi/Persian, French, German, Greek, Gujarati, Hindi, Italian, Japanese, Polish, Portuguese, Punjabi, Russian, Serbian, Somali, Spanish, Swahili, Turkish, Urdu and Vietnamese. According to the Department for Education and Skills, at least 3m people living in the UK in 2001 were born in countries whose national language was not English. In 2007, 13.5 per cent of all primary school children and 10.5 per cent of secondary school children had a first language other than English. America is much the same. The US speaks a total of 311 languages, of which 162 are indigenous, and 20 per cent of people aged over five speak 'foreign' languages. This adds up to 14m households. *A political unit consisting of an autonomous state inhabited predominantly by a people sharing a common culture, history, and language*? Clearly, in the most advanced societies, the old notion of nation state no longer applies. From out of this lumpy clay something very different will have to be formed.

Gordon Brown's search for 'Britishness' therefore is not quite the stunt it might appear to be. The who-are-we question is a real question needing a real answer, not just a spasm of neurotic whimsy. As Abraham Lincoln put it, society – any society – needs principles 'applicable to all men at all times'. We need liberty and opportunity. One cannot imagine a prime minister prefacing a speech with 'My fellow Britishers'. And yet this is what American presidents, Democrats as well as Republicans, do as a matter of course. *My fellow Americans.* It harks to the founding principles of the Bill of Rights. To declare yourself American is to buy into an ideal. So it is to declare yourself French: *liberté, égalité, fraternité*. It is often suggested that our indistinct sense of Britishness is explained by the lack of a French- or American-style founding ideal, and that all we need to rediscover our patriotism is a US-style Bill of Rights. But it is not that straightforward. America, too, is struggling with its identity and facing precisely the same kinds of conflict – traditional Anglo-Protestantism versus multiculturalism; the immutable 'creed' of the founding fathers against the cultural mongrelism of the world's most diverse nation. Even America can feel threatened by the tide of Spanish-speaking immigrants from the south. The question, *Can Mexicans and South Americans adopt the 'core values' of the Anglo-Protestant pioneers of the USA?*, precisely mirrors the dilemmas of Europe. *Can Muslims be real French people? Can they be real English? Can Turks be real Germans, or Indians real Scots?* And what does 'real' mean? Even if the answer to 'can' is yes, what about 'should'?

Multiculturalists follow the Rousseauesque line that all cultures are created equal, and that it is wrong to assert WASP values *über Alles*. This is not actually a very good argument. Charles R. Kesler, professor of government and director of the Henry Salvatori Center at Claremont McKenna College, California, put it succinctly. 'The problem with this argument,' he said in a lecture in 2005, 'is that it is self-contradictory. For if all cultures are created equal, and if none is superior to any other, why not prefer one's own?' And of course, as he went on to say, multiculturalists trim their case to exclude cultures they disapprove of – those that oppose multiculturalism, disrespect the environment and deny equal rights to women and homosexuals. He reminded us, too, that the US in its early years (how different they were from today!) had naturalization laws but not immigration laws – 'so that, technically speaking, we had open borders'.

On immigration, the founders taught that civil society is based on a contract, a contract presupposing the unanimous consent of the individuals who come together to make a people. When newcomers appear, they may join that society if they and the society concur. In other words, from the nature of the people as arising from a voluntary contract, consent remains a two-way street: an immigrant must consent to come, and the society must consent to receive him. Otherwise, there is a violation of the voluntary basis of civil society.

Any individual has, in Jefferson's words, the right to emigrate from a society in which chance, not choice, has placed him. But no society has a standing natural duty to receive him or to take him in. Thus, it is no violation of human rights to pick and choose immigrants based on what a particular civil society needs.

Immigrants, in other words, need to be made of the right stuff, and they need to understand what they are buying into. Kesler quotes Benjamin Franklin's essay of 1784, 'Information to Those Who Would Remove to America'. Anyone intending to join the 'Land of Labor', Franklin said, would have to put his back into it. America was not a place where 'the Fowls fly about ready roasted, crying, Come eat me!' Nevertheless, the long history of assimilation in the US *has* built a tradition of national pride and unembarrassed patriotism. Regardless of your roots, you are first and foremost an *American*. In the most perverse and appalling way, 9/11 was the proof of this. The hijackers who steered the jets into the World Trade Center cared nothing for the race or religion of their victims – black, white, brown, Asian, Oriental, Mexican, Muslim, Catholic, Jew, it mattered not. All that counted was that they were American. It is frequently asserted that 9/11 'changed everything', and that 7/7, when the London transport system was attacked by 'home-grown' suicide bombers, changed it a little bit more. Such events have placed a powerful argument in the hands of the anti-multiculturalists, and have emphasized another threat to the integrity of the nation state – the influence of supranational forces (in this case religious fundamentalism) which outrank local citizenship, and which oblige elected governments to negotiate with 'community leaders'.

As a seat of empire, Britain of course had long experience of supranational power, and the 'United Kingdom' of England, Wales, Scotland and Northern Ireland allowed it to develop an idea of Britishness that did not depend on ethnicity. But there is nothing in either the collective memory or the historical record that can provide a ready answer to the question Gordon Brown asked – a question given further twists by the devolved assemblies of Scotland and Wales and the strength of Scottish nationalism. What does it mean to be British? What *are* the values that unite us? What are the ideals around which everyone – English, Scots, Welsh, Northern Irish and ethnic minorities – can regroup? In political, economic and cultural terms you can argue for and against the UK's 'special relationship' with America; for or against the European Union. What cannot be argued is that these things have had no effect on sovereignty. Administrative, legal and economic ties with Europe have combined with the Americanization of Britain's culture to fracture yet further our elusive national identity.

Some people think that the answer – or part of it – lies in better history teaching, in creating a 'national story' with which we can all identify. But which version of whose story would it be? We might also feel a sense of connection through our redistributive tax system, pride in the National Health Service and the welfare state. Or through Gordon Brown's emphasis on 'values' – by which one takes him to mean things like fairness, tolerance, charity, freedom of expression and civic responsibility. But these are universal values and we cannot be defined by them as a nation, only as humans. Unless you count the forces of globalism or international terrorism, there is not even a common enemy to unite against, and no 'finest hour' to aspire to. The debate will go on, and I doubt it will yield an answer. The 'citizenship tests' for non-EU citizens wanting to settle in the UK may help people understand a little more about the country they are moving to, but it will not reprogramme them or wipe clean their cultural slates; and what could be more unBritish than the school-children's oath-swearing ceremonies envisaged by Gordon Brown's patriotism commissar Lord Goldsmith?

Multiculturalism may not have delivered nirvana, but for millions of people in Britain it is, and for more than a generation must surely remain, the reality of their daily lives. It is the same for all nation states in the developed world. There is no way forward that does not involve diversity and multi-ethnicity. We can let our worst instincts – jealousy, bigotry, selfishness, greed – turn it into a nightmare of ghettoization, second-class citizenship and oppression in which young men conceive violent hatreds for the countries of their birth. Or we can look for a new concept of nation state that builds on shared experience and is bound together by something more than distrust of strangers. Of all the stations at which greed makes obeisance in its outflow from the self, the boundary of the nation state – the line on the map – is by far the most dangerous.

7

Turning on the Power

A motion approved by the National Union of Teachers in March 2008 called for representatives of the armed forces to be banned from visiting schools. The proposer argued that 16-year-olds were too impressionable to be exposed to 'glamorized and untruthful' accounts of military life, and that they would be seduced into fighting 'deeply unpopular' wars in places like Iraq. This tells us something about the politicization of the teaching profession, but something also about the decline in respect for military careers. Earlier the same month, airmen from RAF Wittering were ordered not to wear their uniforms while off duty in Peterborough, where they had been abused by people opposed to the Iraq and Afghan wars.

Both incidents were symptomatic of a wider truth. Military actions by British and American troops, pursuing our national interest in faraway countries at the cost of thousands of lives, have been so completely stripped of glory that no political leader now would dream of repeating Margaret Thatcher's call to 'rejoice' in victory. Tony Blair very early in the Iraq campaign veered away from the word 'crusade', though many on the other side have no such problem with *jihad*. As it was in the 11th, 12th and 13th centuries, so it is now. The advancing armies are mainly Christian, and the bodies piling up are mostly Muslim.

Self-censoring news media, sensitive to images of death, protect us from the bloodier realities of what is being done in our name. Many years ago I visited the British and German military cemeteries in Crete, where the message repeated endlessly in the visitors' books was 'Never again'. And so, in a way, it has been. The insanities of 9/11 and 7/7 were committed by young men, religiously schooled in violence, who thought they could surf to paradise on a rip-curl of infidel blood. But it was precisely the rarity of such events that made them so shocking. Violent death did not end in 1945. It just stopped happening in the cities of the victors. For as long as our bombs, bullets and rockets were delivering democracy in other latitudes, we could call it 'peace-time' and go on writing 'Never again'. Wars against evil were acts of peace.

Look anywhere in history and you will find city states, countries or empires killing each other's people. Some of the wars will have been 'holy'. Many will have been retributive – aggression answered by aggression. Most will have ended with the transfer of wealth, land and blame from the vanquished to the victor. Soldiers will have been brought to arms by coercion, bribery and rhetoric. Future historians looking back upon the 21st century may conclude that nothing much had changed beyond the power of national armouries and the language used to justify them. Holy wars these days tend to be freelance affairs trading on terror – anathema to secular sophisticates who categorize them as medieval. Western governments are no longer driven to battle by angry gods, but by moral codes in support of peace. In place of 'holy' we have 'just'. I owe to the BBC's Religion and Ethics department this six-point checklist which such a war must satisfy:

The war must be for a just cause.
It must be lawfully declared by a lawful authority.
The intention behind the war must be good.

All other ways of resolving the problem should have been tried first.

There must be a reasonable chance of success.

The means used must be in proportion to the end that the war seeks to achieve.

It doesn't take a lawyer to spot the routes for coach and horses. 'Just cause', 'lawful', 'good', 'reasonable' and 'in proportion' are interpretive highways of infinite breadth, like 'pretty', 'nasty' or 'nice'. Beating up Tibetan Buddhists is 'in proportion' if you think Chinese communism is a 'just cause'. The rhetoric of the old Soviet Union as it sent in the tanks was full of stuff like this. Modern Russia doesn't sound much different. Its May Day parade in 2008, with cocked missiles and soldiers stiffened in almost erotic ecstasy, would have made even Brezhnev smile. Its subsequent 'disciplining' of Georgia by its own definition was both 'reasonable' and 'lawful'. Nor did the speeches of George W. Bush do much to lighten the mood. Buddhists of course believe that anger is self-destructive, and expect to find the proof of it in future lives. Pope Gregory I in the 6th century excoriated it as a deadly sin, along with pride, envy, avarice, sadness (later to transmute into sloth), gluttony and lust. Others believe anger is hard-wired into our natures. Evolutionary psychologists see it as essential to the 'fight or flight' response that ensures our survival, and therapists argue that 'letting it out' is vital to our mental stability. Whether exemplified by possession of nuclear warheads, or by the belligerent reaction of an individual whose rights or property have been violated, the threat of anger is a powerful deterrent against transgressive behaviour. Hence the anxiety of the nuclear 'haves' to keep the 'have-nots' in their place. Nations are super-organisms composed of people whose instincts and behaviours are driven by their genes. You can believe that the seven deadly sins delineate the fall of man, or that they are tools in the workshop of a highly competitive species, forged by evolution. Either way, avarice, envy and pride guarantee that anger will always have a cause, and that enemies will not be far to seek.

Force of arms is not the only way strong countries oppress the weak. In place of colonels plotting troop movements on charts, businessmen and economists now track machine tools, sugar and bananas. Enemies are no longer blockaded by the fleet. In the ultimate agony of a consumerist world they are excluded from international markets. Economies wither, inflation spirals and people queue for bread. The banished have no tractor parts or medicines; no buyers for their crops. If invasion is like the bite of a cobra, then trade-war is the squeeze of a python. Nor does the predator simply glide away when the crisis passes. It just marginally loosens the squeeze.

The trade embargo is a powerful weapon, but trade itself is mightier still. Greed in the modern world wears many labels – 'free trade', 'economic growth', 'laissez faire', 'the market' – and the line between need and greed has been rubbed away. Western governments speak of the 'need' for new airports with the same certitude that Africa cries out for something to eat. Economists are the shock troops of the new world order, but their aim is erratic and collateral damage always likely. Economics is not an exact science, and so not really a science at all. Better call it informed speculation. By tweaking taxes or tariffs, raising or lowering interest rates, wealth and poverty are squirted up and down like ping-pong balls on fountains. It can look clever, spectacular even, but it is inherently unstable. An earthquake here, a tsunami there, wildfire, drought, disease, war, flood, famine, a change of government, the entire panoply of 'events' – all these can turn the neatest of calculations into number soup. This is why we get Black Monday, Black Wednesday, Northern Rock, Freddie Mac, Lehman Brothers, AIG, HBOS and all the rest. It is also why we get obesity in England and starvation in Ethiopia. It's why most Africans can expect to die before they are 48.

Economics is more than just a church. It is a theological war zone of clashing orthodoxies in which swivel-eyed cultists denounce each other for errors of faith. But they are also paid servants of their masters. There is a reason why half the world's population subsists on less than two dollars a day, and it has nothing to do with the fertility of the earth. When people starve it is not because there is insufficient food in the world. It is because their countries are too poor to buy it. 'Free trade' is the economist's best attempt at a moral precept. A tariff-free world, so the theory goes, is a fair world in which prices and incomes become equalized across the globe. The reality of the market, however, is that it has no more sense of justice than a rattlesnake, a tapeworm or a gene. The price of corn is the price of corn. Take it or leave it.

And of course we do not live in a tariff-free world. Rich countries patrol the supply lines like border guards in Soviet-era Berlin. Their weapons are import tariffs, trade barriers and subsidized agricultural overproduction, which ensure they will go on getting richer while the poor stay behind the wire. The economists who write the rules are the Mikhail Kalashnikovs and J. Robert Oppenheimers of the spreadsheet wars. Aid agencies say that 128m people would be lifted out of poverty if Africa, Latin America and eastern and southern Asia could increase their share of world exports by just 1 per cent. This would be worth 70bn dollars to Africa alone. But of course rich countries are no keener on empowering poor ones economically than they are on giving them the nuclear bomb. Tariff barriers faced by poor countries exporting to the rich are four times higher than those faced by the rich selling to the poor. Oxfam in 2002 reported that 'developing' countries – what used to be called the Third World – account for more than 40 per cent of the world's population but less than 3 per cent of the trade. Put another way, it means that 97p out of every £1 generated by world exports goes to high earners, and 3p to the poor.

At the polar extremities of economic debate are two irreconcilable views of the relationship between trade and poverty – 'globophobia' and 'globophilia'. *Globophobes* argue that international trade is a system of economic warfare that rewards aggressors and leaves victims even worse off than they were before. They believe poor countries should aim for self-sufficiency and so place themselves beyond the predators' reach. Only mavericks now think this, though 200 years ago it was the prevailing orthodoxy. Import barriers then were regarded as signs of hostile intent, and international trade seen in terms of victory and defeat. It was not until 1817, when the British economist David Ricardo published his *Principles of Political Economy and Taxation*, that the theory of 'comparative advantage' – the trade equivalent of reciprocal altruism – impressed itself on the political mind, and it was accepted that both parties in a transaction might enjoy a benefit. This now is the orthodoxy of the *globophiles*, and is as close as we get to a worldwide creed. The economic papacies of the World Bank and World Trade Organization are committed entirely to the belief that the cure for poverty is trade, and Ricardo is quoted more often than Moses. It is why some of us who write about 'the environment', unlike some organic fetishists, tend to tread carefully on the issue of air miles. Those imported beans are African livelihoods. It is why there is little demand for an outright ban on Asian sweatshops. Those bags and trainers at least put bread in mouths. The international community is supremely good at moral fanfares. This was the declaration issued by the UN General Assembly following the Millennium Summit in September 2000: 'We will spare no effort to free our fellow men, women, and children from the abject and dehumanizing conditions of extreme poverty, to which more than a billion of them are currently subjected. We are committed to making the right to development a reality for everyone and to freeing the entire human race from want.'

Never mind Tony Blair with the hand of history on his shoulder ... The UN wants to twist history's arm behind its back and make it change its ways. In the entire span of existence, no sovereign power has attempted anything like it. Global inequality since 1945 has widened from a chasm into a rift so wide that you can't see one side from the other. In 1950 the average income in the world's richest countries was 35 times higher than it was in the poorest. By 1992 the differential was 72:1, and by the end of that decade it was 86:1. More and more countries now are involved in global trade, which the high priests tell us should fling open the doors to equality and wealth. For some people it has done exactly that. For many of the world's poorest, however, the experience has been more of the same, a rolling programme of disasters as predictable as night: famine, disease, civil war, failed aid programmes, low life expectancy and economic breakdown.

What would confuse a stranger to the planet is that countries with scant natural resources seem to prosper at the expense of those with plenty. Erik S. Reinert, in *How Rich Countries Got Rich and Why Poor Countries Stay Poor*, offers the historical example of Venice. Wobbling on a swamp, and with scarcely as much as a potato to call its own, it nevertheless managed to place itself at the very hub of the world economy. In stark contrast was Naples, which was garlanded with natural abundance but locked in poverty. Reinert recalls the 'theory of uneven development' first expounded by the Neapolitan lawyer Antonio Serra in his *Breve trattato* of 1613: 'The key, [Serra] argued, was that the Venetians, barred from cultivating the land like the Neapolitans, had been forced to rely on their industry to make a living, harnessing the increasing returns to scale offered by manufacturing activities ... Paradoxically, being poor in natural resources could be a key to becoming wealthy.'

So the spiral began, and so it continues. Wealth creates power; power creates wealth. Driven by empires of church and state,

Europe conquered, colonized, enslaved and milked the world. Gold, silver, diamonds, platinum, oil, spices, coffee, tea, timber, muscle power . . . The raw ingredients of economic abundance were torn from their native soils and turned into foreign wealth. Mass poverty is the result. 'The problem,' said Oxfam, 'is not that international trade is inherently opposed to the needs and interests of the poor, but that the rules that govern it are rigged in favour of the rich.' It is not easy to understand quite how a system rigged for the rich could be anything other than opposed to the poor, and Oxfam's attempt at diplomacy, if that's what it is, is short-lived. 'In their rhetoric,' says the same report a few lines further on, 'governments of rich countries constantly stress their commitment to poverty reduction. Yet the same governments use their trade policy to conduct what amounts to robbery against the world's poor.'

In theory (and 'theory' here is right), trade stimulates employment, and it does so especially in the kinds of labour-intensive industries upon which poor countries depend. Thus it follows that the principal beneficiaries are the poor themselves. As everyone who has ever opened a newspaper must know, theory and fact are distant kin. Wages paid to workers in developing countries are a fraction of what they are in the north. Reinert points out that a bus driver in Frankfurt earns 16 times more than his equivalent in Nigeria. The *Financial Times* reported in 2003 that a British shoe manufacturer shifting its production from the UK to China had cut its per capita wage bill from an average of 490 dollars a week to 100 dollars *a month*. Theory says that free trade must lead to the equalization of wages across the world. Experience says it does no such thing. In the mid-1980s more than 1.1 billion people had to survive on less than a dollar a day. In the first year of the 21st century the number remained exactly the same. The fact is that freedom to trade and freedom to eat are not linked in any simple linear process in which the former leads always to the latter. As Oxfam says:

In the absence of redistributive measures, it is very difficult to close income gaps as wide as those ... in the world economy ... If developing countries were to increase their average incomes by three per cent a year, and average incomes in high-income countries were to increase by one per cent a year, it would still take approximately 70 years before absolute incomes in both sets of countries increased by an equal amount.

There is danger, too, in lumping together all developing countries in a single homogeneous group. During the 1990s, for example, East Asia improved its market share by 4 per cent. This sounds good, but Oxfam points out that this was the *entire increase* recorded by all the developing countries added together. Over the same period, sub-Saharan Africa lost a quarter of its markets, shrinking its global share to just 1.3 per cent. Percentages, too, are dangerous. Exports from developing countries during the 1990s actually grew faster than those from high-income countries – 7 per cent against 5.6 per cent – but the problem of course is that 7 per cent of very little is worth exponentially less than 5.6 per cent of a vast amount. Per capita income from exports in the developing world during the '90s went up by 51 dollars a year. In high-income countries it went up by 1,938 dollars a year. Even East Asia, whose exports grew at twice the high-income average, pushed up the per capita value of its export businesses by only 234 dollars. Southern Asia and Africa between them hold a third of the world's population and three-quarters of its poor. As the 21st century began, they accounted for just 2 per cent of its exports.

Various factors conspire to keep poor countries poor. Many of them rely for their exports on the same 'primary commodities' – unprocessed food crops and raw materials – for which their former colonial masters farmed them. As colonies, they were not involved in the industrial revolution. Their commodities are subject to fluctuating but generally low prices on world markets, and all the 'value added' goes to foreign processors and manufacturers. For as long as this continues, the predicted equalization of wages across a 'borderless' global economy will be marginally less likely than the second coming of Beethoven. 'In today's world economy,' says Oxfam, 'dependence on primary commodities offers an almost automatic route to a diminishing share of world exports and world income, with its attendant implications for living standards.'

Nor should we mistake manufacturing industries for fairy godmothers. It's not stardust they sprinkle but pragmatism (aka extreme cynicism). Shoes, 'designer' bags and clothes are knocked out in Third World ghettoes that pay no more than they need to keep their workers alive (and sometimes not even that). High-tech industries similarly can look glamorous and progressive, but the 'miracle' they offer is low-skilled, low-waged assembly work for the advantage of foreign investors. The benefit to local economies is marginal. Tourist infrastructure, too, is often foreign-owned, and the only benefit to local people is low-paid work as cleaners and porters. In many places not even the food served in the hotels is locally sourced. In the case of fish in Africa, they may even have to reimport what has been stolen by foreign fleets illegally raiding their territorial waters. The really heavy hitters in the oil, arms, tobacco and minerals industries advance like conquistadors, bribing and colluding with corrupt politicians and evicting those whose labour they do not want. When local governments try to intervene – by insisting on a proportion of local ownership, for example – they are cursed by globalism's high priesthood in the World Trade Organization, to whom 'performance conditions' are blasphemy. It is a subject to which we shall return in Chapter 9. Free trade means what it says. Hands off! But as everyone's grandmother knows, 'free' markets marginalize those without bargaining power, as well as those who cannot pay the price. When water on South Africa's eastern seaboard was privatized in 1999, thousands of slum-dwellers couldn't afford the bills and had to find other sources. Result: the 21st century announced its arrival with the worst outbreak of cholera in the country's history – 250,000 infected, 300 dead.

Even where investments are called 'aid', they may be tied up in string. America's African Growth and Opportunity Act (AGOA), for example, offered African manufacturers 'privileged access' to American markets. But the privilege is heavily qualified. To compete for American custom, African countries must develop 'a market-based economy that protects private property rights', must eliminate 'barriers to United States trade and investment' and must create a political environment beneficial to US 'foreign policy interests'. What this means is that Africans can sell clothing to the US only if they use 'fabrics wholly formed and cut in the United States', and do not compete with American products. Elastic, for example, is permitted only if it is 'less than 1 inch in width and used in the production of brassieres'. A paper in the trade policy journal *The World Economy* in 2003 estimated that the act had delivered an 8–11 per cent increase in non-oil exports from Africa, but that this 'would have been nearly five times greater if no restrictive conditions had been imposed on … market access'. Just to make sure aid is not at the expense of trade, the AGOA's steering committee is run by the Corporate Council on Africa, a lobby group representing US corporations – Halliburton, ExxonMobil, General Motors *et al* – with interests in Africa. With the directness for which his speechwriters have made him famous, President Bush spelled it out: 'No nation in our time has entered the fast track of development without first opening up its economy to world markets. The African Growth and Opportunity Act is a road map for how the United States and Africa can tap the power of markets to improve the lives of our citizens.'

So we see exactly what the Third World is up against. American self-interest is a gale against which house-of-straw economies have no defence. A similar gale – some would say a stronger one

– blows from the European Union, whose entire *raison d'être* is economic firepower. And Africa of course stirs local eddies of its own. The Commission for Africa under the chairmanship of Tony Blair in 2005 revealed that the continent was inefficient even at trading with itself. Only 12 per cent of its goods are sold to other African states. Bureaucracy and anarchy quite literally block the roads. Bribes must be paid, or complicated paperwork filled out, checked and approved by officials. Exports from Europe are agreed at the speed of mouse-clicks, and can be shipped on Day One. Until time travel is perfected, this is as fast as trade will ever get. Large parts of Africa, by contrast, would struggle to keep pace with a mule-train. It takes *30 days* to get customs clearance for goods leaving Ethiopia. The Commission for Africa reported: 'An average customs transaction in a developing country is estimated to involve 20 to 30 parties, 40 documents and 200 data elements, 30 of which have to be repeated at least 30 times. Costs and inefficiencies like these make it extremely difficult to get goods to market at competitive prices.'

And then – infective, poisonous and paralysing – there is corruption. It can be small and petty (a dollar here, a bottle of whisky there) or gross (presidents and ex-presidents of some of the world's poorest countries live like Bond-movie oligarchs). The African Union in 2002 reckoned it cost the continent 150 billion dollars a year, inflating prices by an average 20 per cent and frightening investors away. In 2004, patients at public hospitals in Cameroon complained that money was being demanded before doctors would even see them. Bribery, not hard work, earned top grades in school exams, and it was neither qualifications nor experience that settled the outcomes of job applications. Public funds were a jam-pot for anyone who could get their fingers in, and more was lost than just what stuck to them. Corruption has been one of the biggest obstacles to the Live 8 and Make Poverty History campaigns. Investors and aid agencies, who are called upon to put their money where the campaigners' mouths are, want to feed hungry children, not kleptocrats' bank accounts.

The rich world of course is not exactly *virgo intacta*. It did not get rich by being over-fastidious about moral hygiene. The abolition of slavery didn't cancel an injustice; it merely curtailed it. Coercion continues by other means. The effective ownership of the US political system by the tobacco, pharmaceutical, oil, automobile and power industries, and the stooges it shoves on to the political stage, are not good advertisements for elective democracy. The UK behind its wigs and gothic architecture may put up a better front but it is no maiden aunt. We have had cash for questions, cash for peerages, false justifications for a foreign war, political interference with the processes of law, and threats to the national broadcaster. Lobby firms sell access to ministers, and large parts of Gordon Brown's speeches when he was chancellor of the exchequer could have been drafted for him by the Confederation of British Industry. Indeed, cynics say the CBI now is more likely to be lobbied by the government than vice versa. An increasingly centralized planning system is manipulated by retail chains and developers whose financial, legal and political power is unmatched by local democracy, and the Private Finance Initiative, giving private investors ownership of public services, has creamed more whiskers than any other government-backed scam since the Enclosure Acts.

Africa therefore is not a vacuum. Corruption is not a self-seeding life form that exists in the dark without nourishment. It has to be nurtured. There would be no point in ministers or officials holding out their hands unless there were someone ready with the silver. Travelling with world-weary film crews, I've seen how bribery opens doors, dissolves queues, buys access. Sometimes it's petty cash; sometimes it's cars, women, airline tickets, medical treatment – small beer in comparison with what happens higher up the chain, but still integral to the local economy and compliant with its mores. American, British,

European, Russian, Indian and Chinese companies prosper in the developing world because they know how to work the system. This is what the business community calls 'living in the real world', aka 'pragmatism', and it is condoned by governments who place the jobs and incomes of their own taxpayers ahead of foreign peasants. That is, after all, what governments are supposed to be for, and 'the national interest' always wins. We shall return to this in Chapter 9.

If, as we shall see, their home countries are disinclined to curb the buccaneers, then there is even less chance of their being prosecuted in Africa. Corrupt governments do not punish those who furnish their palaces; nor do institutions in the world's financial capitals turn away 'legitimate' business from criminal regimes. According to a leaked report by the international risk consultancy Kroll, many of the millions of pounds looted by the former Kenyan president Daniel Arap Moi and his family found their way to London banks and thence to the purchase of expensive properties in Surrey and Knightsbridge. One of the leading campaigners against institutionalized corruption is Transparency International (TI), a Berlin-based NGO which has 'chapters' in more than 90 countries, including the UK. Its aim is to 'combat corruption at the national and international levels through constructive partnerships with governments, the private sector, civil society and international organizations'. On International Human Rights Day, 10 December 2007, its managing director Cobus de Swardt joined Desmond Tutu, Mary Robinson and other world figures in Cape Town's old slave quarter to launch its Every Human Has Rights campaign. 'Corruption has greased the wheels of exploitation and injustice since time immemorial,' said de Swardt. 'And the great human tragedies of recent history – genocides and institutionalized racism – have likewise been welded to abusive systems that twist public trust for private gain . . . Human rights are predicated on the belief in human dignity and political equality, and corruption corrodes both.'

A TI survey of more than 63,000 respondents in 60 countries showed that, time and again, poor people – it was always the poor – were forced to pay for services that were supposed to be free (a money-raising stunt which, irony of ironies, is routinely pressed upon indebted governments by the International Monetary Fund). More than one in ten said they had to pay bribes for public services. In the very worst countries – Albania, Cambodia, Cameroon, Macedonia, Kosovo, Nigeria, Pakistan, Philippines, Romania and Senegal – the rate was nearer one in three. Shockingly, police and judiciary usually were among the worst offenders. In a survey in 2002, 96 per cent of respondents who had either petitioned or been summoned before the courts in Pakistan said they had met 'corrupt practices'. In Russia it is estimated that 210m dollars is paid every year in bribes to the courts. Elsewhere, as in Cameroon, the medical or education services may stand out as more venal, but in every state where corruption reigns there is one unvarying constant. Year after year when TI asks people which institutions they find most corrupt, the answer is always the same – politicians and parliaments. Yet these are the regimes, rotten in head and heart, that companies from the rich world court for their business. In 2006, TI drew up a 'Bribe Payers Index' to measure the propensity of companies from 30 top exporting countries to illegally exploit the greasy palm. The scores – marks out of ten – were calculated from the responses of more than 11,000 business people from 125 countries who took part in the World Economic Forum's Executive Opinion Survey. A perfect ten out of ten means zero corruption, a land of paragons. Nought out of ten means economic anarchy, a land of pimps and pariahs. The 30 countries, in rank order from best to worst, were:

Switzerland, 7.81; Sweden, 7.62; Australia, 7.59; Austria, 7.50; Canada, 7.46; UK, 7.39; Germany, 7.34; Netherlands, 7.28; Belgium, 7.22; USA, 7.22; Japan, 7.10; Singapore, 6.78; Spain,

6.63; United Arab Emirates, 6.62; France, 6.50; Portugal, 6.47; Mexico, 6.45; Hong Kong, 6.01; Israel, 6.01; Italy, 5.94; South Korea, 5.83; Saudi Arabia, 5.75; Brazil, 5.65; South Africa, 5.61; Malaysia, 5.59; Taiwan, 5.41; Turkey, 5.23; Russia, 5.16; China, 4.94; India, 4.62.

It may be no surprise – certainly it is no comfort – to see the emerging powers of India and China (already the world's fourth largest exporter) stashing their piles in the moral basement. Those versed in commercial *Realpolitik* may not be surprised, either, to find that business people in the poorer quarters of Africa name France and Italy as the two most persistent grafters. But even Switzerland, up there alone on the dusted mantelpiece, is far from perfect, and it would be less perfect still if the definition of bribery could be extended to include the blandishments of its famously discreet banks, where the three wise monkeys have been given mahogany desks. All these countries, by succouring crooks, are doing their bit to make poor people poorer. For those who gain, it is the 'win-win situation' of economic theory. For those who lose, it is a double whammy. On the shady side of the street, in the spinners' netherworld of sleaze and double-speak, the prime cuts go to the rich and powerful. On the sunny side, where the law is observed with rigorous transparency, right down to the last sub-clause and caveat, the carve-up is exactly the same. Unlike water, gravy always flows uphill.

To this already uneven playing field is added another angle of tilt. It is commonplace to cite 'trade barriers' as the vipers that rip African infants from the breast, and commonplace to believe their eradication would deliver a decisive blow for good against evil. The World Trade Organization says so. The World Bank says so. National governments on both sides of the economic divide say so. Never in the history of the world economy have so many lips paid so much service to one straightforward ideal. And yet . . .

Trade liberalization in practice is just another kind of

inequality. Poor countries heeding the World Bank and WTO have dropped their tariffs with reckless speed, but with scant reciprocation from the rich. Trade theory's central tenet is that the income gap will not be narrowed until all the fences have been taken down and poor countries can race on the flat. This means having unrestricted access to rich countries' markets. According to Oxfam in 2002, trade restrictions were costing developing countries around 100 billion dollars a year – double what they got in international aid. The annual cost to sub-Saharan Africa alone was 2 billion dollars, and of course this was just the headline figure, not the bottom line. Loss begets loss. 'The longer-term costs associated with lost opportunities for investment and the loss of economic dynamism are much greater,' Oxfam said.

The damage is especially severe because the barriers are targeted at labour-intensive manufacturing industries and agriculture. There are parts of Africa where crops such as sugar and cotton can be grown more easily and more cheaply than anywhere else in the world. Natural advantages, however, can be made valueless by economics. The European Union, for example, caused fury in the developing world by subsidizing its farmers to produce sugar much less efficiently from beet, with the result each year that 4.1m tonnes of cheap European sugar flooded the market and crushed African competition. It was the same with cotton. Local subsidies meant that farmers in the US received twice what their crop was worth on the world market. The fact that West African farmers could produce cotton at a fraction of the price – 21 cents a pound in Burkina Faso, against 73 cents in the US – was thereby made irrelevant. Oversupply and dumping from the US sabotaged the livelihoods of more than 10m people in West Africa. The Commission for Africa complained of 'disgraceful protectionism' against Africans in world markets. 'Those barriers and subsidies,' it said, 'are totally unacceptable; they are politically antiquated, economically illiterate, environmentally destructive and ethically indefensible. They must go.'

The figures seem astonishing. Agricultural products entering the US face an average tariff – effectively a border tax – of 14 per cent. In Europe it is 22 per cent. But that is not the worst of it. Some 'sensitive' market sectors are not so much protected as barricaded in trade-proof bunkers. The Commission for Africa reported that tariffs on imported fruit and nuts in the US exceeded 200 per cent. On meat in the EU they were 300 per cent. Schemes allowing preferential access have blunted the impact of some of these tariffs on the world's very poorest in sub-Saharan Africa, but barriers still remain and the schemes themselves are so complex that, as the Commission for Africa put it, they 'undermine entry'.

Manufactured goods are hit even harder. In the EU and Japan, tariffs on processed foods are double what they are on raw commodities. In Canada they are 13 times higher. Orange juice entering the US faces a 30 per cent tariff, and peanut butter 132 per cent. Although, again, African countries to some extent do benefit from preferential access, 'sensitive' products still find the drawbridge raised against them. In the US these include soya bean oil, sugar, cocoa, tobacco and cotton, all essential to African economies. One of the most extreme examples is cocoa in Japan. Raw cocoa beans entering the country have a zero tariff; cocoa paste is levied at 5 per cent, defatted cocoa paste 10 per cent, cocoa powder 13 per cent and manufactured chocolate more than 280 per cent. The term economists use to describe this process is *tariff escalation*. Its effects are twofold. On the one hand it protects manufacturers in the client country; on the other it discourages poor countries from developing industries of their own. The result is that the precious 'value-added', from which fortunes are made, is concentrated in the rich countries, while the poor have to scrape by on raw ingredients.

It doesn't stop even there. Exporters face yet more hurdles in the 'product standards' set by client countries to ensure the efficacy of what they import. Most are what they claim to be – health and safety regulations necessary for public protection. But this is not always the case. Sometimes the cost to producers is so disproportionate to the benefit, and the standards so difficult to meet, that it is little more than a disguised form of protectionism. In 2001 the World Bank reported that new EU standards for the naturally occurring carcinogen aflatoxin would cost African exporters of nuts, cereals and dried fruits 670m dollars a year with no significant benefit to European muesli-eaters. This is why some authorities in Africa and South America are showing so little enthusiasm for a proposed international certification system designed to ensure the sustainability of biofuels. It's not that they want freedom to poison the planet. They fear it is just another way of rigging the market.

Even rich countries find it difficult to comply. American fruit exporters, for example, complain that EU standards are so impossibly high, and so rigorously applied, that they are tantamount to trade barriers. Mirth may greet the sound of bully crying to matron, but it is a serious point. If the US finds the going hard, how is Africa supposed to manage? Standards are applied to just about every stage in food production from field to plate – pesticide residues, additives, handling and hygiene, processing and packaging. Having been drafted by lawyers briefed by scientists, they often have great precision but little clarity. Oxfam spells out what this means: 'Monitoring and enforcing compliance with these standards requires a level of scientific and technical expertise not often available in poorer countries. Meeting standards is not cheap: the cost of complying with legislative requirements, including testing and certification, can be as high as 10 per cent of the overall product cost for some agricultural goods.'

In a jungle like this the protectionist wolf slips easily into the skin of the health-and-safety sheep. Vietnamese fish farmers, for example, established a profitable business selling catfish to the US. America's response? In November 2001 its farmers persuaded Congress to change the definition of 'catfish' to exclude the Vietnamese imports – a fiddle conducted in spite of advice from the US Department of Agriculture that it had no basis in science. 'This dubious restriction,' said Oxfam, 'threatens the livelihoods of 15,000 Vietnamese families who had invested their life savings in buying the floating cages needed for production.' In a remote part of central Mozambique not long ago, I was surprised to meet a couple of villagers in full beekeeping kit. Their hives, which hung from trees in the forest, were of a standard pattern supplied by one of the several charities and fair-trade organizations that promote small-scale honey production in rural Africa. It was – still is – a perfect way of bringing low-level technology, food and income to some of the world's poorest people. The potential for export, however, was drastically reduced by EU rules on the monitoring of pesticide residues – something for which tribal languages have no words. For death and disease, on the other hand, they have plenty. In a continent where health care still often means the witch doctor, and where life expectancy struggles to exceed forty, the caution of northern governments can seem not so much excessive as paranoid. In 1997, following a cholera out-break, the EU banned all imports of fish from East Africa. It did eventually take notice of the World Health Organization's insistence that the fish were safe, but not before Kenya had lost 33 per cent of its trade.

The problem with free trade is that freedom is proportionate to wealth. It is of equal benefit only when both parties are at the same stage of economic development so that deals are not imposed by market power. You could argue, for example, that a deal struck by a small apple-grower with a supermarket was voluntary, free and fair. His signature was not extracted at gun-point; he could take or leave it as he wished. The truth is that the bargaining positions are grossly unequal and that supermarkets exploit their power with ruthless amorality. Their double triumph – high dividends for shareholders, low prices for customers – is either the free market's finest flowering or its worst abuse, depending on your angle of view. International trade is precisely similar. Sharks and squid swimming together may have equal rights, but equality of outcome is about as likely as ice in the Namib. You might say this is the way the world works. Selfish genes flowing through selfish organisms into selfish communities produce exactly the result a biologist would predict. The strong outlast the weak – or, in economy-speak, the 'imperfectly competitive' – and the economic bloodline is all the stronger for it. Of course the world is not quite as cruel as that. It is not likely that the priest and the Levite in the parable of the Good Samaritan were economists, but their passing by on the other side would have been based on a careful assessment of costs and benefits, not on any particular wish to see the victim dead.

One of the most damaging aspects of international trade is the below-cost 'dumping' of (often subsidized) goods on world markets. It depresses prices, drives local firms out of business and creates monopolies. Even some free marketeers acknowledge the need for government intervention to prevent it. 'Anti-dumping policies', as they are called, work by imposing tariffs against the dumpers, and most countries now have them – indeed, they are a condition for membership of the World Trade Organization. 'Dumping' occurs when products are sold abroad more cheaply than they are at home. But not all dumping is the same. For all the slowness and, in some cases, reluctance of countries to comply, trade barriers *are* coming down, which is increasing the incentive for companies to compete in foreign markets. Competition inevitably pushes down local prices, which is exactly the benefit to consumers that free markets are supposed to deliver. And it is not necessarily unfair. The exporter might simply be pricing his wares in relation to the local market – ie he could be charging less than he does at home (where he might benefit from a near monopoly), but still be selling at above the production cost and making money. This is 'fair competition'.

Nor is this the only circumstance in which 'dumping' might be condoned. It can happen, for example, that a worldwide surplus depresses prices and producers are forced to cut their losses by selling below cost. They have no choice. Prices ordinarily are fixed by world markets, so that producers become 'price takers' rather than 'price setters' and must take what they can get. Here again common sense follows economic theory in finding no fault. Mischief is done only where the price-cutting is predatory, and where market power is used to destroy local businesses. This is what anti-dumping policies are supposed to prevent. You could say that here is the point at which free and fair trade meet, in a concerted effort to stop trade liberalization for the many turning into world domination by the few (the sound of hollow laughter is coming from Chapter 9).

That is, or *was*, the theory when Canada became the first country to apply anti-dumping laws in 1904. By late 2001 more than 90 countries had followed suit, but with a drastic change of purpose and in very different mood. 'Fair' competition is a tender plant in the icy winds of international trade. Fair's fair when you're on the attack, but it's a different matter when you're under siege. The result was predictable. With old-fashioned tariff barriers infra dig, anti-dumping measures were put in their place and became just another form of protectionism. Any importer undercutting local producers – particularly when the flow was from Third World to First – would be accused of dumping. Clare Short, then UK Secretary of State for International Development, spelled out the risk in a speech to the United Nations Conference on Trade and Development (UNCTAD) in March 1999: 'The Anti-Dumping Agreement now risks becoming a WTO-endorsed route for protecting domestic industry – a very real danger, especially in the wake of the Asian financial crisis.'

Scandalously, it was the rich countries – the US, EU, Canada and Australia – who led the rush to law, and the poor who were their targets. During the 1980s, according to an academic source, they were the only 'active and heavy users' of this particular form of protectionism. Between 1995 and 2002, the EU and US between them brought 234 anti-dumping actions against developing countries. The US in particular, said Oxfam, had 'developed some of the most imaginative strategies for abusing the letter and the spirit of the WTO's anti-dumping provisions': 'Under legislation known as the Byrd amendment, customs authorities are mandated to collect anti-dumping duties and then transfer them to US firms alleging damage – in effect providing them with a subsidy.' It went on: 'The procedure for establishing that dumping has taken place is complex and costly, and therefore many developing countries have difficulty in challenging anti-dumping measures imposed by industrialized countries. Yet the impact of anti-dumping duties on a developing-country exporter can be devastating . . . There can be knock-on effects in the wider economy.'

As 'leader of the free world', the US could hardly be surprised if those lower in the food chain were influenced by its example. The developing world soon began to return fire. In the next decade, the 1990s, the most prominent accusers were Brazil, China, South Africa and, more recently, India, and their targets were the US and the EU. Two things became obvious. First, anti-dumping law was being used as a substitute for import tariffs. Second, countries formerly targeted by the rich were now getting their own back, tit for tat. China even made retaliation a principle in law: '. . . the People's Republic of China,' it ruled in 2002, 'may adopt corresponding measures against any country or region adopting discriminatory anti-dumping measures against its exports'. The reek of double standards was not new. It had been made explicit a year earlier by a resolution of the US Congress which required its negotiators at the WTO to:

preserve the ability of the United States to enforce rigorously its trade laws, including the antidumping and countervailing duty laws, and avoid agreements which lessen the effectiveness of domestic and international disciplines on unfair trade, especially dumping and subsidies, in order to ensure that United States workers, agricultural producers, and firms can compete fully on fair terms and enjoy the benefits of reciprocal trade concessions; and ensure that United States exports are not subject to the abusive use of trade laws . . . by other countries.

Thus did Congress make the best possible use of anti-dumping laws to protect its own interests while denying the right of others to do the same. This is not economics: it is politics. Raw politics, at that – politics stripped to its Darwinian essence of power to the strong and weakest-to-the-wall. Political parties serve many masters. They must appeal to the voters who elect them, and they must reward their corporate sponsors. The price of the former is populist policies designed to ensure, or at least to make it seem, that there are enough winners to outvote the losers. (The Labour Party's political meltdown following the abolition of the 10p income tax band in the spring of 2008 shows what happens when you get it wrong.) The price for the latter is schmoozing. Companies do not support the Labour, Republican, Democrat or any other party because they want to Make Poverty History, or to accelerate UN health and education targets. They want their interests looked after, and protectionist trade policies are part of the deal. This is why anti-dumping laws grow in direct proportion to the removal of tariff barriers. New barbed wire for old.

Economists always seek 'equilibrium'. There is a theory, redolent of the Cold War, that once every country has anti-dumping policies, then no one will dare to use them. It is not a theory that travels well. The EU, US and China may bluff each other into simmering truce. For the poor, however, unequal economic firepower gives them no more influence than they had in the Cold War proper. It's still flintlocks against ICBMs. The only difference is the semantics. As ever, agriculture is the best example. In rich countries it accounts for a much smaller proportion of GDP, yet looms disproportionately large in the public and political psyches. There are several reasons for this. Farmers are not just food growers: they are curators of the landscape. We want them not just to work the land but also to preserve it and enhance its beauty. This is a high priority in northern Europe, where people walk for pleasure, but rather less so in, say, Ethiopia, where people walk because they have to. Increasingly, too, we are concerned with 'food security' – ensuring the regularity and quality of supply, and minimizing the risk of disruption by external forces. The Dig for Victory campaign in the Second World War was not just a bonding exercise. Food security was, and is, the first line of national defence. Add to this the suddenly passionate 'green' antipathy to (and, often, misunderstanding of) 'food miles', and you can see why African exporters want for encouragement. Farming in developing countries has to support a much higher proportion of the population than it does in the industrialized world – more than 70 per cent in the poorest countries, against less than 10 per cent in the rich. And yet it is the industrialized countries that take the lion's share of the export trade. Even so, half of all developing countries still rely on agriculture for more than a third of their export income, and are intensely vulnerable to shifts in the market. 'Global markets,' says Oxfam, 'are dominated by industrialized countries for whom farming represents a negligible amount of GDP, employment and export earnings, largely by virtue of heavy subsidies. So producers in developing countries suffer low prices, lost market shares and unfair competition in local markets.'

For them it is more than just a few pence at Tesco. It is the roof over their heads; their health; their children's education. And yet rich countries spend five times more on subsidizing their farmers than they do on international aid, and go on spending more even as they promise to spend less. So it happens that farmers in the developing world have to compete not just with foreign agribarons but also with their sugardaddy governments. An African smallholder will have to survive on 400 dollars a year; US and European farmers are pocketing subsidies worth an average 21,000 and 16,000 dollars respectively. Or look at it another way: the member states of the Organization for Economic Co-operation and Development (OECD) spend more on farm subsidies each year than the 1.2 billion poorest people in the world have to live on.

What makes it all possible is the verbal dexterity of lawyers. A way with words. A way of redefining 'subsidy' so that it doesn't sound like a subsidy at all, but more like a way of protecting the environment or preventing wasteful gluts. The World Trade Organization licenses what it calls 'Amber Box', 'Blue Box' and 'Green Box' support schemes. The Amber category (amber for 'warning') is for schemes that 'significantly distort the market'. In rich countries these are capped at 5 per cent of the value of farm outputs. Blue Box schemes are uncapped, but permit governments to pay subsidies only to farmers who agree to restrict production. (Prime example: the European set-aside scheme, which pays farmers to keep land fallow.) So far, so clear. It is in the Green Box – colour-coded for sustainability – that most of the trickery is done. To qualify, payments must be given in return for environmental or social improvements, or for 'rural development', and they must *not* involve price support. This is not so much a loophole as a six-lane highway. The WTO aims to cut subsidies that allow farmers to sell below cost and distort the market by dumping. *But this does not include the Green Box.* As subsidies in this category are meant to be 'non or minimally trade-distorting', they are regarded as neutral and unthreatening. There is no restriction on their number, and the definition of 'minimally' is left to member states.

In November 2005, four leading aid agencies – ActionAid

International, Caritas Internationalis, Coopération Internationale pour le Développement et la Solidarité (CIDSE) and Oxfam International – complained that the US and EU were playing dirty: 'Instead of complying with their WTO commitments, [they] are simply shifting subsidies from the Amber and Blue Boxes and hiding them in the Green Box. This allows them to maintain, and even increase, the high levels of support they provide, which largely goes to agribusiness. In other words, it is the richest countries, not the poorest, who will be getting [the benefit].'

This is more pernicious even than it looks. Transferring subsidies from the Amber and Blue Boxes allows rich countries to claim that they have actually *reduced* trade distortion, and to argue that developing countries should show good faith by cutting subsidies too. Thus was President Bush able to announce that the US would drop all trade barriers if other countries did the same. Europe's justification for continuing with subsidies is not so much ingenious as casuistic. What matters, it says, is not the over-all level of support but rather the *structure* of the payment schemes. It argues that it is meeting both the spirit and the letter of WTO policy by scaling down subsidies that encourage higher production and directly supporting farm incomes instead. In other words, the NGOs were right. Money is being siphoned from the Amber and Blue Boxes and laundered in the Green. The sums are huge – 50 billion euros a year in the EU, over 50 billion dollars in the US. Some of this is genuinely needed to help the American and European rural poor, but much of it – especially in the EU – is putting *foie gras* into the mouths of the wealthy. You could forgive the developing countries for not being overly impressed. 'If you are a poor farmer in Burkina Faso,' said the NGOs, 'the technical categorization of the payments makes little difference if you are still facing unfair imports. It is the same money, going to the same place – it just has a different name.'

The box schemes are still supporting farmers who grow more than they would otherwise be able to sell. This makes dumping inevitable and wrecks the livelihoods of African farmers. The Australian government calculated that if the US and EU were to halve their subsidized dairy exports, then the prices available to Third World farmers would be 34 per cent higher. US cotton subsidies, it said, cost Burkina Faso 1 per cent of its GDP. US and European wheat prices are respectively 46 per cent and 34 per cent below the cost of production; the US maize price is 20 per cent below; EU skimmed milk 50 per cent below and white sugar 75 per cent below. Thus prices on the world market are set by state-subsidized 'dumpers' insured against risk. The NGOs spelled out the consequence: 'farmers and exporters in developing countries receive prices for their crops at or below the artificially low prices set by the powerful industrialized countries' policies'.

According to the World Bank in 2001, part of the cost to the world's poor was an annual welfare loss of 20 billion dollars. The imbalance means also that manufacturers of food products – confectionery, for example – in rich countries can buy their ingredients far more cheaply than Third World competitors paying local prices. So food processing industries, too, have to play uphill and are forced out of business. And so the spiral continues. Local sugar producers lose their biggest customers, and more rural jobs are lost. Let them eat Mars bars, as Marie Antoinette might have said.

Of course there will be a rethink. There are always rethinks – fresh rounds of world trade talks, reform of the EU's Common Agricultural Policy, the dreaded multicoloured boxes – yet the benefits to the poor, and the concessions by the rich, tend more towards the theoretical than to the actual. This is the world as it is seen from desk or computer screen, not as it looks from the *mashamba*. Men with PhDs crowd around moribund African economies like doctors around a patient – but old-time doctors from a bygone age, without diagnostic aids, not knowing whether their prescriptions will kill or cure. As Peter Griffiths revealed in

The Economist's Tale, his first-hand account of the World Bank's catastrophic involvement in Sierra Leone's food crisis in the late 1980s, African statistics tend to pass through numberless prisms of corruption, inefficiency and imagination. Crop yields and consumptions; the volume, value and destination of food aid; the true extent of hunger and starvation; birth and death rates – all have the substance of smoke. You might as well read the entrails of a goat.

The traditional rich-country response to Third World hunger is food aid. But even here the shining light of altruism is dimmed by self-interest. The US in particular has a dismal record of dumping agricultural surpluses and looking for trade deals in return, thus threatening the livelihoods of yet more local farmers. It is not at all coy about this. In the words of the former Secretary of State for Agriculture Dan Glickman, food aid was 'a useful market development tool' for the US. In most people's minds, 'food aid' conjures an image of the international community at its best, coming together in times of war or famine to feed the starving. Sometimes it really is like that. Emergency food aid, when the right supplies are brought to the right people at the right time, is welcomed by all but thwarted tyrants. But it is not always like this. There are other kinds of food aid, too, in which the 'donors' show all the moral scruple of jackals.

'Programme food aid' is the term used for routine shipments of food from rich countries to poor. For most donor states this is straightforward grant-giving – an international version of the kind of good-neighbourliness that sees surplus beans being passed across the garden fence. The difference is that very often the food is 'monetized' – ie sold on local markets for the benefit of the receiving government. In the case of the US, there is another difference too. The aid is not given but *sold*, and sold moreover on the basis of 'export credits' – in effect, money lent by the US to enable its customers to buy American goods. In plain language, they are export subsidies.

You see it plainly if you measure food aid against the recipients' actual need. Common sense says they should peak simultaneously, with aid flowing fastest when food stocks are low and prices are high. What really happens is the exact opposite. In the peak aid year of 1999–2000, says Oxfam:

US food-aid donations of wheat and wheat flour increased when prices were low, the very time when recipient countries could most easily afford to obtain supplies in the world market. Conversely, when prices were high and the need for food aid may have been expected to increase, levels of US donations fell. Over half of US wheat-flour exports in this period were sent in the form of food aid, compared with less than 10 per cent for other exporting countries. Furthermore, these US wheat-flour exports were destined for a number of countries where there was no food emergency, or which have the resources to purchase food.

This had the same effect that dumping always does. World prices went through the floor and poor farmers were ruined. It happened again in 2000 when America grew a bumper rice crop. By dumping the surplus on Jamaica, it robbed Guyanese growers of their export market. Dharankumar Seeraj, general secretary of the Guyana Rice Producers' Association, observed: '[US food aid] was meant to boost food security . . . It was supposed to assist in the elimination of poverty, not in creating it. And we have seen a direct effect whereby in the very process of eliminating poverty [in one place], we have poverty being created in another . . .'

Again in 2003, donors 'overreacted' to a food deficit in Malawi, which received almost twice what it needed. Rice, maize and cassava prices all crashed, inflicting 15m dollars' worth of damage on the Malawian economy. 'Monetizing' food aid generally has the same effect. The flood of food on to local markets depresses prices, displaces local produce and crushes competition. This does not happen by accident, or because

American economists are too stupid to understand cause and effect. Dan Glickman was not speaking out of turn. It is a legislative requirement in the US that food-aid programmes should prioritize countries likely to develop into export markets. This is why the United States Agency for International Development (USAID) in 1996 was able to report that 'nine out of ten countries importing US agricultural products are former recipients of food assistance'. The law even extends to transport. Seventy-five per cent of US 'in-kind' food aid has to travel on American-registered ships. Never mind the hunger: count the dollars.

The WTO does not approve of this. It 'requires' its members not to link food aid to exports, and says aid should be given and not sold. But there is no enforcement, and no stick in the world is big enough to beat the US with. At the same time, ordinary financial aid has struggled to keep pace with inflation. G8 leaders at the Gleneagles Summit in 2005 pledged themselves to double their aid by 2010. Well . . . they are cutting it fine. In each of the next two years, according to the OECD, financial aid was actually *cut*. In real terms in 2007 it fell by 8.4 per cent, enough to suggest that the 2010 target could be missed by £30bn. According to Oxfam, this is the cost of five million lives. Putting it another way: in 2006, rich countries spent 0.31 per cent of their gross national incomes (GNI) on overseas aid. In 2007 it fell to 0.28 per cent. The UN also has a target – an average 0.7 per cent of GNI to be spent on aid by 2015. This, too, is creaking under the weight of half-heartedness, and in no country is the international development minister a political big-hitter. A few countries, mainly those with small populations, are leading the way (Norway in 2007 achieved 0.95 per cent, Sweden 0.93 per cent, Luxembourg 0.90 per cent), but the supposed economic powerhouses are left patting their pockets. The UK's contribution in 2007 slipped from 0.51 per cent to 0.36 per cent, and the US's bottom-of-the-league 0.16 per cent was challenged only by Japan's 0.17 per cent and Italy's 0.19 per cent. One reason for the decline is that contributions previously were ramped up by creative accounting – debt relief was counted as 'aid'. With one-off debt relief now mostly a done deal, the real level of aid – what Oxfam calls 'the crumbling credibility of the Gleneagles promises' – is stripped of its packaging and revealed for the economic runt it really is.

Nor is this the only sphere in which fine words have run ahead of action. Rajendra Pachauri, head of the UN's International Panel on Climate Change (IPCC), warned in April 2008 that the rich world's failure to lead by example was jeopardizing agreements on emissions control. Without evidence that the old polluters of North America and Europe were making some meaningful progress towards wiping themselves clean, the new industrialists of India and China could see no reason to stop heating the greenhouse. 'Protocols' would come and go – and so, in time, would humankind. We would leave the planet to insects and salamanders.

Never has the world been so joined in disunity. Science does not make policy. It quotes the odds and we place our bets, but of course we want to have our stake and eat it. We live in an age of payment deferred, when 'credit details' are the core of our identity and APR counts more than price. In any apparent conflict between present and future, the present always wins. That is the reality of politics. The unborn have no vote.

The problem with climate change is that it reverses the polarities of the consumer economy, which promises immediate gain and never-never long-term cost. Arresting global warming would mean the opposite – immediate cost for never-never long-term gain. So long-term, in fact, that the gain will be enjoyed not by ourselves but by some unknown people in the faraway future. This is the cue for economists to preach the indivisible truth of numbers. The Danish statistician and political scientist Bjørn Lomborg not long ago was named by *Time* magazine as 'one of the 100 most influential people in the world'. In 2006, after the success of his best-selling book *The Skeptical Environmentalist*, he followed up with *Cool It: the Skeptical Environmentalist's Guide to Global Warming*. In this he argues that the cost of fighting climate change cannot be justified by the likely benefit, and that there are more pressing problems for the world to throw its money at. He calculates, for example, that many more people now die from winter cold than might perish in future from summer heatwaves, and that climate change therefore would save more lives than it costs. He reckons that warming by 2050 will bestow an annual cost benefit of 1.4m lives, but omits the not altogether insignificant detail that the 2003 European summer heatwave – cool by comparison with what is likely by mid-century – slowed plant growth by a third and cut cereal crops by 36 per cent (though he looks forward to a bonanza of fruit and veg). His calculator tells him that applying the Kyoto protocol would cost 23 dollars for every tonne of CO_2 saved, and would return only two dollars' worth of 'good'. 'Maybe,' he wonders, 'we could have done more good for the world with those 23 dollars elsewhere?'

Well, indeed . . . A number of 'top-level economists' helped him show that money would be better spent fighting disease and malnutrition, providing sanitation and clean water, and dismantling trade barriers. In Lomborg's hierarchy of global challenges, climate change – described by Tony Blair as 'the most pressing problem the world faces' – ranks only 15th in order of priority. He quotes in support a long list of countries that share his scale of values, 'placing communicable diseases, clean drinking water and malnutrition at the top, with climate change at the bottom'. It takes an economist to argue that one global crisis should be costed against another and that the bottom line should be the decider. (In logic, it is like a climate campaigner arguing that the cost of cutting carbon should be deducted from the AIDS budget.) Anyone unable to accept this economic machismo – the European Union, the IPCC, the overwhelming majority of climate scientists – is, as Lomborg told an interviewer, 'pitiably weak on logic'.

He is halfway right. Communicable disease, polluted water and malnutrition are indictments of every country that does less than it might to fight them off. In April 2008, as price rises for some food staples reached 80 per cent and food price inflation was averaging 40 per cent, the UN's World Food Programme asked rich countries to contribute another 500m dollars (£255m) to help stave off world hunger. Many countries in the developing world – among them India, Mexico, Haiti, Zimbabwe, Egypt, Ivory Coast, Cameroon, Mauritania, Mozambique, Senegal, Morocco, Uzbekistan and Yemen – had already suffered food riots, and the World Bank declared that 33 were at risk of political destabilization. Who would argue that feeding the hungry was less of a priority than climate change? The needle would have to drop off your moral compass before you yielded to the moral reductionism of economic theory. There is only one possible answer to how much we should be prepared to pay to avert tragedy: whatever it costs. But the same is true of climate change. If we want to *ensure* that famine, water shortages, disease and conflicts bring death to Africa, then raising the global temperature is the way to do it. We don't have a choice. It's not either/or. Aid is the palliative, but emissions control is the prophylactic.

Failure in Africa is not something the world can afford. Failed harvests, failed economies and failed states would mount into a human tsunami, a surge of refugees that would overwhelm every country in its path. Even the logic of self-interest – *economics* – must drive us to the same conclusion. It's not just Africa. As glaciers shrink, so rivers will cease to flow and people right across the world will lose their water. The average global temperature has to rise by only between one and two degrees to plunge the nuclear-armed India and Pakistan into a fight for survival. Every continent will face the threat of upstream states sucking the life out of their downriver neighbours, and of the ultimately self-defeating grab-it-while-it-lasts greed of the rich. We see it already, starkly illustrated in the lop-sided relationships between the US and Mexico, and between Israel and Palestine. Swimming pools on one side; dying donkeys on the other.

The willingness of the haves to bully the have-nots is exemplified by the political control of Russia's energy giant Gazprom. In 2006 it cut off supplies of gas to Ukraine, ostensibly in a dispute over debt payments. The real reason, many observers thought, was that the Ukrainians had elected a pro-western government. In March 2008, after the victory in Russia's own presidential election of Gazprom's chairman, Dmitri Medvedev, the company again cut supplies to Ukraine. Like a May Day parade, it was an ostentatious display of Russian power. Unlike a May Day parade, it caused a genuine frisson of panic throughout the rest of Europe, which receives 80 per cent of its vital Russian gas supplies by way of pipelines through Ukraine. The other 20 per cent comes via Belarus, which in the summer of 2007 was similarly threatened by the Russians, who steeply increased their prices. All this prompts frowns in European capitals and, in London, urgent talk of 'fuel security' and of a looming 'energy gap' which will be used to justify the rebirth of nuclear power.

For Africa, and for parts of South America and Asia, such troubles seem almost frivolous, like worrying about what to wear to a party, or which SUV to buy. Their problems by comparison are elemental – about getting something to eat, not about how to heat their ovens; about survival, not about political or commercial advantage. No one from the north visits Africa and comes away without a sense of shame. 'Fairness' is a dry husk of a word tossed about by politicians to justify tax increases. It is meaningless because it is immeasurable and indefinable, lost somewhere in the confusion between 'egalitarian' and 'meritocratic', and unfailingly subjective. Some things are so hugely and manifestly wrong that they require an entirely different language. Inequalities in the world – the rewards and penalties for accidents of birth – are so extreme that 'fairness' is scarcely even an ambition. In April 2006, a letter to the *Guardian* afforded a moment of bleak amusement. Signed by a coachload of Fabians, academics and trade unionists, and of sufficient importance to be reported by the BBC, it declared: 'The core mission that should underpin progressive politics is that we should not inherit our life chances at birth.'

And what was the signatories' big idea for bringing this about? Reforming world agriculture? Abolishing trade barriers? Technology-transfer from rich nations to poor? Ah . . . no. What 'progressive politics' actually means is . . . not reducing UK inheritance tax. This came in the very same month that Robert Mugabe dismissed Gordon Brown, and by implication the UK, as 'a little tiny dot on this world'. It is a perfect encapsulation of Africa's grief. Local corruption and malfeasance; international hesitancy; northern parochialism. 'Progressive politics' may begin at home, but it has a hell of a road to travel.

Part Four

The Wider World

8

Stroking the Cat

The bald and lobeless Bond villain Ernst Stavro Blofeld did not need a face. His identifying features were his fingers, forever smoothing a fluffy white cat. As head of SPECTRE (the Special Executive for Counter-Espionage, Terrorism, Revenge and Extortion), Blofeld's aim was straightforward. Beams launched from a diamond-encrusted satellite would wipe out national defences across the globe. His power would be more than godlike (for no one could doubt his existence), and his wealth would be infinite.

No one wastes much time searching for allegorical significance in Bond movies. Insofar as they have a moral message, it is that good guys get more sex and villains are blown into eternal torment. Cowboy movies were much the same, though the black-hats chasing the stagecoach never aimed to rule the world. It is this extra dimension in Bond – the force that crushes all other forces – that furrows M's brow and stokes the tension. It's not just Bond himself that's at risk: it's the entire world. And here it is that we find just the tiniest, spider-thread connection with reality. Nothing rocks the political boat more shockingly than the threat of supranational agencies that put people, events and economies beyond the reach of their governments.

The oldest and most inextinguishable supranational force, the enemy of kings and progressive governments, is the church. The world might have been spared much grief if Pontius Pilate had played a cooler hand and let the prophet from Nazareth die more forgettably. More probably it would not. Like rising damp, god would have found another outlet and the clash of holy with temporal power would have resounded just as violently. In England it took that martyr to self-indulgence Henry VIII to snatch himself and his people from the papal grasp. His motives might have been personal – ignoble, some might say – but people on the whole were undismayed by the insult to Rome. Then as now, the Roman Catholic Church was sickeningly rich and it controlled the turnstiles to heaven. Fees were payable to it for marriage (to avoid the sin of fornication); for baptism (without which there could be no passport to heaven); and for burial in consecrated ground (ditto). The treasuries of the church bulged like the waistlines of its priests.

Rome didn't like the Reformation, and it still doesn't. Still less does it like the sound of rationalists who look to the heavens and see nothing but empty clouds. Astonishingly for a body with the Inquisition in its curriculum vitae, it complains of persecution. In May 2008, Britain's senior Roman Catholic, Cardinal Cormac Murphy-O'Connor, delivered a lecture in Westminster Cathedral which continued a theme he had already made familiar – the (entirely regrettable, in his view) secularization of society and the unwillingness of governments to accept the leadership of the church. 'You cannot banish religion to the church premises,' he said, 'and I am unhappy about the various attempts to eliminate the Christian voice from the public forum.'

He was having no truck with unbelievers. 'As always, the interesting question about atheism is "what is the theism that is being denied?" Have you ever met anyone who believes what Richard Dawkins doesn't believe in? I usually find that the God that is being rejected by such people is a God I don't believe in either.'

This was the thousand-and-first resurrection of the argument that the mitred classes always level at Dawkins: that he does not understand 'theology'. They might as well accuse him of failing to understand the metabolic rate of airborne reindeer or the needlework of fairy seamstresses. It doesn't matter what gods are meant to look like, how often or in what language they expect to be worshipped, or what they think about sex. Atheists do not believe in them, and their disbelief applies just as much to Murphy-O'Connor's god ('the God revealed to us by Jesus, who is the father who forgives us, accepts us, and loves us . . . the God who speaks to us about who we are . . .') as it does to anything else that goes bump in the night. His assertion that Dawkins is simply rejecting the wrong kind of god, and that 'modern atheism is the product of a distorted kind of Christian theism', is . . . well, how can one put it? A bit over-sophisticated? The cardinal archbishop perhaps is best left undisturbed with his spells, to enjoy in peace the knowledge 'that I stand in an unbroken line of teaching and holiness that goes back to the first apostles who knew Christ'. He is welcome to his beliefs if they comfort him. Secularists are not evangelists: they do not roam the aisles in search of converts.

But Murphy-O'Connor does not reciprocate in kind. He complains that the church is being caricatured as 'some heartless, insular institution that wants to deny people their freedom'. But this is exactly what it *does* want. And not just the Church of Rome but all churches and all sects within them; not just Christianity but all religions. They may differ – and differ enough to kill each other – over the particulars of liturgy, idolatry, 'transubstantiation' and sexual health, but they share an appetite for 'hearts and minds'. They believe that they speak for god, and that god's word outranks all others. If this is 'freedom', then it's a kind of freedom apparent only to the jesuitical mind. Some of the influences are subtle. For example: as I type this paragraph, the computer software wants to insert capital letters every time I come to words like god, church or jesuitical. For the BBC, today as on all days, 'Thought for the Day' has meant a simplistic religious homily and not a challenging new idea. Other incursions into the secular world are more blatant.

There are sects within Islam that claim the right to slaughter in god's name any who choose freedom instead of faith; the right even to kill indiscriminately in public places. Many of those who stood before Murphy-O'Connor in the 'unbroken line of teaching and holiness that goes back to the first apostles who knew Christ' thought the same. This is why the word 'crusade' is a no-no in international relations, even though foreign policy awakens the echo of medieval popes. In the mind of President George W. Bush, as he licensed carnage in Iraq, what was it that stood in opposition to the Axis of Evil? (Clue: he declared he was on a mission from God.) We might wish it otherwise, but it is for reasons like these that agents of the almighty like Murphy-O'Connor need to be taken seriously.

The Vatican's opposition to condoms in the African AIDS epidemic earns the disgust of all who put human life ahead of dogma. The falsification of evidence on the permeability of latex by the late Cardinal Alfonso Lopez Trujillo, head of the Vatican's Council for Family, was a crime for which 'faith' is no defence. (He said that condoms had holes in them through which the HIV virus could pass – a claim wholly repudiated by the very scientists whose work he misrepresented.) Also well documented, in the Catholic press if nowhere else, is the pre-eminence of sexual pleasure in the church's hierarchy of sin. Some liberal theologians in making a case for condoms have tried a 'lesser of two evils' line. To take a life (by transmitting HIV), they argue, is a greater sin than preventing one (by blocking conception), and is an obvious violation of the fifth commandment – *You shall not murder*. Conservatives hit back with a commandment of their own – the sixth, *You shall not commit adultery*. This blackest of all sins is not just a matter of avoiding pre- or extramarital sex: it embraces any coupling, inside marriage or out, that fails to 'honour the fertile structure that marital acts must have'. In other words, as Pope John Paul II reiterated, a man commits adultery with his own wife if he acts merely to gratify his own 'sexual concupiscence'. It might take an omniscient god to track down a normal human being unvisited by such a sin, and contraceptive pills might be tumbling down Catholic throats as freely as they are down Protestant and atheist ones, but it changes nothing, and nor should it. You can't half-believe the word of god. You either do or you don't. God is not a follower of social trends. If cruel and medieval is what he wants, then cruel and medieval is what he must have. That is the law.

As a religious society, the Roman Catholic Church enjoys unique privileges. Its temporal home is Vatican City, which contains all the apparatus of the Holy See – the pope, the Roman curia and the College of Cardinals – by which the worldwide church is governed. The status of the Vatican in international law is 'city state' – in effect an independent country of 108.7 acres whose permanent population of around 500 are all officers of the church. As a 'state', it maintains diplomatic relations with other states. Its 'apostolic nuncios' serve as ambassadors, and it is pushing for full membership of the United Nations. Any trip by the pope to another country counts as a full-tiara 'state visit', paid for by the host. In the course of his 27-year pontificate, Pope John Paul II managed to get his ring kissed in 130 different countries. Alone among religious organizations, the Holy See is a 'Non-member State Permanent Observer' at the UN, a status which until recently it shared with Switzerland (which was admitted to full membership in 2002). This gives it a powerful voice in the international political arena and direct influence over policies that affect the entire world, not just the 1bn members of the Catholic Church. It was not something the UN itself deliberately invited – it was more a freak of history, which the church exploited with some typically sharp diplomacy. The sequence of events was this:

To its deep regret, the Holy See was refused membership of the UN's precursor organization, the League of Nations, on the grounds that its 'statehood' was more of a technicality than a geographical or demographic actuality (Vaticanese is not a nationality), and that it might exercise too much control over the voting behaviour of Catholic countries. Experience has shown this to be a valid concern. Centuries before SPECTRE, SMERSH and the Coca-Cola Corporation, and with the ink scarcely dry on the New Testament, the Roman Catholic Church already was an energetic pioneer of globalism. Being active in all five continents, its appetite for power was, and is, exceeded only by the god whose estate it manages. Not by accident has it survived to become the oldest institution in the western world. Instead of beams from diamond-studded satellites, it fires off bulls and encyclicals. Instead of piranha tanks it holds the threat of hell. More importantly, it identifies and exploits tactical openings with the skill of a Grand Master. Smarter by far than SPECTRE, it prospers politically not because of its statehood but because it owns a post office, the Poste Vaticane, and a radio station, Radio Vaticana. God does indeed move in mysterious ways.

Shortly after it was founded, the UN invited members of the Universal Postal Union and International Telecommunications Union to attend its sessions on an ad hoc basis – an invitation upon which the Holy See pounced like a conquistador upon a silver mine. The slippered foot-in-the-door was followed in 1964 by chasuble, alb and stole when the Holy See sent to the UN a 'permanent observer', whose status was accepted by the then Secretary General U Thant on the grounds that the Vatican belonged to two specialist agencies (the postal and tele-communications unions) that were internationally recognized. As a result, and despite its presence never having been voted upon by the General Assembly, the Holy See is entitled to speak and vote at UN conferences – a right it exploits with sectarian partiality. Its representation extends into the UN Organization for Industrial

Development, the Food and Agricultural Organization, the Educational, Scientific and Cultural Organization, the Organization of the American States and many other policy-making bodies within the UN. With no population of its own to feed, house or defend, and with nothing to trade but tickets to heaven, its guiding principles are very different from those of the other participants. It has multiple opportunities to involve itself in the internal affairs of other states, which have no such influence over its own. More: because its policies are defined by the dogmas of the church, it cannot be persuaded ever to change its position – a fact which undermines (indeed, flatly denies) the very purpose of international diplomacy.

Aside from AIDS victims, the principal sufferers are women, whose right to control their own bodies is flatly denied where it amounts to anything beyond the church's idea of 'the responsible use of sexuality within marriage'. 'Family planning', as it is still quaintly called, is 'morally unacceptable'. The church will not sanction the morning-after pill or abortion even for victims of rape, and cannot agree that safe abortion has anything to do with public health. By constant lobbying and formal dissension from the majority view, it strives to erode women's rights and – though the sophisticates of the north are mostly beyond its control – it scores easy victories against the weakest and poorest in South America and Africa, whose earthly miseries it soothes through the balm of early death. Because doctrine permits no alternative, it continues to insist that condoms invite promiscuity and therefore increase the spread of AIDS rather than preventing it. By the same logic, seatbelts must encourage reckless driving (an easy thing to believe in Rome) and confession must be a licence to sin (ditto).

If anything, the church is even more confused about its own sexuality than it is about women's. Its public horror of gay sex is as good a joke as hypocrisy has ever provided, though there is nothing funny about its record on pederasty. The cover-up and protection of paedophiles in the American priesthood was as vile as anything ever perpetrated in the name of Christ. Literally thousands of cases of sexual misconduct by priests have now come to light, in scores of countries including Canada, Ireland, Italy, Poland, Mexico, Germany, France, Australia and the UK. The nearest any of this got to levity, which was not very near at all, was in September 2005 when a Texan court scheduled a lawsuit accusing Pope Benedict of conspiring to cover up assaults against boys. Of course it didn't happen. What we got instead was the US Justice Department panicking like an altar boy before a trouserless cardinal. As a sitting head of state, said Assistant Attorney General Peter Keisler, the Holy Father was above the law, and suing him would be 'incompatible with the United States' foreign policy interests'. Note: not 'vexatious', 'unlikely to succeed' or 'unjust'; just politically inexpedient. And this is the nub of it. In most of the developed world, clergy are preaching to empty churches, and the verdict of society is that they are out of touch with the public mood. This is inevitable. The church is rooted in orthodoxy, fixed and immutable. If Leviticus says homosexuality is a sin, then sin it will remain until Armageddon. The rest of the world meanwhile has moved on.

There is a new, liberal orthodoxy that puts life ahead of theology. This orthodoxy says women *do* have a right to choose. It says that what consenting adults do in their own bedrooms is no sin, and no business of anyone else's, and that people should be as free to enjoy sex as the archbishop is to pluck an apple from his garden. All the church can do as the world moves forward is to grab its shirt and try to pull it back again. As I write, a group of Anglican bishops is meeting in Jerusalem, indignantly peeling away from the Canterbury mainstream and voting to restore 'the word of God' – by which they mean driving homosexuals out of the temple and barring the door to bishops without penises. They are viewed from afar with the indulgent good humour reserved for the harmlessly daft. But the dear old C of E (famously 'not a proper church' in the opinion of John Paul II) is no threat to anyone but itself, and has no more idea of world domination than Blofeld's cat. For all that its congregations are disappearing into the cemetery, the same cannot be said of the Church of Rome.

In its dual role as a state and a world religion, it has huge lobbying power. In the poorer Catholic countries of the south, the pope fills the space between head of state and god. Catholics believe that the former Cardinal Ratzinger, like every pope before him, is the direct descendant of the apostle Peter. His authority is absolute, his judgement infallible. By way of 'apostolic succession' – the doctrine by which spiritual power has been transferred by 'laying on of hands' from Christ to the disciples and thence to every subsequent generation of bishops – he and his representatives receive their credentials directly from Jesus. If you believe this, then the pope is a hard man to say no to.

An officer of the Methodist Church (no believer in apostolic succession, he) once ticked me off for using the word 'sophisticated' to mean refined rather than perverted or corrupt. Sophistication to him was an adjunct of sophistry, and sophistry meant jesuitism. I took little notice at the time but now I think I see what he meant. The Church of Rome is the most sophisticated lobbying machine the world has ever known. It expects special privileges not available to others, including direct access to governments and broadcasting organizations. Senators, congressmen and parliamentarians are petitioned, and Catholics urged to vote with their 'conscience' rather than with the party whip. A classic current example is the church's opposition to embryonic stem cell research – a position it shares with the right-wing, born-again evangelical Christian movement that exercised so much influence over George W. Bush. As it was with AIDS, so it is again. We meet not just principled objections based on Christian belief but also casuistry, misinformation and the kind of Frankenstein's-monster scaremongering that is guaranteed to grab the attention of tabloid newspapers. The technique is sophisticated indeed. The church first impedes stem cell research, then argues that it has failed to yield any tangible benefits and should be banned, which is a bit like slashing the tyres and then complaining of slow progress on the road. Just to be on the safe side, it simultaneously raises the spectre of the vehicle's running out of control and careering towards a nightmare future of half-human, half-cow hybrids that won't know whether to mow the lawn or eat it.

If propaganda fails, it brings out the big stick. In 2006 the arch medievalist Cardinal Trujillo (the same who lied about condoms) threatened excommunication to any Catholic who strayed from the papal line. 'Destroying human embryos is equivalent to an abortion,' he told the Vatican magazine *Famiglia Cristiana*. 'It is the same thing. Excommunication will be applied to the women, doctors and researchers who eliminate embryos [and to the] politicians that approve the law.' It prompted a leading Italian geneticist to compare the Vatican with the Taliban.

Early in 2008, while the UK parliament was debating the Human Fertilization and Embryology Bill (which Catholic MPs were told to oppose), the pope returned to the attack. Addressing the Vatican's Congregation for the Doctrine of the Faith, of which he was formerly head, he said that marriage was the only forum within which human life could be transmitted. 'When human beings in the weakest and most defenceless stage of their existence are selected, abandoned, killed or used as pure "biological matter",' he said, 'how can it be denied that they are no longer being treated as "someone" but as "something", thus placing the very concept of human dignity in doubt?'

Lisa Jardine, chair of the UK Human Fertilization and Embryology Authority, in turn accused the church of pressing 'fatal dogma' to prevent all forms of embryonic research. These are not easy arguments for laymen to follow – a point of great convenience to churchmen, who can cut factual and philosophical corners, beg questions and rely on emotive language. The scientists, or 'Doctor Frankensteins' as they are characterized, need a bit more meat on their arguments. It takes time just to explain what an embryonic stem cell is, and some effort from the reader or listener to understand. The following account is lifted verbatim from a thoughtful and balanced report, *Looking at the Ethics of Technology for a New Millennium*, from the Church of Scotland.

> Embryonic stem cells are special cells which exist just before the embryo begins to differentiate. At this point they have the potential to form any type of cell in the human body, and they can also be kept in the laboratory in a cell culture for very long periods. In November 1998, after many years of searching, these were isolated for the first time. In principle, you could now take a human embryo, extract these cells, and chemically direct them into becoming any particular type of human cell – skin, heart, nerve cells and so on. Certain tissues in adults also produce stem cells, which could also be reprogrammed, but so far they seem much more limited in which cell types they can produce.

'Differentiation', when the embryo forms outer and inner cell masses (which will develop to become the placenta and the foetus), happens around five or six days after the fertilization of the egg. This is the stage at which scientists isolate the stem cells from the inner cell mass and, in the Catholic view, murder a child. It cuts no ice that the cells are, in effect, clinical waste taken from embryos unused after in vitro fertilization treatments – the church opposes IVF too, and it only deepens the horror. To scientists, these microscopic fragments have the potential to *become* human but at this stage are just bundles of undeveloped genetic material – building blocks, not human bodies. Because they have the capacity to develop into any kind of cell in the body – heart, skin, nerve, brain, whatever – they might be used to repair or re-grow diseased or damaged organs or tissue. Very obviously, this has profound implications for the future treatment of, for example, heart disease, diabetes, Parkinson's and Alzheimer's diseases and many other common killers and debilitators. Our understanding of cell biology will be greatly improved; so will the design and validation of new drugs. Lives will be saved, suffering relieved. While it would be fair to say that scientists vary in their degree of optimism, and that some of them are frankly sceptical of the more extravagant claims (a fact frequently quoted by the church), this does not mean that they oppose the research (a fact never quoted by the church). And it certainly does not mean that they would credit a stem cell with a 'soul', or that they would follow the polished sloganeering of Peter Smith, Catholic Archbishop of Wales, for whom a stem cell is 'not a potential human life, but a human life with potential'. If churchmen do draw back, it is only to step forward again with another jesuitical thrust. This is not a conflict between religion and science, they say; it is a question of ethics. Well, so be it. Let us ask an ethical question. What is likely to be of greater benefit to the greatest number of people? Stem cell research, or dogma?

It will be argued that the Catholic Church has a right to campaign in its own cause. This cannot be gainsaid. What cannot be admitted is that it deserves special access to secular authority, or that it should interfere with the lives of people who do not share its beliefs. A peripatetic pope should be received as head of a church, not as a head of state, and the ring-kissings, 'Holy Fathers' and genuflections left to members of his own congregation. The rest of us owe him nothing save the courtesy ordinarily due to strangers. The church's entanglements with the Mafia and the IRA, its anti-Judaism and concordat with Hitler, the sumptuousness of its palaces and cathedrals, all testify to the primacy of its self-interest. Guenter Lewy, in *The Catholic Church and Nazi Germany* (1964), quotes the Führer:

We should trap the priests by their notorious greed and self-indulgence. We shall thus be able to settle everything with them in perfect peace and harmony. I shall give them a few years' reprieve. Why should we quarrel? They will swallow anything in order to keep their material advantages. Matters will never come to a head. They will recognize a firm will, and we need only show them once or twice who is master. They will know which way the wind blows.

No one should be condemned by the word of Hitler. Nor should we underestimate the pressures that church leaders faced in living next door to a psychopath, or imagine that our own instincts under stress would have been any different. As torturers throughout the ages have known, self-preservation is the default mode of our genetic programming. But that is exactly the point. As the ructions in the financial markets during the autumn of 2008 so forcefully reminded us, greed under stress turns to fear. Greed is a human condition, and the megalomania of tyrants is greed gone mad – a genetic malfunction that puts reason under terminal stress. It doesn't matter whether it's Ernst Stavro Blofeld or the pope, the piranha tank or exclusion from paradise. It doesn't matter whether it is the Jewish lobby forcing the US government's hand on Israel, or Pakistani madrassas training young men for murder. Democracy is the victim. Without consent there is only tyranny. Without consent we have innocent women, men and children abandoned to AIDS; we have in the Middle East a tinderbox, fanned by sectarians who believe they are answerable only to god and that democracy is blasphemy; we have bombs in cities; we have a cross-border criminal economy that floods the world with narcotics; we have economic meltdown. We have Africa.

Governments always fear invasion by alien ideologies. Hence the loathing of communism and the improbable alliances (the pope with Hitler, for example) that were ranged against it. But subversive influences are often subtler than this. The global pre-eminence of the English language is a good example. Without its influence on culture and thought, we would be living in a very different world. In an essay for the *Sunday Times*, the novelist and biographer Peter Ackroyd described Geoffrey Chaucer's decision to write *The Canterbury Tales* in English rather than Latin or French as 'perhaps the most significant moment in our national culture' – the point at which English became the language of literature. Other significant moments followed. In 1620 the Pilgrim Fathers made English the language of America. In 1621, Shakespeare's first folio made it the language of genius. In 1763, victory over France in the Seven Years War made it the language of international relations. In 1974 the *Protocol for Packet Network Intercommunication*, by Vinton Cerf and Robert Kahn, made it the language of cyberspace. Among all these, the most crucial was 1620. When the earth's most powerful nation speaks, the rest of the world listens and understands. Indeed, the language of internationalism now might better be described as American rather than English – it's asses, not arses, that get kicked now. When you travel the world and marvel at the fluency in English of waiters and taxi-drivers, the inflection is pure New York. On the Greek island of Samos, a waiter is reading Kerouac and intends to return to Athens 'in the fall'. In Amsterdam, Barcelona, Rome, English vowel sounds are burred by familiarity with Uncle Sam – *No prarblem!* Once we were 'sir' and 'madam'. Now we are 'you guys'.

Like a movie, the whole world is being dubbed in American. Even in their colonial majesty the British never achieved as much. They were more likely to bring back what they found – tea, spices, bungalows, the tango – than they were to take out plum duff and the songs of Marie Lloyd, though they were generous with their technology. You could argue that the entire modern world, global economy and all, came off Britain's drawing boards in the 19th century. The greatest of its gifts was the mainline rail-way, which governments across the globe recognized as a vital stimulus to economic development. Wherever lines were built – in the Middle East, South America, India, Australia – it was British engineers who led the way. By the time he died in 1871, a single British contractor, Thomas Brassey of Chester, had built 12.5 per cent of the world's entire railway mileage. And it wasn't just transport. William Lindley, for example, built not only Hamburg's railway system but also most of the water and sewerage networks in central and eastern Europe. Britons built major canals in Sweden and India, and bridges wherever there were rivers to cross. Budapest's iconic Szechenyi suspension bridge was by William Tierney Clark, and Kiev's bridge over the Dnieper by Charles Blacker Vignoles, both in the early 1850s. And so it continued into the 20th century: Aswan Dam by Benjamin Baker, Sydney Harbour Bridge by Ralph Freeman, Sydney Opera House by Ove Arup, a new Cairo sewerage system by Gwilym Roberts, replacing the original by Carket James nearly a hundred years earlier. But it did not turn the world into a little England. As any visitor to India will testify, railways have always reflected the character of their native countries. You knew where you were. From the farts in the carriage to the music in the street, even at the height of empire, the sounds and smells were peculiarly local. Coca-Colanization is changing all that. Now every major city in the world, and most minor ones, can offer you an American cheeseburger with a free side order of western popular music. This is the world of the selfish meme. The survival of the loudest.

Cultural cross-fertilization has a long and vital history, the give-and-take of art, technology and science marred only by the interference of religious and political zealots. Always among the displaced there is a hunger for familiarity. The first act of a group of migrant white Zimbabweans I met in Mozambique was to found a cricket club. The second was to light a barbecue. English expatriates in the Costa del Sol oil their nostalgia with all-day breakfasts, Irish pubs and grey Sunday roasts with 'all the trimmings'. The German sectors of Greek holiday islands welcome their guests with *Schweinfleisch*, *Koteletten* and *Wurst*. In themselves these are examples of small significance, but they are details in a much larger picture. Cultural greed says the only taste that matters is my own: I will impose it wherever I go. 'International cuisine' is one regrettable result. 'International wine' is another. Distinct local flavours are stirred into international blends whose dominant characteristic is bland American-Englishness. Perhaps it doesn't matter too much: you don't have to eat in McDonald's or a Sheraton-a-like unless you want to. There is (almost) always an alternative, though you may have to forgo the essential international requirements of consistency and 'convenience'. But homogeneity is not confined to the palate. It hits the ear and the eye just as hard. Take a taxi from any international airport to the city centre, and what do you see? International architecture; international brand names; international vehicle types; international advertising. You have to check your ticket to remind yourself where you are. Amsterdam? Palermo? Manchester? Tokyo?

There have always been supra-national movements in art, architecture and philosophy, and governments have always distrusted them. 'Sedition' or 'apostasy' is literature's crime against entrenchment, and the *fatwa* is just the Muslim version of a tendency as old as writing. It is no accident: when dictators dictate, it is always intellectuals who are first against the wall, and books that feed the bonfires. Art and music when they challenge the party are invariably 'decadent'. Even so, I was astonished to find the following on the website of the Union of International Associations, under the heading *World problems*.

Claim:
1 Whilst it is true that good music is still heard and even still written, the evil influence of musical perversions cannot be overstated. Modern music has resulted in the ruin of an entire generation.

2 Crime and violence in society are partly due to the pre-
ponderance of aggressive (rock) music and to the lack of classic
music with its soothing powers. Aggressive music alienates the
body from its natural emotional climate and evokes its most
primitive reactions. In rock concerts, for example, the high volume
of the music, the mechanical hammering of its rhythm, its sheer
physical impact and total lack of nuance, leave an audience in a
state of complete mental stupor, drugged, numbed and impervious
to feeling. The repetition of music which is totally unemotional in
its effect dis-educates the emotions. A synthesized rhythm section
with an immaculate, mechanical beat is totally unnatural and
estranging. It breeds automata, or worse still, causes people to
suppress unexpressed emotions, and the frustrations stemming
from this can burst out in otherwise inexplicable violence. There is
a danger of pornography in sound, whereby the raucous, throaty
delivery of many pop singers bases itself, albeit unwittingly, on the
sound of lustful ejaculation.

Counter-claim:
History of violence is considerably longer than that of rock music.
In earlier times, the Church objected to the lasciviousness of much
dance music and the profane tunes in sacred works. Even Bach was
accused of excessive elaboration. In the 1920s jazz was seen as a
threat to the civilized European society. In the 1960s the Beatles
were thought subversive. Music has a powerful impact on
emotions and senses, but the arousal achieved by rock music or
Wagner are not different from each other.

Reading such a 'claim', you feel the oniony breath of the risen
Stalin on your neck. 'In the music of Comrade Shostakovich,' said
his cultural hatchet man Tikhon Khrennikov, secretary of the
Union of Soviet Composers, 'we find all sorts of things alien to
realistic Soviet art, such as tenseness, neuroticism, escapism and
repulsive pathology. In the work of Comrade Prokofiev natural

emotion and melody have been replaced by grunting and scraping.' There is, just, a faint mew of encouragement in the thought that the commissars of Stalin's evil empire could believe themselves threatened by symphonies. Prokofiev's career as a composer was effectively ended by Khrennikov's denunciation in 1948, and with terrible irony he died on the same day as Stalin in 1953 – much too early to enjoy history's verdict on his and Khrennikov's respective merits as composers. Khachaturian and Schnittke, too, will long outlast the philistine who persecuted them. Stalin's attitude to architecture was pretty much the same. Beautiful old houses and churches made the supreme sacrifice for the sake of 'patriotic' visual banalities in the style of his favourite music – portentous, slabby, monumental and lying through its teeth (for what could be more deceitful than the approved decorative motif of smiling farmworkers?). The international modernism so fashionable in the West was as unwelcome as the 12-note scale. The one thing you might positively say about the designers who gambled with their lives every time they sketched a façade is that they were required to satisfy the tastes of 'the people', not impress their fellow architects.

To this extent you could say that Stalin had a point. Outside politics and religion, few groups of men and women have shown more persistent symptoms of megalomania than planners and architects. In Britain, no less than in Hitler's Germany or Stalin's Russia, planning has always been tangled up with social engineering. First came the garden cities – Letchworth and Welwyn Garden City – with their utopian vision of *rus in urbe*; then the post-war New Towns which applied social and political idealism to the problems of metropolitan overspill. 'New' was the buzz. In the period of post-war reconstruction, planner-visionaries like Patrick Abercrombie declared war on historic city centres and saw wholesale reconstruction as the recipe for a brave new egalitarian world of high socialistic seriousness (literally 'high' in its enthusiasm for streets in the sky).

The legacy was city centre blight and a depressing rash of kit-form, everywhere-and-nowhere New Towns – Stevenage, Crawley, Hemel Hempstead, Basildon and the rest. In 1948 Lewis Silkin, minister for planning in Clement Attlee's Labour government, declared with utter conviction that 'Basildon will become a city which people from all over the world will want to visit. It will be a place where all classes of community can meet freely together on equal terms and enjoy common cultural and recreational facilities.' Yes, well ... The madness resurfaced in 2008 with the government's proposal to parachute a number of gigantic housing estates into the countryside and call them 'eco-towns'. But this is 'building', not 'architecture'. It's not housing that makes reputations in the architectural world: it's towers and terminals, offices and piazzas, monolithic not intimate spaces.

The business is transnational. British-based firms busy themselves in Madrid, Dallas, Dubai, Kazakhstan, Florence, Rome, Shanghai, Washington, New York, Paris, Berlin, Barcelona, Tokyo, Seoul, Zurich ... Dutch and American firms at the same time are working in London. Many of their creations are of supreme beauty – clean (or, in the case of Frank Gehry, crumpled) sculptural forms that might have come from the studio of Brancusi. Others are more like fashion designs, striving for weirdness or cutting-edgeness. The current fashion is for shiny metallic skins. You'll see them in Bilbao (Gehry's Guggenheim Museum), Berlin (Daniel Libeskind's Jewish Museum), Glasgow (Foster and Partners' Scottish Exhibition and Conference Centre, aka the 'Armadillo'), Salford (Michael Wilford's Lowry Arts Centre), Hong Kong (Rocco Design Partnerships' MTRC Central Station), Amsterdam (Kisho Kurokawa's extension to the Van Gogh Museum), Lima (Atelier Hollein's Interbank), Manhattan (G TECTS' Issey Miyake showroom), California (Charles Walton's Cerritos Millennium Library), Denver (Hardy Holzman Pfeiffer's Denver Museum of Nature and Science; Libeskind's Denver Arts Museum Expansion), Jakarta (Arkdesign's Sun

Plaza), Normandy (Chamberlain Architects' Juno Beach Centre), Vancouver (Bing Thom's Surrey City Centre), and on and on around the world. Titanium is the new concrete. Glossy is the new matte. Stand-out is the new discreet. Greed is the new socialism. Look at me, *look at me*, LOOK AT ME.

In 2007 the winner of Britain's most prestigious architectural award, the Stirling Prize, was David Chipperfield's Museum of Modern Literature at Marbach am Neckar in Germany. The design is formal, restrained, neo-classical in a pared-down kind of way, with not a shiny surface in sight – a building lost in thought. Having observed that Chipperfield's architecture 'perhaps wears its angsty gravitas and subtlety too pointedly on its sleeve', a writer in *The Times* nevertheless found it 'a blessed relief to encounter in this dumbed-down age, like switching to Goethe after Dan Brown'. Chipperfield himself seemed to agree. This was the second consecutive year in which the 'building that has made the greatest contribution to British architecture' was built on foreign soil (in 2006 it was Richard Rogers's Barajas Airport in Madrid). How could it have happened? 'Simple,' Chipperfield told *The Times*. 'Britain gets the architecture it deserves. We don't value architecture, we don't take it seriously, we don't want to pay for it and the architect isn't trusted . . . We are a country that values money and individualism. Architecture becomes glorified property development, not valued culture . . . All people want now is delivery. Sod the quality. Just make sure it's up on time and in budget. Nobody takes a risk . . . Actual architecture isn't valued, just this beauty parade of fizzy buildings that look good for the cameras.'

It is easy to sympathize with some of this. In a risk-averse age, creative thinking is reserved for cost control. But 'the architect isn't trusted'? Whose fault is that? Did the public wake up one morning, rack their brains for someone to despise and cry 'Architect!'? Or did they perhaps look at the rape of their city centres, the multistorey misery of the 'streets in the sky', the stained and forbidding concrete of modernism's brutalist nadir and – the ultimate betrayal of human genius – the conflation of 'housing estate' with 'eyesore'? Architects were not solely responsible for all this (they got away with it only because we let them, and clients and governments were in it too), but it was they who came up with all that 'machine for living' cobblers; they who conned us with 'artists' impressions'; they who knew better than us how we ought to live; they who turned architecture into politics; they who wanted to possess the very sky. And they are doing it still, building new orthodoxies from old, ism upon ism, still knowing best. The result, in this titanium-clad sub-period of the post-modern era, is as we see it now on every continent. In favoured locations, a shimmering chorus-line of architectural bling, like silos dressed for the ballet, hogs the skyline but gives nothing to the earthlings in the street. Everywhere else gets bland, medium-rise uniformity or, on the urban margins which seem everywhere to have been disqualified from entitlement to care, frank tram-shed ugliness. Regrets? We've had a few. We did it their way.

The Blofelds of the architectural establishment are as tyrannous in their stranglehold over taste as the Turner or Booker juries in art and literature. Anyone taking a different line, particularly a traditional or populist one (as in, say, Quinlan Terry or the Prince of Wales), can expect to be denounced in terms that would make Tikhon Khrennikov squirm with pleasure. The world's architectural elite do produce work of stunning originality and beauty, but we do not need just international masterpieces. We need men and women of talent to attend to our common experience of everyday life – the buildings in which we live and work, the buildings that make the townscapes we pass through. Above all we need to rediscover and retain a proper sense of place, to recognize and appreciate the value of 'local' as well as 'global'. To set aside greed and realize the value of humility.

*

It is no accident that many of the most spectacular world build-ings are sports stadiums, and that the most spectacular of all have been for the Olympics. The Olympic movement is among the richest and most influential supranational forces on earth. Fuelled by vast broadcasting, sponsorship and advertising budgets, it is richer than many countries and more powerful than their govern-ments. No regime on earth is too proud to beg, plead and, ultimately, pay for its blessing. The world's biggest corporations fight with their chequebooks to be glorified by association. It is an arena in which million-dollar deals are for wimps: real men talk in billions.

The first Olympians would be no more likely to believe this than they could comprehend a human landing more than 19 cubits from his point of take-off. The ancient Games were held for approximately 1,000 years from 776 BC, at Olympia in the north-west Peloponnese (not Mount Olympus, as is sometimes erroneously believed). Historians find it difficult to describe them without using the word 'homoerotic'. Women and slaves were excluded from the stadium, wherein the chaps stripped to the buff, oiled and powdered their bodies and enjoyed a little manly racing and wrestling. For all their campness, however, the ancient Games did hold some portents for the modern. After a golden age of aristocratic amateurism, the serious competition devolved to professionals; and nemesis, when it came, arrived in the form of politics. Theodosius the Great finally killed the Games in AD 394 when, in fear of a barbarian influx, he banned all religious festivals.

The line of descent from Classical Greece to the 'father' of the modern Olympics, Baron Pierre de Coubertin, followed an improbable dog-leg via *Tom Brown's Schooldays*, the Cotswolds and English public schools. Coubertin was a diminutive Frenchman, pop-eyed and with the kind of moustache you could see from behind, whose passion for exercise amounted almost to a fetish. His aim was to reform the French education system to place more emphasis on sport, which he took to be the secret of English success. He read Thomas Hughes's classic, *Tom Brown's Schooldays*, and found a lifelong hero in the headmaster of Rugby School, Dr Thomas Arnold. The little Frenchman was further inspired by rustic revivals of 'Olympick Games' at Chipping Campden in Gloucestershire and, more particularly, by the Wenlock Games at Much Wenlock in Shropshire. Everything that is best about modern sport, and everything that is worst about it, can be traced back to Coubertin and what he liked to call *le régime arnoldien*. It was all there in 1896 when his lobbying finally yielded the prize he had been striving for – the first modern Olympic Games at Athens. They were nothing if not high-minded. 'Olympism,' said Coubertin, 'is a philosophy of life, exalting and combining in a balanced whole the quality of body, will and mind. Blending sport with culture and education, Olympism seeks to create a way of life based on the joy found in effort, the educational value of good example and respect for universal fundamental ethical principles.'

By 'joy', he meant exactly what he said. 'Many sportsmen,' he wrote in 1913, 'will swear that this pleasure [of athleticism] reaches in certain circumstances the characteristics at once imperious and stirring of sexual passion.' No wonder they took cold showers.

Compared to the bloated wealth-digester cranked up during each four-year 'Olympiad' now, Coubertin's Athenian effort was hardly more than a village fete. There were just 211 competitors from 14 countries (by comparison, the figures for 2008 were 10,500 and 205 respectively, competing in 28 different sports). Yet the infant was already exhibiting many features of the giant it would become. An Alexandrian businessman sponsored the rebuilt stadium. Ticket touts bought blocks of seats and sold them at inflated prices. There were squabbles about eligibility and status. (Two staff members from the British Embassy faced fierce opposition to their participation in the cycle race because they were 'servants' and thus not proper amateurs.) And, as the national flags of the winners rattled up the flagpole, there were ostentatious displays of nationalism – most particularly by the Americans.

And so it went on. By the time the fourth Games came round in 1908 the cost of staging them had escalated so dramatically that the scheduled host, Rome, could not face the bills and the event was shifted to London. By now the original right of individual entry had been rescinded, and only members of national teams were permitted to take part. Coubertin's 'universal fundamental ethical principles' found their outlet in endless track-side feuds. Stan Greenberg, in his epic *Olympic Facts & Feats*, recalls that trouble began even before the starter raised his gun. America and Sweden complained that their flags were not being flown; the Finns refused to march behind the flag of Tsarist Russia; the American flag-bearer refused to dip the Stars and Stripes to Edward VII. The actual racing only made things worse. American officials protested about fixed heats and biased judging, then ordered a boycott of the rerun 400 metres final after the original American winner had been disqualified for impeding the lone Briton, Lieutenant Wyndham Halswelle. As the other two finalists were also American, it gave Halswelle the only walkover in Olympic history. It was not, however, the last time the Olympics would hear the word 'boycott'.

When did the Olympics lose their innocence? A cynic might say they never had any, or that they left it behind on the fields of Much Wenlock. By the Mexico Games of 1968 they had pretty much given up all pretence. The first lesson of the modern Olympics is that nothing sells like a winner. Kit manufacturers had been paying athletes to wear their products since the 1950s, and by 1968 the notorious 'shoe wars' were at their height. At Mexico the winning margin for Adidas was wider even than Bob Beamon's in the long-jump. Eighty-three per cent of the gold medallists wore its kit.

It was not just *le régime arnoldien* that died. Ten days before the opening ceremony, students opposed to the Games held a rally in Mexico City's Plaza of the Three Cultures. Estimates of how many of them were shot dead by government troops vary between dozens and 300, with thousands more injured or imprisoned. However many it was, they were not enough to divert the juggernaut from its path. The show had to go on. The show *did* go on. At Munich in 1972 the Games lost some of its own. Arab terrorists of the Black September group killed 11 members of the Israeli team and ensured two things:

First, that all subsequent Games would take place within a steel ring of armed security. Second, that they would be of exponentially greater interest – and, hence, value – to world television. Until now, the Olympics had excited remarkably little interest among television's most powerful paymasters, the American advertising industry. All that was about to change. ABC in 1972 paid 7.5m dollars for the American broadcasting rights. By the next Games in Montreal the price had more than trebled, to 25m dollars. And there was another fatal wounding. The idea, implicit in Coubertin's 'universal fundamental ethical principles', that the Olympian ideal was somehow aloof from politics, took a javelin straight through the heart. The International Olympic Committee (IOC) and the Canadian government could not agree on what exactly the Taiwanese team should call itself – the Canadians would not permit 'Republic of China' – and the Taiwanese went home. Their withdrawal shrank into insignificance against the absence of black Africa, which stayed away in protest at the presence of New Zealand, whose rugby players had toured apartheid South Africa. Like a mad parrot the IOC went on squawking its mantra, that politics had to be kept out of sport. 'Ethical principles' of course are all things to all rogues. They are the very sluice-gates through which politics will flood – and flood they did.

Moscow in 1980 and Los Angeles in 1984 were Cold War

battlefields. The response of the US and British governments to the Soviet invasion of Afghanistan was to discourage their athletes from competing in Brezhnev's Olympics. Margaret Thatcher's government tried persuasion and lost (the British team, aided by sudden surges of generosity from trades unions and Labour local authorities, returned with five gold medals). The Americans preferred coercion and got their way. None of this devalued the Games commercially. In 1983 the chairman of Adidas, Horst Dassler, was appointed to run the IOC's international marketing effort, selling advertising rights worldwide. Dassler had already bought influence with the international federations of individual Olympic sports – underwriting their programmes, helping friends to rise within their hierarchies – so that the IOC appointment was little more than *Realpolitik*. By the time of his death in 1987, insiders recognized him as the single most powerful figure in international sport. His support for Barcelona as host city for 1992 was said to be worth 30 IOC votes.

Los Angeles in 1984 was the tit-for-tat Games, with the political football hoofed to the other end of the stadium. This time it was the Soviet bloc that stayed away, but all those extra gold medals for home athletes (83 in all, plus 61 silvers and 30 bronzes) ensured that the 'Free Enterprise Games' were a fabulous festival of the dollar, a medallioned altar of American self-love. Television rights fetched 287m dollars, and the global audience reached 2.5 billion. Even the torch relay legs were 'sold'.

Four years later in Seoul, television itself tried to seize the flame. Stupendous bids were made (up to 750m dollars, by one account), but on condition that box-office events would be timed to run between 9am and 11am, local time, for the convenience of America's prime-time audience. The inevitable compromise reduced NBC's winning bid to a 'mere' 300m dollars. The Americans protected their investment with 40,000 troops along the border between North and South Korea and two aircraft carriers in the Yellow Sea, but still had to stomach the Soviets and

East Germans heading them in the medals table. These were the Games at which the Canadian sprinter Ben Johnson was disqualified for drug-taking after winning the 100 metres in a then world record of 9.79 seconds. Here, then, was the final clause in the Olympics' compact with the devil. Professional athletes were dependent on their sponsors, who expected results. The pressure to win was enormous. If it was dope that made the difference, then 'ethical principles' were in a race they could not win.

The competition to host the Games now is beyond extreme: it is wild-eyed and messianic. The IOC's mission statement, 'to contribute to building a peaceful and better world by educating youth through sport', still holds the echo of *le régime arnoldien* but, like male nipples or Darwin's Points, it's a vestige of some bygone evolutionary stage. When a successful candidate leaps up and down in triumph, it is not to celebrate an opportunity to educate the world's youth. It is to welcome a seat on the gravy train. Winning cities anticipate not just a gloss on their reputations but tangible assets: massive inward investment, redevelopment programmes kick-started by new stadiums, athletes' villages and other enduring legacies of the Olympians' visit. If the application process itself were an Olympic event, then it would be called hardball. Technical excellence is essential, but on its own it will not be enough. The IOC has 111 voting members, and winning a majority takes more than writing a good proposal, smiling sweetly and saying please. Before Atlanta, there was only suspicion, not proof, that Coubertin's ethical principles were being warped by personal greed. Christopher R. Hill, in his comprehensive study of Olympic political and economic history, *Olympic Politics*, said he had no direct evidence that IOC members had been influenced by gifts or inducements, though he recorded the suspicions of others. 'Bidding committees,' he said, 'have been said to offer jobs to relations of undecided members, or to hold out such inducements as free surgical operations.' Members who saw it as their duty to visit each of the bidding cities could travel in first-class, five-star luxury around the globe and enjoy the kind of hospitality usually reserved for monarchs and popes. Hill reported, for example, that as well as 'trinkets and brochures', Seoul quietly handed out two first-class return air tickets to each IOC member, redeemable for cash.

And then came Salt Lake City, whose bid for the 2002 Winter Games stands as a benchmark in the history of institutionalized corruption. The IOC's 'Board of Ethics' implicated 24 individuals – approximately a fifth of its membership – who had variously received support for their children, profited from land deals and international aid, accepted donations to political campaigns or simply pocketed cash. Only those within the IOC bothered to pretend surprise. Former Olympic competitors said such things had been going on for as long as they could remember. It was, inevitably, 'just the tip of the iceberg'. The legacy of all this is, on the one hand, a gift to cynics who believe every deal is corrupt and every medal won by drugs. On the other hand (more fuel for the cynics), the inflationary spiral has continued. It is not just business as usual but business on an unprecedented scale. In the name of universal fundamental ethical principles, political expediency (blind eyes turned to Chinese human rights abuses) is dressed up as political non-involvement. And the gravy train is hooked to an even bigger engine. High among the IOC's objectives is 'To prohibit the uncontrolled commercialization of the Olympic Games', which you might think has a nice *arnoldien* ring to it. Rampant profiteering would be a strange way of 'educating youth through sport'. The idealism, however, is thinly spread and carefully applied. By 'uncontrolled commercialism', all the IOC means is any enterprise not licensed by itself. Megabuck sponsorship deals are done with companies across a wide spectrum of product categories. To preserve the value of exclusivity, only one sponsor – ideally, the global brand leader – is allowed from each category. In return, depending on their level of entry (international or local), they can make promotional use of the IOC's five-ring symbol or of national Olympic emblems. For the right to use 'Olympic marks, imagery or themes', a licensee must pay between 10 and 15 per cent of its sales revenue – a deal that covers even commemorative coins and stamps.

The real Olympic elite are the so-called 'TOP VI' – the 11 multinational corporations that enjoy exclusive global rights as 'worldwide Olympic Partners'. For Beijing in 2008 these were Coca-Cola, Atos Origin, Manulife, GE, Kodak, Panasonic, McDonald's, Samsung, Omega, Lenovo and Visa International. So tight was the control exerted by and on behalf of these sporting titans that, for example, Visa was the only credit card accepted for the purchase of tickets. Mastercard? Get a life!

Another 11 corporations, the 'Beijing 2008 Partners', enjoyed the benefits of sponsorship within the host itself. These included the Bank of China, Air China and six other Chinese companies, plus Volkswagen, Johnson & Johnson and, yes, Adidas (which will also sponsor the London Games in 2012). All these were shielded by the IOC's principled opposition to 'uncontrolled commercialization', which in China went as far as advising local media organizations to refuse advertising from non-Olympic sponsors. Cats, however, may be skinned in many different ways. The world's biggest sports shoe and clothing company is not Adidas. It is Nike, which also is possibly the world's most skilful exponent of what is called 'ambush marketing' – the art of capitalizing on an event without coughing up a multimillion-dollar official sponsorship deal. Nike does it by sponsoring individual sportsmen and women, whom it pays to wear its kit and appear in its advertisements. In Beijing, no fewer than 22 of China's own Olympic teams were contracted to wear Nike; so were leading track stars. On the back of all this, the company launched an advertising and promotional blitz which, sure enough, true Olympians found offensive to the ideal of 'universal fundamental ethical principles'.

This, then, is the essence of Olympic sport – the IOC, national governments, global corporations and broadcasting organizations locked in a quadrennial gravy-fight that has as much to do with *le régime arnoldien* as nandrolone does with a sucked orange. Educating youth through sport? Well, yes . . . though the lesson in raw marketing power is possibly not the one the founders intended. The budgeted cost of the 2012 London Olympics started at £2.4 billion. Two years on, the latest figure to have zipped past on its perpetually upward trajectory is £9.3 billion. No one knows where it will stop – least of all, it seems, Tessa Jowell, whose task as Britain's 'Olympics minister' combines the role of Blofeld's cat with that of a fruit machine permanently stuck on three cherries. For the gentlemen and ladies of the IOC, nothing is too good. In April 2008 the *Sunday Times* reported that, four years ahead of the London Games, the organizers already had made the most expensive hotel block-booking in Olympic history – 1,925 rooms for international delegates and their spouses at a cost of £10m. For the benefit of the most senior officials, these included 345 suites at up to £3,000 a night at Park Lane hotels including the Dorchester, the Hilton and the Grosvenor House. To smooth their way to the venues they would have the use of 3,145 chauffeur-driven cars whisking them along routes cleared of other traffic. All this despite the IOC's own warning against the evils of 'overspending and gigantism', and the supposed new Spartanism of the post-Salt Lake age.

Snouts in troughs; noses up bottoms; governments in thrall to the blazered Blofelds and their star-fleet of commercial giants. It may sum up the 'mutual understanding' prescribed in the Olympic charter, but it puts a whole new spin on its much-quoted and frequently satirized motto. *Citius, altius, fortius* – faster, higher, stronger. No one knows how long this eternal progression can continue. Is there really no limit to what the human body can achieve in trimming seconds or adding inches? What we *do* know is that nature is no barrier to avarice, or to the capacity of priest-hoods to confuse ethics with sectarian interest. This will continue until mankind itself falls over the finishing line and evolution ceases. There will always be winners, and for every winner a billion losers. Very probably Dr Arnold knew this too. It's the way the game is played.

I am looking at an X-ray image of a woman's abdomen. It looks like the body of a caterpillar attacked by ichneumon flies, filled with parasitical eggs. 'Parasitical' perhaps is right, but eggs they are not. The woman is from Trinidad, and was persuaded to repay a 'favour' to some men who had helped her financially. The favour involved swallowing 100 latex-covered packages, each containing more than the 1.2 grams of pure cocaine that would have killed her if it leaked. She was caught when she flew into Heathrow and later sentenced to five and a half years in prison, followed by deportation. Her case was no big deal. The bellies of drug 'mules' are just one delivery system among many, a some-times efficient but always risky overnight courier service in the most complex, comprehensive and uncrackable network the criminal world has ever seen.

But we lounge-bar moralists have a problem. Discounting juvenile naughtiness (I was a two-a-week man at the age of ten), I have never had a tobacco habit. Despite the health warnings, though, many others do go on risking cancers and heart disease, and ignore all the attempts of the health lobby to cast them as pariahs. One of my friends lights up sixty times a day. Smoking in public places may not be allowed, but then neither are a whole lot of other pleasures enjoyed by adults in private. Smokers are easy targets for disapproval, but we are nowhere near criminalizing them. 'Binge culture', too, comes in for plenty of hand-wringing, but alcohol is no more likely to be banned, or even effectively controlled, than country walks. Ignoring the late John Junor – 'Only poofs drink white wine' – I drink at least half a bottle of the stuff a day, usually more, and have it delivered in bulk. No social event passes without alcoholic lubrication. Dinners are a libationary progress from Manzanilla to Cognac. In inclement weather a pint in the pub will replace the walk on the marsh. Birthdays and Christmas bring gifts of wine, to which I like to claim a modest degree of connoisseurship. Alcohol has been part of my life since my middle teens, but I avoid drunkenness and (so far as I am aware) nobody regards me as an addict. And yet my habit is a killer. Alcohol causes the deaths of 2.5m people worldwide every year, and tobacco twice that number. Illegal drugs by contrast kill just 200,000. These figures obviously look a bit different when they are expressed as percentages of users but, nevertheless, the moral high ground is far from solid. In its judgement of what is or is not an acceptable social drug, and in its attitudes to those who use them, the law can seem as arbitrary as the wind.

The twenty-sixth of June 2008 was the United Nations' International Day Against Drug Abuse and Illicit Trafficking. The UN Secretary General, Ban Ki Moon, took the opportunity to deliver a message in stark contrast to earlier resolutions of the UN General Assembly. Ten years earlier, intoxicated by good intentions, it had pledged itself to 'eliminating or significantly reducing the illicit cultivation of the coca bush, the cannabis plant and the opium poppy by the year 2008'. Some hopes! Ban Ki Moon's message on the unfulfilled target date was all about human rights, and sounded oddly similar to the case for smokers. 'No one should be stigmatized or discriminated against because of their dependence on drugs,' he said. Member states should 'ensure that people who are struggling with drug addiction be given equal access to health and social services'. But it was a plea for understanding, not tolerance. Drugs continued to 'destroy lives, generate crime and threaten sustainable development . . . We still have much work to do to reduce our vulnerability to drugs. States with weak criminal justice systems and limited law enforcement capabilities need assistance to reduce illicit drug trafficking, which spreads crime, corruption and instability . . .'

Later the same day, the UN Office on Drugs and Crime (UNODC) released its 2008 World Drug Report. It calculated that 4 per cent of the world's population between the ages of 15 and 64 were cannabis users – a total of 165.5m. Amphetamines had 24.7m takers worldwide; cocaine 16m; heroin 12m and Ecstasy 9m. Altogether in the previous year 4.9 per cent of 15–64-year-olds – 208m in all – had taken some kind of illegal drug. Every measurable trend was upward. The appetite for opium and heroin was such that the area of land cultivated for poppies had increased by 17 per cent. Most of this was in Afghanistan, which produces 92 per cent of the world's supply; the rest was in south-east Asia. The area under coca cultivation in Bolivia, Colombia and Peru had also expanded by 16 per cent. In the ten years during which the UN had pledged to 'eliminate or significantly reduce' the cultivation of opium poppies and coca, opium production had risen by 102 per cent and cocaine by 20 per cent. It would be difficult for any drug-control agency to claim this as success, yet this is exactly what UNODC tried to do. Its senior researcher, Thomas Pietschmann, bizarrely asserted that drug controls had 'undoubtedly helped stabilize the world drug situation'. Evidence? The world is consuming much less of the hard stuff than it was a century ago. 'The problem is still not eliminated,' he said, 'but . . . we have a decline of 40 per cent in prevalence over 100 years.' UNODC rated this 'an impressive achievement when considering that the world's population increased fourfold over the 20th century'.

This is not so much casuistic as frankly dishonest. What mind-altering substance could have persuaded UNODC to claim credit for declining opium use in China (for that is what its figures reflect)? Or to imagine that such comparisons are of any value in the context of international drugs trading in the 21st century? Opium in China was like alcohol in the West – the social drug of choice. Even so, UNODC has only the tendentious and self-serving claims of 19th-century missionaries to support its assertion that China was 'once a country where perhaps one in four men was a drug addict'. This version of history is strongly challenged by the Transnational Institute, whose report *Rewriting History: a Response to the 2008 World Drug Report* dispatches it 'to the realm of fantasy'.

Instead, studies show that most of the opium smokers used only moderate amounts and were able to regulate both the quality and quantity they used. There were (and continue to be) many smokers using only limited amounts and on certain occasions only, who were able to control their use, including reducing or stopping it if needed. There were also different qualities of opium, and different strengths. Sweeping statements about massive opium addiction problems in China are a myth.

Furthermore, traditionally opium smoking in China has been a ritual, performed with social functions, often consumed in teahouses rather than in dark and dirty opium dens, offered at home as a welcome gesture to visitors, or at colourful festivals and rich traditional ceremonies.

UNODC also fogs the picture by suggesting that opium use in China was always recreational and thus directly comparable with heroin. In reality much of it was medicinal, and better compared with aspirin and antibiotics.

In the absence of affordable analgesics for common people [says the Transnational Institute], opium was often used as a painkiller and also as a household remedy for all kinds of familiar ailments such as diarrhoea, dysentery, cough relief, bronchitis, asthma, and against the symptoms of cholera, malaria and tuberculosis. It also helped to overcome tiredness, hunger and cold.

Evidence to the Royal Commission on Opium in London in 1893 led it to the entirely reasonable conclusion that 'the relief of pain and sickness was a major reason why people took up smoking'. For UNODC's comparison to have any meaning, medicinal use would have to be discounted and there would have to be some trustworthy statistical base for the calculation to rest upon. There is no such thing. UNODC's source was a report by Chinese delegates to the International Opium Commission in Shanghai in 1909. Even at the time, nobody believed it. 'The statistics in this report are of very little value,' declared the *British Medical Journal* in January 1910: 'They were challenged by the British delegates, with the result that the Chinese delegation has represented to the Government the necessity of obtaining more reliable data. The figures dealing with the growth of the poppy and the consumption of opium are, as a rule, nothing more than rough estimates or mere expressions of opinion.'

For all its bluster and revisionism, UNODC is no closer to its ten-year target than it was in 1998 when the target was set. The emphasis on criminality – jail for offenders in most countries, death in some, and destruction of coca and opium crops – has allowed enforcement agencies to crow about gang-busts and 'record hauls'. But it is empty boasting. Against the super-heavies of international crime, the law is fighting above its weight. It doesn't matter how many you knock over; they just keep coming. In a £320m business, vacancies for drug lords don't stay vacant for long. And it doesn't matter where in the world you live. If you want drugs, you can get them. Pushers start in school. Ask at any bus stop.

A survey for the BBC in 2006 revealed that 75 per cent of people in Britain believed drugs were 'a problem' where they lived, and 31 per cent thought the problem was 'large'. In the prosperous south-east, where cocaine gets up more noses than Ant and Dec, 26 per cent confessed to using drugs themselves. Overall, 16 per cent said they were (or had been) users, and 37 per cent of these specified cocaine. According to the police, a drug 'hit' in some parts of the country cost less than a pint of beer, and

Ecstasy was changing hands at £1 a pop. Like silk and spices in earlier centuries, drugs follow well-worn trade routes. Forty per cent of the cocaine reaching Europe still comes by way of the Caribbean, but more and more is being smuggled through West Africa. Opiates from Afghanistan travel via Pakistan, Iran and central Asia. The 2007 report of the UN's International Narcotics Control Board (INCB), published in March 2008, identified Britain as the crack capital of Europe, and despaired of 'celebrity endorsement'. If it's shampoo you want to sell, putting a famous face in your advertising will cost you a fortune. If you're a drug baron, you get the favour for free.

We used to hear a lot about 'the war on drugs'. If it's still being fought, then it is a war with so little strategy that it makes the invasion of Iraq look like a lesson from Clausewitz. No one in the command bunker seems to know whether to order targeted assassination or carpet bombing. Specifically, the INCB complained that a disproportionate amount of effort was being invested in pursuit of low-level offenders and drug users, and nowhere near enough in nailing the men who matter:

Bringing to justice powerful drug traffickers and dismantling their networks are resource-intensive, painstaking and dangerous undertakings. The traffickers are usually careful never to touch the drugs and are difficult to convict unless they are caught red-handed. The cases can be complex to investigate; they often involve transactions made abroad in an effort to disguise or hide wealth derived from drug trafficking. Strong laws targeting criminal associations and conspiracies are usually needed to ensure the conviction of the persons involved and the confiscation of their criminally derived wealth. Such cases can also require substantial international law enforcement and justice system cooperation because of all the sensitive intelligence, evidence and operational action needed for success. By comparison, smaller cases involving drug trafficking are typically more easily proved and less ably defended than cases involving major drug traffickers. Add to all that demands on justice systems to be more accountable for their budgets and performance, and the result can be strong pressure on the authorities to focus more on low-level offenders and less on persons higher up in the drug trafficking chain.

Such is the tick-box accountancy of modern politics. What matters to the target-setters is the number, not the strategic importance of the convictions they obtain. Grazing on minnows costs less than hunting sharks and is easier to dress up as 'firm action' or 'zero tolerance'. The upshot of this target-driven craving for 'results' has been a grotesque loss of proportion and a distortion of perspective. 'Many states,' said the INCB, 'impose unconditional imprisonment of drug abusers for lesser offences, such as possession or purchase of drugs for personal use, and these typically make up a significant proportion of growing prison populations . . .' Its plea to governments therefore was that they should 'apply the law proportionately when prosecuting drug offenders, as not doing so could undermine efforts to effectively implement the very conventions that these laws seek to enforce'. Hence Ban Ki Moon's emphasis on human rights. Hence, too, the comfortable billets of the criminal officer class as the infantry takes the hits.

The UK charity DrugScope chastised the INCB for not daring to name and shame the countries where the worst abuses were taking place. These included most obviously China, where officials planned to compulsorily 'detoxify' a million drug users before the Beijing Olympics, and where the UN's International Day Against Drug Abuse provides the excuse for mass public executions (in 2002 there were 64). Altogether, 64 countries retain the death penalty and half of these apply it to drug offenders. Not all the killings are judicial. 'Despite a recent visit to Brazil,' says DrugScope, 'the INCB report does not mention the 449 people who were shot and killed in the first half of 2007 in drug enforcement operations by police. Brazilian children, recruited into drug gangs, are considered legitimate targets by police and are shot at frequently in incursions into Rio's *favelas*.'

I wouldn't dare to suggest that Tesco will ever offer two-for-ones on heroin and cocaine ('Every little helps'). If it did, however, it would have an instinctive grasp of the way the market functions. Low-paid peasants do the hard work; middle men cream off the profit; consumers pay what they must. Such markets have their own ethical standards. For moralists they are a labyrinth within a minefield. 'In the past decade,' says the Transnational Institute, 'international drug control emphasized eradication of illicit crops, before having alternative livelihoods in place. Hundreds of thousands of peasants have been condemned to poverty and robbed of a life in dignity . . .' It goes on:

> Apart from causing immense suffering to local communities, these campaigns have significantly contributed to the growing insecurity in the country. In Colombia, ten years of indiscriminate aerial spraying of coca crops have failed to reduce coca cultivation, while creating a vicious circle of human, social and environmental damage, displacement, human rights violations and fuelled the decades-old civil conflict in the country.

In Afghanistan, too, record production levels have led to 'more aggressive forced eradication of opium crops'. It's the same story in the Golden Triangle of Burma, Thailand and Laos, where those paying the price are 'the opium farmers, who need the income from opium to buy food and medicines'. The Transnational Institute asks whether such campaigns are 'morally justifiable'. It is difficult to imagine the moral arbiters of the English Home Counties rising up and crying No! 'Immense suffering to local communities' comes in many forms, not least the misery, violence and crime brought about by the end products of the peasants' endeavours. They may not intend to cause this, but cause it they do. The Transnational Institute advocates 'a rights-based approach and a pragmatic stance towards all those currently involved in the local drugs economies while protecting their economic, cultural and social rights'. But pragmatic stances, too, come in a variety of poses.

Let us not forget that coca and opiates in other societies are accepted social lubricants, and remember that alcohol in the Muslim world is stigmatized just as 'hard' drugs are in the West. An argument on purely moral grounds would have to treat all mind-altering substances equally. This is possible only if you are an extreme libertarian, an indiscriminate drug-and-booze fiend happy to ride whatever cloud blows along next, or a total abstainer who stops at coffee. For the rest of us, who flirt with hypocrisy, the question is more cultural than moral, and the 'moral' component is comparative, not absolute. It would not be unreasonable to suppose that a middle-aged Colombian is as entitled to chew his coca leaf as I am to sip my Sancerre, and that it is only an accident of history that herbicide is sprayed on coca crops and not on the vineyards of the Loire. The wine may make me happy, but it does not make me morally superior. Hence the campaign for 'cultural and social rights'.

But the citizens of Middle England, Middle America, middle-anywhere-you-like in the western world, are not going to renounce their cultures and become consenting liberals. For as long as there are laws, heroin and cocaine will be illegal. For as long as there are poppy and coca crops, the business will be driven by criminal oligarchs who live outside the moral universe and whose supranational penetrating power exceeds the power of governments to keep them out. From the Mafia downwards, there is not a criminal network in the world that does not run on drugs. They have the use of ships, yachts and private aircraft, and the services of financial technicians who know their way around company law and the world banking system like rats around a sewer. They live in a parallel world, a parallel economy, that exists outside the structures of visible society. The more of them you catch, the more there seem to be.

Common sense of course says otherwise. What's obvious to Middle England is that without pushers you have no addicts and no drug-related crime. Without suppliers you have no pushers. Without crops, you have no suppliers, so that the whole criminal pyramid dissolves into dust. The peasant farmers who have 'migrated into illegality' will then migrate back again and we can all drink to a safer, cleaner world. But the failure of the eradication programmes is proof that common sense is not so much a bold initiative as a naïf abroad. Banning, criminalizing, destroying and imprisoning are not going to get the job done. Unilateral actions by national governments will only move the counters to different squares on the board: the game will go on. The Transnational Institute is right to argue for 'a more rational pragmatic and humane approach'; right to insist that farmers should be helped into new livelihoods and not just given a choice between crime and poverty. Perhaps it is there, in the poppy fields of Afghanistan and the coca fields of Colombia, that bleeding-heart liberalism and tough-skinned, stand-to-reason common sense can drink from the same bottle. Unless they do – unless governments, acting together, shift their focus from punishment to prevention – then greedy men with dirty money, abetted by an international banking system whose only virtue is secrecy, will burrow their way deeper and deeper into the 'legitimate' economy and make accomplices of us all.

The workers of the world never did unite. They tried, but the world is a bazaar in which price is all and buyers move from stall to stall without a backward glance. Technological revolutions, hardball politics, free markets and globalization (of which more in the next chapter) have knocked the wind out of the labour movement. In the UK, the grand old days of union bosses ended with the miners' leader Arthur Scargill's mistaken belief that he was a bigger man than Margaret Thatcher. Once upon a time, news bulletins regularly were topped by shots of 'strike action', with pickets massing like besieging armies. Union officials, even local 'shop stewards', were public figures as recognizable, and as powerful, as Cabinet ministers, and the labour correspondents who followed them were the aristocrats of Fleet Street newsrooms. Now most people would be hard pressed to name more than one or two unions, and would have no idea who their leaders were. Labour correspondents have gone the way of hot metal and green eyeshades. Everything these days has its price on the global market, and that includes labour.

In July 2008 the UK's biggest union, Unite, and the largest private sector union in North America, the United Steel Workers (USW), signed a pact to create 'the world's first global union', with three million members in Britain, North America, Ireland and the Caribbean. There was a queasy symbolism in the choice of venue for the signing – not Detroit, or Cleveland, or Sheffield or Manchester; nor any other of industry's historic hubs. Instead, in the manner of men who know where the world is heading, they took themselves to the new global capital of legitimate aspirations, Las Vegas. They did their best to sound bullish, but it came out as more of a bleat than a roar. Derek Simpson, Joint General Secretary of Unite, said this: 'The political and economic power of multinational companies is formidable. They are able to play one nation's workers off against another to maximize profits. They do the same with governments, hence the growing gap between the rich and the rest of us. With this agreement we can finally begin the process of closing that gap.' Leo W. Gerard, president of USW, blew the trumpet even harder: 'This union is crucial for challenging the growing power of global capital. Globalization has given financiers license to exploit workers in developing countries at the expense of our members in the developed world. Only global solidarity among workers can overcome this sort of global exploitation wherever it occurs.'

These are good examples of what old-school union men would have called 'wind and piss'. No hush fell in the boardrooms of global corporations or in the labour ministries of governments. No blue-collar victim of the US mortgage collapse woke up with new hope. No news editor cleared the front page. Without hesitation, deviation or a second thought, employers held to the Tesco principle, sourcing their labour wherever it was cheapest. Maybe one day the pendulum will swing back again. It was brave and principled opposition by exploited workers against greedy and oppressive employers that brought the labour movement into being. It was the greedy and oppressive demands of their later beneficiaries that stripped it of political support and public sympathy. Greed again may inspire a backlash – it has already blown the financial markets off their feet. But, as Leo W. Gerard himself observed, only 'global solidarity' can make it happen. Is there some East Asian Spartacus who, for the benefit of his British and American brethren, will lead the sweatshops in self-annihilating revolt? Is there any British or American union leader who will do other than fight his corner? Any alternative to 'divide and be ruled' as the self-denying ordinance of workers disunited? History says not. Here is the Labour MP Denis MacShane, musing in the *Guardian*:

A few years ago I was giving a talk at the Pittsburgh head office of the USW with whom I have worked for a quarter of a century. It was a grim time for American steelworkers. Their answer was to launch a political charter to keep jobs safe. They asked me to sign it. I looked at the first clause. It called for a complete ban on imports of steel into the US. I had to say: 'Sorry, guys. I represent Rotherham, which makes the world's best engineered steel and exports tonnes here. How do I go home and say I have signed a protectionist pledge to block my constituents' exports to America?'

President George Bush did support USW and imposed a ban on

British steel being exported into America. It was reversed after a bitter battle in which the EU did the heavy lifting for British steelworkers.

So it will be fascinating to see how the new Unite-USW alliance deals with the first instinct of embattled American industrial workers, which is to demand import restrictions.

It will not be the first global ideal to founder on the rock of American protectionism, and it won't be the last. At a time when the White House holds US jobs to be more important than global warming, what chance is there of American workers doing other than fight those whose interests conflict with their own? Maximum probability: zero.

If governments do now fear any supranational movement, it is not the card-carrying battalions of labour but the bomb-carrying cadres of international terrorism. In the West now we have 'home-grown' militants of murderous intent whose loyalties owe their origins to ancestral homelands far beyond the countries of their birth. The network that links them ironically is the same that empowers all the mechanisms of western commerce and culture that they so despise – the internet. Governments fear it too, and curse their inability to control its content or to lay hands on those who offend. Liberalism as ever is its own worst enemy, the problem most acute for countries that value freedom of expression. Totalitarians in a way have it easier. They perceive no need to treat the internet any differently from the way they treat the printed and broadcast word. What they do not like, they ban. The 'Great Firewall of China' is the best example of the kind of propaganda-by-default that keeps inconvenient truths out of sight. The violence of Chinese security forces against Tibetan Buddhists in March 2008 was a textbook example of co-ordinated repression. Among the websites denied to China's 210m internet users were YouTube, the news pages of Yahoo!, the *Guardian*, the *Los Angeles Times*, Wikipedia and parts of *The*

Times. Given that China has only a small number of internet service providers, through which all web traffic from the West has to pass, it is easy for the authorities to instal keyword-filtering software that blocks access to any site containing forbidden words such as 'Tiananmen Square', 'Tibet' or 'Dalai Lama'. In its backhanded way, this is a full and frank acknowledgement of the internet's potential to inform, educate and influence.

A few days ago (I am writing in July 2008), I was surprised to hear a former BBC channel boss insist that it would take another 20 years for the internet to have any measurable impact on tele-vision sales. No head was ever pushed further into the sand. University students – the next generation of potential TV owners – habitually view programmes on their computers. The laptop is their window on to the world, replacing libraries and newspapers as fast as it is supplanting old-fashioned tele-viewing. News-papers, too, are putting more and more emphasis on the web, as energetic in their pursuit of 'hits' as they are of old-fashioned readers. The internet is the world's noticeboard, its coffee-house, its marketplace, its den of thieves. Almost every day I am emailed by banks or building societies seeking to check various of my personal details 'for security'. These are fakes – fishing (or, irritatingly, 'phishing') expeditions by criminals trying to steal my identity. Sleazeballs in Canada and the US pester me daily, offer-ing to cure my nicotine addiction (I don't smoke), increase both the size of my penis and its circle of acquaintance. 'Hot chicks in your area are dying to meet you,' offers someone apparently in Florida. In rural north Norfolk, where I live, we have 'hot chicks' like Florida has icebergs, and none of them is going to melt over a white-haired 62-year-old. 'Rescue a married woman from her boring life' sounds a bit more plausible, but – god almighty! – who in this sedate village of middle-aged matrons do they have in mind? And are they included in, or extra to, the 'wild hot dates that await you this week'? No matter how often I hit the 'block sender' tab, the same cloned messages pour in, seemingly from all over the world. Others offer prescription drugs, special offers in American department stores, 'hot tickets' for 'hip-hop stars' I've never heard of, electronic gizmos I don't know the purpose of, electronic spying devices to keep tabs on my (bored?) wife, free access to 'explicit' television channels, factory-price wetsuits and flippers, opportunities to make a million overnight. Wherever people gather, they will attract chancers, shysters and crooks. The internet is like a Derby-day crowd for pickpockets, but without the risk of recognition and arrest. It is almost organic in the way scams perpetuate themselves in a mushroom cloud of cyber-spores from an electronic mycelium. It helps itself to whatever it wants. Intellectual property is lifted and dished out for free. A whole chapter of one of my earlier books is there, with no per-mission sought. Days', weeks', months' worth of music is there, stolen from its creators. It is the hot housewife of cosmic gossip, an insatiable engine of greed. And yet . . .

It is generous too. In democracies at least, it gives us un-precedented access to the machinery of government. It delivers news. It provides a public forum in which the idiot may take issue with the genius. It plants flowers in cultural deserts and is the implacable, uncrushable enemy of secrecy. Pixel by pixel, it leaks even through the bamboo curtain. The manipulators of the global economy feed on the ignorance of those they seek to dispossess, and it is only knowledge that will thwart them. Woody Guthrie's guitar famously bore the legend, 'This machine kills fascists'. Were he alive now, he might stick the same message on his laptop.

Part Five

Globalism

9

Starship *Enterprise*

Years ago I had an elderly relative, a man of generally pacific temperament who was prone to sudden outbursts of frightening rage, usually brought on by something he had read in the *News Chronicle* or heard on the wireless. At such moments his voice would crack into a mad falsetto that seemed only to underline the impotence that so frustrated him. He wrote what he called 'smiting letters' to the managing directors of businesses that had sold him short, complained to the council about every imperfection in local services and always 'stood up for his rights'. Nothing ever happened as a result. The managing directors and council officials passed his letters to minions who sent pro-forma replies. He would complain about these but only get another identical one by return. Luckily he died long before the age of the call centre could drive him mad, and he never knew the meaning of 'computer'. But I have always remembered him, and have always been cautioned by his example. Usually this keeps me from pointless rage, but not always. Sometimes when I am displeased I hear in my own voice a thread of that same impotent shrillness. Worse, I catch echoes of it in what I write. Whingeing. Always something to moan about.

But I remember also that the old man got great pleasure from life – a long and happy marriage, a garden he cherished, landscapes he loved to explore and music he loved to hear. He would play bowls in the park and then come home to aggressively beat me at table tennis and gracefully lose at darts. Being an active chapelgoer he pretended to teetotalism, but I soon learned the meaning of the brown paper parcels that appeared occasionally from his raincoat pocket. Sherry often would be the prelude to some riotous parlour games or practical jokes that would leave him weeping with laughter. As a boy, I found it difficult to reconcile the opposing halves of his character, as if two quite different gods were fighting for his soul. It was at a time when the word 'schizophrenic' was commonly used in everyday speech to describe anyone whose moods or attitudes seemed inconstant, and I certainly thought he qualified. As an adult, with decades of personal inconsistency all too literally under my belt, I understand him perfectly.

Oilmen and the lazier kind of libertarian like to characterize environmentalists as either Luddites and killjoys (for denying life's pleasures) or hypocrites (for enjoying them). In the bear garden of popular debate these can sound like points well made, but they hit the target only at the margin. No one could deny that self-righteous bean-eating twerps are a visible minority within the green legion, but they are not its heartbeat. It has its hedonists, too, and their philosophy is so simple it could qualify for 'Thought for the Day'. Take all the pleasure you can, but do it in such a way that you create some benefit for others and don't deny the same pleasure to anyone else. Like all ideals it is impossible to realize absolutely, but it is not a bad working principle. Reciprocal altruism with gravy on its chin. Real conservationists are not so much killjoys as kiss-of-life-joys, defending the right to enjoy. We should raise a glass to them.

We must remember nevertheless that change *is* always resisted. The resolve of churchmen to maintain the moral standards of the first century is an extreme but not untypical example of what might be called 'golden ageism'. Somewhere in the past – 10 years ago, 20 years ago, 'before the war', in biblical times – was a period of sublime perfection which we have betrayed with our philistinism/short-sightedness/faithlessness/swinish greed. We distrust and despise our own genius, and lapse too easily into fundamentalism. Nothing can be 'art' that does not conform to some bygone prescription. Nothing can be wholesome that is not the unadorned work of nature. Nothing can be honourable that is performed for profit. 'Modern' is a cuss-word whose targets include everything from ethnic cleansing to *Big Brother*, body-piercing, SUVs, blank verse and Turkey Twizzlers. But 'modern' in the western world also means shoes on our feet, fat on our bellies and (fingers crossed and bird flu notwithstanding) no dread of epidemic disease. If we had the power to transport ourselves back to some earlier century, it is only those with royal blood in their veins or a thirst for holy vengeance who would take the trip.

The present is the sum of all things past, and the past is immutable. Scientific discovery will not go back into the box; we cannot restore our ignorance, forget what we know or inhabit any other age than the one we now find ourselves in. Like so many of our forebears, we face a clash of theologies in which 'truth' huddles in the crossfire. It was ever thus. But the difference in an age of mass literacy and instant communication is that *everyone* is engaged, not just a classically educated elite. We are courted for votes and custom more desperately than any other people in history. Talented men and women are paid vast salaries to seduce us with slogans and catchy tunes. Buy this cereal; endorse that party leader. The result is a whole new form of disenfranchisement, giving us banners to follow in place of ideas. Like designer handbags, entire creeds and philosophies wear stick-on labels that disguise their complexity. I remember a comedy sketch, probably in *The Fast Show*, which had two straw-sucking yokels sitting in a field. I don't remember the exact dialogue, but it went something like:

'Wodger fink o' the real-time tax smoothing based fiscal policy
rule?'

Brief pause for thought, then: 'Bollocks, innit.'

I thought of this every time I heard one of Gordon Brown's
budget speeches. *Demand side, supply side, fiscal policies,
monetary policies, prudence, the Golden Rule . . .* Economics is a
swamp in which comprehension drowns like a convict on the run.
Much has happened since I began this book, and much more will
have happened since I laid down my pen. The blow-by-blow
account of the world financial meltdown will be written by
others, but it is a story through which the word 'greed' will throb
like the bass drum in a military march. Banks have behaved like
hormonally deranged teenagers unable to control their own lusts.
Like teenagers, too, they have expected the grown-ups to dig into
their savings and bail them out. But there the parallel ends. Unlike
the young, bankers are not easily loved, forgiven, or even understood. In pursuing their college-taught conviction that the only
thing better than debt is more debt, they created a market in
worthlessness that threatened the livelihoods of everyone who
trusted them. As bank shares collapsed, so feral gangs of financial
speculators moved in all too literally to make a killing. There may
be 'ethics' – rules of engagement, honour among thieves – but
they breed in a bog far below the high peaks of morality and
altruism. No one outside the gangs really understood what 'short-
selling' was until the UK banking giant HBOS, worthy custodian
of ordinary families' savings, saw its share price crash and the
wide-boys tiptoe away with bulging pockets. Short-selling did not
cause the banking collapse, but it helped it on its way and
brilliantly illuminated the moral vacuum through which our
money has to pass. It is like backing a horse to lose, with the
difference that the very act of betting makes the loss more likely.
This is how it works:

An investor, typically a hedge fund or an investment bank,

calculates that shares in a company are heading for a fall. It then *borrows* shares in that company from, say, a pension fund or an insurance company, and sells them. When the shares fall, it buys them back at the lower price and returns them to the owner. It will have to pay a fee for the borrowing, but still registers a handy profit. Sometimes the entire transaction is a phantom, with no stock changing hands at all. Share deals often have a time delay, so the short-seller can buy back what he has 'sold' before he has even borrowed it. As wheezes go, it's a belter. It is also highly damaging. As HBOS found to its cost, the market responds to rumour like brushwood to flame and the financial heartwood turns rapidly to ash. The *Independent* newspaper calculated that hedge funds betting against HBOS made a billion pounds in two and a half months, and that a single fund profited by the same amount from the earlier collapse of Northern Rock. We have seen hubris and must face nemesis, but catharsis still seems a long way off. The 'credit crunch', as we knew it before the global meltdown, was the consequence of banks feeling they could no longer trust each other sufficiently to lend each other money. In the US and across Europe, the money men successfully argued, faith could be restored only at the expense of guarantees from the taxpayer. As these people have been taught to believe that it is their destiny to rule the world (a point to which I shall return in Chapter 10), the portents for a globalized economy are written in dust.

I believed when I planned this book, and I believe now, that globalization is the ultimate manifestation of human greed, and that it will remain so until such time as we colonize Mars and tap the power of the stars. There is no turning back. Even now, with smoke still rising from the ruins of the banking industry, who can conceive of any viable future for a world without a global economy? The difficulty arises over what such an economy should be designed to achieve, and for whose benefit it should be run. Should it prioritize the welfare of the poor, aiming to stimulate employment, good health and education for the economically dispossessed? Or should it be an instrument of the free market? Understand this: it cannot be both.

As I wrote in Chapter 7, trade liberalization, which is the very essence of global economics, means different things to different people. The governing institutions of globalism – the World Bank, the World Trade Organization and the International Monetary Fund (IMF) – are dominated by the developed countries, and most particularly by America. The authors of their policies are rich-world economists whose priorities differ somewhat from those of dollar-a-day Africans, Asians and South Americans. Western banks and corporations have grown rich beyond the fantasies of Mammon. So too have corrupt dictators siphoning off IMF loans, and Russian kleptocrats vulturing the old Soviet economy. For ordinary Russians, the effect of 'capitalism' was even worse than the diehard communists with pictures of Brezhnev over their beds had said it would be. Others had it even harder. In the 1990s, as globalism accelerated and world income increased by 2.5 per cent annually, so another 100m people faced life on less than a dollar a day. The managements of international corporations meanwhile awarded themselves bonuses, share options and golden parachutes that mocked any notion of decency and shame. There is, be assured, a connection.

First, it is important to understand the way power has shifted since Marx and Engels challenged 'capitalism' to a revolution. I have added the quotation marks because it is not a word you hear much now, least of all from economists. Somehow it has a bad odour to it – 'free trade', 'the market economy' or 'the market system' all smell sweeter. They are, of course, exactly the same thing, though the ownership of capital now is much less important than the management of it. Modern owners – the shareholders – do not wield the power that old-time proprietors did. There will be no more Fords, Rockefellers or Carnegies. In modern corporations it is the *managements* that count. Any consumer (I laugh at the idea of the old gentleman with whom this chapter began) now wrestling with the tentacles of a major company will understand every implication of the word 'bureaucracy'. Government departments by comparison can seem like havens of intimacy and models of human scale. Transnational corporations may not have armies, navies and air forces but they have power over people who do. In the economics, for which also read 'politics', of globalization, they are the ultimate controlling force.

There has been another shift too. The first principle of old-fashioned market economics was that power was vested in the consumer. 'Economic democracy' meant the market would produce only what consumers required of it. This ensured that supply and demand always would be in balance and that the market would be like an attentive servant – on hand to stock the shelves but never presuming to make decisions of its own. Fewer people now believe this than believe Homer Simpson is a real person. The servant does not ask us what we want – it *tells* us. Corporations develop products first – Pot Noodles, Prada, heat-seeking missiles – then persuade us that we need them. They advertise, they lobby, they insinuate their names into sporting arenas, films and television programmes – every way they can think of to pummel the consumer into shape. Olympic sponsorship, discussed in the previous chapter, is a perfect example. In his extended essay *The Economics of Innocent Fraud*, the late J. K. Galbraith put it like this:

> In the real world, the producing firm and the industry go far to set the prices and establish the demand, employing to this end monopoly, oligopoly, product design and differentiation, advertising, other sales and trade promotion . . . Reference to the market system as a benign alternative to capitalism is a bland, meaningless disguise of the deeper corporate reality – of producer power extending to influence over, even control of, consumer demand.

In her devastating polemic on the institutionalized greed of American corporatists, *Pigs at the Trough*, Arianna Huffington observes that Washington has 38 lobbyists for every member of Congress. Those from the pharmaceutical industry alone outnumber elected members by 623 to 535. The most notorious outcome of their lobbying was the denial of affordable life-saving drugs, and particularly AIDS medicines, to the poor of Africa. Worldwide revulsion forced them to back off, but it's a telling example of the way 'free' markets abuse their freedom. The notion that they automatically default to the common good is the most pernicious distortion of the truth. Another fallacy, high-lighted by Galbraith, is that there is some clear and meaningful distinction between the public and private sectors, and between business and government. The infestation of Washington, London and other seats of government by lobbyists is proof in itself that public and private are limbs on the same tree, all swarming with the same parasites. Galbraith pointed out that nearly half the total discretionary spending by the US government in 2003 was on 'defence' – ie buying weapons. Like the pharmaceutical industry, the weapons trade is aggressive in its own cause. Selling armaments to governments is much like selling Pot Noodles to the public. First you design the product, then you persuade the customers to want it. With weapons, however, the relation-ship is somewhat cosier. Galbraith again: 'In an impressive flow of influence and command, the weapons industry accords valued employment, management pay and profit in its political constituency, and indirectly it is a source of political funds.' Result: a vital area of public policy is dominated by a pri-vate sector industry whose political voice is loud enough to influence not just defence policy but foreign policy and war. As the *New York Times* reported in October 2002:

[Corporations now provide] stand-ins for active soldiers in every-thing from logistical support to battlefield training . . .

Some [firms] are helping to conduct training exercises using live ammunition for American troops in Kuwait, under codename Desert Spring ... Others have employees who don their old uniforms to work under contract as military recruiters and instructors in R.O.T.C. classes, selecting and training the next generation of soldiers.

In the UK, the strength of the public-private umbilicus is such that the government itself halted the Serious Fraud Office's inquiry into British Aerospace, which had been accused of illegally paying bribes to a member of the Saudi royal family. 'National security,' said Tony Blair. Now look at the fuel and energy industries. Look at agriculture. Look in particular at the financial sector, and you will see public policy and private gain tripping across the globe like Tweedledum and Tweedledee. On a broadly typical day, 24 July 2008, several things were happening. A motley of Anglican bishops and archbishops was taking time off from the Lambeth Conference to parade through London in a 'walk of witness', calling upon governments to keep their promises to the world's poor; the former Bosnian Serb leader Radovan Karadzic was pictured in every British newspaper after his arrest in Serbia; the US Democratic presidential nominee Barack Obama was speaking on 'transatlantic relations' in Berlin. The single thread that connected these seemingly very disparate eventualities was globalism. The churchmen in their mild way were protesting at the slow rate of progress towards the eight 'Millennium Development Goals' declared by the UN in September 2000. (These were: to eradicate extreme poverty and hunger; achieve universal primary education; promote gender equality and empower women; reduce child mortality; improve maternal health; combat HIV and AIDS, malaria and other diseases; ensure environmental sustainability; develop a global partnership for development.) After eleven years on the run, Karadzic was picked up because of Serbia's desire to develop closer ties with the international community. And Obama was following a well-worn trail of US presidents and presidential hopefuls setting out their foreign policy credentials. Ronald Reagan famously stood by the Brandenberg Gate and called upon the Soviet Union to tear down the Wall; and John F. Kennedy in 1963 even more famously declared '*Ich bin ein Berliner.*' For Obama and his planeload of journalists, Berlin was just one stop-off in a 12,000-mile world tour taking in Afghanistan, the Middle East and Europe. It's what the pope does. Even Gordon Brown had a bash at it, though fewer people noticed.

But these men are just the 'faces'. They are not the power. Prime ministers and presidents vary in their grasp of economics, just as they vary in their grasp of everything else. When they speak, it is the distillation of thousands of words written for them by lawyers and policy advisers. The real powers have no faces or names that are known to the public. Two institutions face each other across Washington's 19th Street – on one side, the headquarters of the World Bank; on the other, the International Monetary Fund. Between them they represent probably the densest concentration of economics PhDs on the planet. Between them they hold the power of life and death over national economies across the globe; the power of life and death over local industries and the people who depend on them. It is their policies that will determine whether or not the Millennium Development Goals are met– whether children will be taken out of poverty, whether girls will be educated, AIDS overcome, the environment preserved.

The World Bank – full title, the International Bank for Reconstruction and Development – is not in any ordinary sense a bank, but rather an agency of the UN funded by its member governments. Created in 1944, its initial purpose was to drive the economic recovery of Europe after the war. Having been set up by mainly American officials, and being based in Washington, it was ideologically opposed to protectionism and committed to free and competitive markets. It now has 184 member states but all its presidents have been American. In the early years, most of its lending was for specific items of infrastructure – roads, dams, power stations, gas and electricity supply systems, etc. – but over time it has diverted its attention to poverty. Its declared aim now is to 'turn rich country resources into poor country growth', which means fighting disease, preventing corruption and fraud, protecting the environment and improving education. All this sounds admirable, but there are snags. Long-term loans are not always beneficial to developing economies, and aid-dependent countries are extremely vulnerable to pressure from the lenders. The same is true of the World Bank's neighbour across the street, the IMF – itself a 'lender of last resort' – which functions as a kind of fiscal fire brigade, charging around the world rescuing stranded economies. It looks like a Good Samaritan, but many countries now are more inclined to see it as a wolf. The conditions attached to its loans can seem more important, and may have a deeper and longer-lasting influence, than the loans themselves. It is the particular conceit of economists that they are the possessors of formulae that can transform politics into a science as exact as chemistry. It is a conceit so tenacious that no amount of contrary evidence can dilute it. So tenacious, indeed, that worsening poverty, unemployment and recession can be held up as successful outcomes if the result is low inflation and a free flow of capital; so tenacious that any critics of the World Bank or IMF not in possession of a higher degree in economics (and particularly any who speak for redevelopment charities) can safely be dismissed as 'naive'.

There is an old joke (or at least, I'm told it's old – it's new to me) in which economists are congratulated for having successfully predicted six out of the last three recessions. An even better joke is that recession was supposed to have been eradicated by economics as surely as smallpox was conked by Edward Jenner.

Jenner, however, had the benefits of genius and scientific proof. Any epidemic of a preventable disease in the developed world now would terminate the career of the chief medical officer who let it happen. Failure to spot America's sub-prime mortgage crisis, by contrast, was passed over as if it were a force of nature beyond human control. The same applied to Russia's transition from soviet to criminal economy; the same to the East Asian financial meltdown of 1997–8; the same to the collapse in 2008 of New Labour in the UK, where supposedly hard-nosed economists in Gordon Brown's Treasury worked their own spin on their master's beloved 'prudence'. Because politicians cannot admit error, economic failure (unlike economic success) always must be the work of external forces. They do not blame themselves, and therefore cannot blame the experts whose advice they took. Even if they did, the experts would only say they were working to order. Teflon by comparison is like contact adhesive.

I would bet that most people reading this paragraph will know the name of Britain's current chancellor of the exchequer or America's treasury secretary, but I'd give very long odds against their knowing the president of the World Bank, the managing director of the IMF, the director general of the WTO or any others of the sacred college whose city state is the global economy. Economics is another of those subjects that escape public scrutiny because they are so boring, and because their practitioners dwell deep within castles of jargon. It is because the 'experts' can so easily denigrate the ignorance, or well-meaning naivety, of those who confront them that they can maintain their pretence of omniscience. Apostates from within their own congregation are excommunicated, and external resistance characterized as 'anarchy' or 'terrorism'. Anti-globalism as a result has become a focus of violent protest and riot.

Seattle in 1999 was a flashpoint. June that year had seen a mini-rash of protests around the world, including one in Eugene, Oregon, where rioters successfully fought police for possession of a park. Seattle in November was host to a top-level WTO conference that was intended to settle conflicts of interest between rich and poor nations and to set fairer rules for international trade. Its failure to deliver any such accord, like the failure of all such conferences since, was caused by the very conflicts it was supposed to resolve. Then as always, powerful countries were in no hurry to surrender their advantage, and the poor were disinclined to sacrifice themselves to the rich. The then French prime minister Lionel Jospin pinned the blame on 'those countries, some of them very large, which did not seek an attitude of compromise'. That was the reality, but there were others ready to hail the breakdown as triumph, not tragedy, and to claim the credit for it. 'We won,' said one of the thousands of activists who had converged on the city, and for whom any setback to globalism was a victory. The protest climaxed in a riot. Local branches of multinational companies were attacked, and the city's mayor declared a dawn-to-dusk curfew, thus ensuring the clashes between rioters and armed police would continue deep into the night. Protesters tried to blockade delegates inside their hotels, obstructed the conference centre and blitzed walls and police vehicles with graffiti. The police answered with teargas. More than 600 people were arrested and many more injured. Seattle set the pattern for protests wherever globalism was on the agenda – Rostock, Naples, Genoa, Prague, Davos, Washington, Melbourne, Gothenburg, Barcelona, Salzburg ... Some of the marchers were peaceful protesters from environmental groups; others were from anarchist factions with long, self-important names who wanted only to smash capitalism (ie enjoy a good ruck) and hurt policemen. The police themselves responded with varying degrees of proportionality, employing batons, teargas, pepper sprays, water cannon, dogs, rubber bullets and even live ammunition to deter, maim and occasionally kill those who confronted them. In Genoa and Naples particularly, the Italian police seem to have rioted in orgiastic carnivals of mass brutality.

Such things always make headlines, but they seldom make sense.

People oppose globalism for a multitude of reasons, but the common enemies are multinational corporations and the political institutions that promote their interests. Some of the antagonism grows out of cultural distinctiveness. People don't want their identities drowned in a homogeneous global soup of 'consumers'. They don't want to watch the same television programmes in Barcelona as in Bradford; don't want to eat from the same menus in the same restaurants, sip their lattes in the same coffee shops, wear the same clothes, hum the same jingles or study for the same exams. Such things are bound to happen – they already *have* happened – but the process can only go so far. Without a second planet to call upon, the earth simply does not have the resources to raise all its people to American standards of living. There will always be inequality; always a measure of difference. Benign globalism, if it ever happens, may lift people out of poverty but it won't make them rich.

The deeper fear is that globalism and democracy are not compatible, and that human rights and the environment will be its earliest casualties. Much anger is directed at the IMF, which is seen as a tool of the US Treasury Department, which in turn is driven by Wall Street, thus turning the whole bang shoot into a bonanza for bankers and financiers and promising only more poverty to the poor. Greed versus hunger? Greed wins. It is not just anarchists, beardies and bean-eaters who say this. Towards the end of *The Economics of Innocent Fraud*, J. K. Galbraith – former professor of economics emeritus at Harvard, former president of the American Economic Association, *Commandeur de la Légion d'Honneur* and holder of the Medal of Freedom – tosses this little grenade:

[Corporate power] ordains that social success is more automobiles, more television sets, more diverse apparel, a greater volume of all other consumer goods. Also more and more lethal

284

weaponry. Here is the measure of human achievement. Negative social effects – pollution, destruction of the landscape, the unprotected health of the citizenry, the threat of military action and death – do not count as such. When measuring achievement, the good and the disastrous can be combined.

And here is Joseph Stiglitz, co-winner of the 2001 Nobel Prize for Economics, in his scarifying account of the IMF and all its works, *Globalization and Its Discontents*: 'Modern high-tech warfare is designed to remove physical contact: dropping bombs from 50,000 feet ensures that one does not "feel" what one does. Modern economic management is similar: from one's luxury hotel, one can callously impose policies about which one would think twice if one knew the people whose lives one was destroying.'

Stiglitz writes with rare authority. For three years from 1997 he was chief economist and senior vice president of the World Bank, in which capacity he fought mightily against the dogmas and obsessions of the IMF. In the end it would cost him his job, but he was not just tilting at windmills. He was a tireless globetrotter who believed that knowing a country was an essential prerequisite for anyone who intended to tinker with its economy. The one-size-fits-all, rigid theologies of the IMF were apt only to make things worse. 'To what extent,' he wondered in an article for the *New Republic* in 2000, 'did the IMF and Treasury Department push policies that actually contributed to the increased global volatility? . . . Did America – and the IMF – push policies because we, or they, believed the policies would help East Asia, or because we believed they would benefit financial interests in the United States and the advanced industrialist world?'

This is a question to which we shall return. First, a brief digression in response to breaking news. On 29 July 2008 in Geneva the WTO's so-called 'Doha round' of trade talks finally collapsed in recrimination. If anyone was surprised by this, they didn't say so. Disappointed, yes. Surprised that the US couldn't reconcile its interests with those of India and China? No. Amazed that the US delegate, Susan Schwab, with not a hint of irony or shame could describe as 'unconscionable' the desire of developing countries to protect their poorest farmers against sudden surges of cut-price imports? Nah. It's in her DNA. This is the same Schwab who declared herself 'dismayed' when the French president, Nicolas Sarkozy, suggested the EU should impose import taxes on countries that refused to cap carbon emissions; the same Schwab who threatened retaliatory action over European reluctance to buy the genetically modified produce on which American agriculture increasingly depends. Right there you have the answer to Stiglitz's question.

But it did not stay in the news for long. I have to concede: there is no faster way to clear a table of lingering guests than by enthusing about world trade policy. *Wow! Guess what the WTO's done now!* Even the *Guardian*, which in Britain is the newspaper most likely to take an interest in the Third World, packed Doha off to the 'Finance' ghetto on page 22. On the BBC *Today* programme, the 'head of global economic research' for a merchant bank was wheeled on to say that world trade was a jolly complicated issue, no one was much surprised that the wheels had come off, and it didn't much matter anyway. Organizations like the WTO, IMF, World Bank and G8 were outmoded remnants of the post-war order, out of touch with the pace of change. Well . . . it might be so, but it hardly makes them irrelevant. They still hold the keys to the bank, and the lives and livelihoods of billions remain in their hands.

The 'Doha round' began at Qatar in November 2001. Its objective was to make trade rules fairer to developing countries and so close the gap between rich and poor. It was never better than a long shot (the hard realities of 'free trade' were described in Chapter 7). By October 2002 the talks were foundering, and in March 2003 deadlines for agreements on agricultural tariffs and export subsidies passed unmet. Further trouble erupted in September of the same year when developing countries took exception to US and EU farm subsidies. From time to time over the next five years agreements would shimmer briefly like mirages in the diplomatic sun, only to crumble into the political dust. When it came to political risk-taking, there were no takers. The failure of negotiators to agree cuts in subsidies and tariffs blocked agreement on the bigger issues of trade liberalization and fairer markets for the poor. Any observer of, for example, the annual haggle over EU fish quotas, will know that the greater good of mankind is no incentive for ministers responsible to local electorates. Jesus may have deemed it 'more blessed to give than to receive', but he was not a trade minister. If the US and EU were going to cut farm subsidies, then they would want a commensurately bigger slice of Third World markets for their manufactured goods.

All the time, too, a very loud clock was ticking in Washington. No declaration by the WTO is worth a row of beans unless the US signs up to it, and this involves ratification by Congress – a body whose faith in free trade is exceeded only by its passion for protectionism. This meant that the impending presidential election imposed an effective cut-off date – initially June 2007 – and that the very last shred of hope expired in July 2008. Even then, not everyone agreed that Doha was dead. 'It could be just resting,' said one British commentator, inviting comparison with Monty Python's dead parrot sketch, 'until the new president has got his feet under the table and dealt with more pressing matters such as Iraq and the housing crisis.'

While claiming still to be a 'passionate believer in the power of trade to lift people out of poverty', the WTO's director general, Pascal Lamy, declared that the breakdown would cost 130bn dollars (£65bn) a year in tariff savings alone. He did not say how this would affect the lives of the poor, but it was unlikely to mean improved nutrition, health and education. The width of the credibility gap was made clear by Kenya's deputy prime minister Uhuru Kenyatta, who complained that Africa was unrepresented in the WTO's inner circle. 'Unfortunately, as always happens, it is the poorest of the poor who always carry the biggest burden,' he said. 'Most of the key issues of interest to the African continent were not even discussed, especially the issue of cotton. Africa critically needs to realize development and get itself out of poverty through the establishment of fair trade rather than aid. Africa's opportunity to achieve fair trade has therefore been gravely undermined by the lack of progress in these negotiations.'

Looking forward, a new age of protectionism seems a lot more likely than the free international trading floor that the prophets of globalism claim to want. That word 'free' itself is as slippery as an oilman's palm. To the IMF and World Bank it means something very different to what might be understood by the man in the rice paddy. The *Today* programme's 'head of global economic research' was right about one thing – the IMF *is* a relict of the post-war order. But this does not mean it is 'outmoded'. At the age of sixty-plus, it is very different from its younger self and is driven by different priorities. In the beginning, it clearly recognized that world markets were inherently inefficient. They could not guarantee that national economies would remain buoyant, and they could not be relied upon to repair them when they slumped. It was the IMF's task wherever necessary to provide the loans that would rebuild stalled economies, stimulate demand and create jobs. The hell to be avoided was a repeat of the Great Depression that had ravaged the world in the 1930s. Stiglitz typically puts it neatly: 'The IMF was founded on the belief that there was a need for collective action at the global level for economic stability, just as the United Nations had been founded on the belief that there was a need for collective action at the global level for political stability.' This meant persuading backsliders to cut taxes and/or interest rates to force some oxygen into their economies, set the tills ringing and get people back to work.

It's not like that now. The 'neoliberalism' of the Thatcher/ Reagan years heralded a lurch into free-market fundamentalism that turned an ideology into a faith. Adhering to its codes might involve pain, even death, but it was the faith that mattered, not the torments of earthlings. The IMF now is more likely to want to *raise* taxes and interest rates, to contract rather than expand local economies, to create unemployment rather than relieve it, to kill rather than encourage local businesses. To understand how this came about, we have to go back to those 'remnants of the post-war order' that the man on the *Today* programme found so *passé*.

Though the IMF is publicly funded and answerable to the finance ministries and centralized banks of its 153 member states, it has the democratic instincts of a rogue elephant. Those who pay for it, like those who live in its path, have little control over how and where it tramples. It is governance without government. As Uhuru Kenyatta complained in Geneva, not all governments are equal. There is a strong bias in favour of the states that held the whip hand when the IMF was founded after the Second World War. One might say *the* country, for there is only one that enjoys an effective power of veto – the USA. This means that the dominant force in the world economy, particularly since the collapse of the Soviet bloc, has been the 'Washington Consensus' – a term coined in 1989 by the economist John Williamson to describe the tripartite economic Panzer of the IMF, World Bank and US Treasury. To these, lurking facelessly in its command bunker, might be added a fourth: Wall Street. For countries taking World Bank or IMF loans, the price is 'conditionality' – effectively the acceptance of American interference with their national sovereignty and a consequent erosion of democracy. Though many of its critics, like Stiglitz, are themselves Americans with an unshakeable belief in the power of trade to beat poverty, the stock response of the Washington archbishopric is to treat all who oppose them as apostates, heretics or terrorists. Such people are anti-American, anti-globalist, evil-doing agents of socialism whose utter wrongness is as manifest as Washington's commitment to holy order. If the result for many countries has been poverty and a breakdown of social and political order, then that is secondary to the higher purpose of making US economic policy the policy of the world.

It is true that much of the criticism does come from left field. But, just as Stiglitz warns us not to jump to the conclusion that *everything* economists say is wrong, so it follows that political alignments, too, can be of small importance. Critics from all points of the political compass will see the reasonableness of this paragraph by Robert Wade, which appeared in a piece for the *New Left Review* in 2001:

> A central aim of US economic policy since the Second World War has been the worldwide acceptance of free-market ideology – the belief that the free flow of goods, services and capital is to the mutual benefit of all; that corporations should be managed for the maximization of shareholder-value; that stock-markets should be used for buying and selling corporate control; and that governments should intervene only in cases of obvious market failure. If the US can persuade powerful segments of national elites to embrace these goals for themselves, it can achieve its foreign economic policy objectives far more cheaply and effectively than through either negotiations or coercion. Once nationalist elites accept the idea of the mutual benefits of free trade and free capital movements, they can dismiss critics of the free market as defenders of special interests, at the expense of the general good.

You might think this was a good thing or a bad, but you could hardly say it was wrong. The problem with Planet Earth, as anyone who has moved around it must have noticed, is that it is not homogeneous. Russia is not like Brazil. Thailand is not like the Congo. The US is not like anywhere else at all. They have different languages, different cultures, histories and values. They have different climates and resources. Different ethical systems, and different ideas of morality. They are at different stages of economic development. Only an extreme dogmatist would say that a one-size economic policy could fit them all. But this is just what the IMF *does* say. It doesn't need to move around the world, or anywhere at all much beyond 19th Street. Like a pope or an idiot, it just *knows* it's right. The market system is the perfect economic tool, and anyone who can't make it work is a criminal or a nincompoop.

Successful economies are like banquets. Ultimately they will feed many people but they need a lot of ingredients and take a very long time to cook. Advanced industrial countries did not get where they are by shouting the odds in a free-for-all. Through tariffs and subsidies they protected their industries until they were strong enough to face foreign competition. When threatened or disadvantaged by shifts in the market they do it still. America ramps up its support to farmers and is not above resorting to cartels (on steel and aluminium, for example) when it has the wind in its face. We saw in Chapter 6 how it manipulates international trade law; saw, too, that the EU has no claim to moral superiority. The message to developing countries is: do as we say, not as we do.

Any country that needs the IMF is, by definition, a country in trouble. Some have baulked at the IMF's political interference and kept their independence. Many others, to their cost, have felt unable to do other than grit their teeth and take their punishment. Sympathy for the late ex-president Suharto of Indonesia would be as misplaced as sympathy for Stalin. He was a world-ranking crook whose 31-year rule was a masterclass in corruption. Transparency International calculated that the sum he'd embezzled from his people lay somewhere between 15 and 35 billion dollars, putting him top of the all-time corruption league, ahead of even the Philippines' Marcos and Zaire's Mobutu. It is, nevertheless, a photograph of Suharto that supports the critics' most persistent complaint – that the IMF behaves more like a colonizing power than a publicly owned institution working for the common good. In the photograph, taken in 1998, a humiliated Suharto is signing a letter of agreement that would, on the one hand, allow aid for his country's blighted economy, and on the other cede control of it to the IMF. Standing over him, in the classic pose of the victor, is the IMF's then managing director Michel Camdessus. 'To those in developing countries,' writes Joseph Stiglitz, 'the picture raised a very disturbing question. Had things really changed since the "official" ending of colonialism a half century ago?'

The 140 conditions which the IMF imposed on Indonesia included abandoning road, bridge and port projects, ending protection of its dairy industry, cancelling price controls on cement, and taxing state-owned companies. Given the exceptional nature of its problems, Indonesia may not look like a good or even fair example of the IMF in action. But in two important ways it was entirely typical. It involved foreign micro-management of a country's economy; and it suited the interests of external financial institutions better than it served the local people. Every country in the IMF's sights becomes potentially a mini America. It has to flatten its trade barriers, allow free movement of capital in and out, toss pompoms in the air and become a high-stepping, fully fledged cheerleader for the market economy. The cheerleaders are then slipped a dose of rohypnol and date-raped. Stiglitz explains:

Forcing a developing country to open itself up to imported products that would compete with those produced by certain of its industries, industries that were dangerously vulnerable to competition from much stronger counterpart industries in other countries, can have disastrous consequences – socially and economically. Jobs have systematically been destroyed – poor farmers in developing countries simply couldn't compete with the highly subsidized goods from Europe and America – before the countries' industrial and agricultural sectors were able to grow strong and create new jobs.

The results are worsening unemployment and poverty. As it is with goods and services, so it is with money. The abrupt suspension of capital controls does for the currency what exposure to rich-world imports does for manufacturing and agriculture. It is like delivering sharks by parachute. Even in industrialized countries before the meltdown, major commercial banks were having to merge to compete effectively against global giants like Citibank, HSBC and Crédit Agricole. With their defences down, small local banks in developing countries have no more chance of beating the odds than the local lemon-squeezer has against Coca-Cola. The big legions not only lure savers and investors away; their lending policies inevitably favour rapid-growth multinationals who speak the same boardroom language rather than the small local businesses that struggle to keep pace. It creates winners, but they are not to be found in the shanty towns and native villages of Africa. Insofar as managements are answerable to anyone at all, it is to their owners. That, after all, is their bounden duty – to maximize value to shareholders, not to create employment for peasants. The obvious corollary is that where profit potential is low – across large tracts of Africa, to take the most obvious example – corporate investors are as rare as gay Anglican bishops.

The relaxation of capital market controls also puts countries at the mercy of speculators – in effect, ultra high-rolling gamblers who bet on whether a currency is going to go up or down. In an echo of the short-selling that brought down the banks, they will pour money into a country when they think it will go up, take it out again when they expect it to go down, leaving the currency busted and local banks rocking on their heels. There are indigenous predators too. Suharto, Mobutu and Daniel Arap Moi were not the only national leaders to treat their people as pawns in a game of personal aggrandizement. The Philippines was robbed by Ferdinand Marcos, Zaire by Mobutu Sese Seko, Nigeria by Sani Abacha, Haiti by Jean-Claude Duvalier, Peru by Alberto Fujimori, Ukraine by Pavlo Lazarenko, Nicaragua by Arnoldo Alemán . . . People like these present a genuine dilemma for lenders of last resort like the IMF and the World Bank. Bent rulers cannot be straightened by loan conditions – their signatures on contracts are worth no more than any other of their lies. Where a loan is made for a specific purpose – a reservoir, say – the purpose might be met; but there is no guarantee that a matching sum will not disappear from the national exchequer to extend the presidential palace. And when death or democracy does catch up with a crook, the loan does not die with him. It lives on like a malevolent ghost to haunt his people. Very often, corruption within a poor country is connived at by rich countries who would rather see a robber in power than a communist. The classic example was Zaire, or the Democratic Republic of Congo as it now is – a vast country with vast resources (it exports diamonds, copper, coffee, cobalt and oil) but a gross national income of only 115 dollars per head and a history written in corruption and blood. Its first elected prime minister, Patrice Lumumba, was murdered in 1961, a year after independence from Belgium, in circumstances which cast suspicion on both the former imperial power and the USA. The man who took him prisoner was the army chief Joseph Mobutu, who in 1965 would seize power, change the name of the country to Zaire and his own name to Mobutu Sese Seko. In the 22 years of his presidency he would steal 40 per cent of the 12 billion dollars' worth of aid received by his country. And yet his active opposition to the Soviet-backed Marxist regime in neighbouring Angola ensured him the support of the USA, and his country duly was awarded loans by the IMF and the World Bank. Pragmatism in African politics is seldom pretty.

The end of the Cold War all but terminated America's interest in Mobutu. This did nothing to reduce his corruption but, without a superpower to hold his coat, he was vulnerable to attack. In 1993, EU and UN arms embargoes added to Zaire's eggshell fragility, weakened again by cross-border reverberations from the genocide in neighbouring Rwanda. In October 1996, backed by Rwanda and Uganda, Laurent Kabila led a revolt which climaxed in May of the following year when he entered Kinshasa and declared himself president. Mobutu went off to die in Morocco, and the country slid through purgatory into the deepest, most unimaginable basements of hell. Kabila quickly fell out with his former Rwandan and Ugandan allies, who supported a new rebellion against him. Angola, Namibia and Zimbabwe meanwhile rallied in support of the president, igniting a conflict which, by the time the war officially ended in 2003, had claimed at least 4m lives. Looting, rape and murder were standard forms of negotiation and they did not stop with the ceasefire. Kabila himself was killed by a bodyguard and replaced by his son Joseph, whose Transitional National Government, formed in 2003, continued to preside over a land dominated by violence, corruption and humanitarian disaster. The economy, heavily indebted, is a thing of rags and tatters.

The IMF and World Bank have been in and out of the place like bears on a garbage tip. In the Cold War when it suited them, and in full knowledge of where the money would end up, the western powers were happy to fund their criminal ally Mobutu. Later, with his usefulness exhausted, the 'economy' unravelling and debt repayments in arrears, they turned off the tap. None of this impinged much on the consciousness of ordinary Zairians, whose lives of poverty, tension and insecurity were never touched by the Kinshasa slush-pump. But this is precisely the point. They might not have benefited from Mobutu's IMF-backed self-enrichment plan, but they were the ones who inherited the debt. This is the real strength of the case for debt relief. Like all lending institutions, the IMF and World Bank have to accept responsibility for the loans they make. If, for whatever reason, they choose to advance money to corrupt dictators, then they can hardly be surprised when the repayments fall behind. Nor should they expect the swindled populace to pick up the tab.

Surprisingly often, however, justice is not so much overlooked as turned on its head. One frequently suspects that the leader-writers of the *Daily Telegraph* neither travel very far nor suffer from overactive imaginations. Their empathy-free attitude to the African poor was tidily summarized in a leader, 'That's enough debt relief', published in June 2005 just ahead of the G8 summit at Gleneagles: 'If country A does everything by the book, making sacrifices and paying its creditors on time, while country B channels its aid money into its leaders' Swiss bank accounts, it seems hard that country B should be the one to get extra help.'

Do they imagine that the people of country B *asked* to be fleeced? That oppressed people should be held to account for the chicanery of their oppressors and the politically inspired cynicism of those who funded them? Would the *Telegraph* acquiesce so calmly in a scam on the English? As a display of compassion, it ranks alongside the Vatican's denial of morning-after pills to victims of rape. *You've been had, now take the consequences.* The article went on: 'The practical objection is that amnesties encourage fecklessness: countries will be readier to amass new debts in the expectation that these, too, will eventually be written off . . . Let us hear no more about debt relief until the year 3000.'

What really encouraged fecklessness, of course, was the IMF's strategic bankrolling of the feckless. Loans to the Democratic Republic of Congo resumed in 2002, and the promise of debt relief came a year later. 'In recognition of the authorities' satisfactory progress in implementing sound macroeconomic and structural policies,' said a joint IMF/World Bank statement, 'the DRC's total external debt . . . is to be reduced by up to 80 per cent.' In 2005 the finance ministers of the G8 agreed that the debts owed to the IMF and World Bank by the world's poorest countries should be cancelled. This is what had excited the *Daily Telegraph* to its spasm of small-mindedness. No surprise there, but you might have expected the reaction from African relief organizations to be exactly that – *relief*. They had got what they wanted. Instead (to quote a *Guardian* headline), there was angry talk of 'spin, lies and corruption'.

The reason for this seeming ingratitude was the same old spectre that had haunted the IMF and its clients since the very beginning – *conditionalities*. For debt relief, these included the need to 'tackle corruption, boost private sector development' and remove 'impediments to private investment'. In other words, states would have to dismantle their trade and currency barriers and surrender to the market. Red Riding Hood by comparison trod a safer path. But it was the anti-corruption clause that provoked the sourest laughter. Since when had *corruption* disqualified anyone from IMF/World Bank largesse? These were people who had talked turkey with Mobutu, Moi, Suharto and Marcos. True, they had drawn the line at Mugabe, but that hardly established them as moral paragons. Stalin might have drawn the line at Mugabe. They did *not* baulk at the likes of Rwanda's Paul Kagame or Uganda's Yoweri Museveni, whose armies ploughed the killing fields of the DRC, and who plied grateful western nations with stolen goods. A 2003 report by Amnesty International on the abuses perpetrated by these two in the DRC began with a quotation from Salvatore Bulamuzi, a member of the Lendu tribe whose entire family – parents, two wives and five children – were killed during attacks on Bunia: 'I am convinced now . . . that the lives of Congolese people no longer mean anything to anybody. Not to those who kill us like flies, our brothers who help kill us or those you call the international community . . . Even God does not listen to our prayers any more and abandons us.'

The report itself went on to explain how the market system, as it was operated by Rwanda and Uganda, took its mountain of flesh:

> Thousands of Congolese civilians have been tortured and killed during military operations to secure mineral-rich lands. Foreign forces have promoted inter-ethnic conflicts and mass killings as a means to secure mining zones. Combatants of the various forces in the region have killed or tortured independent miners and traders for their minerals or money . . . In eastern DRC, the neighbouring states of Rwanda and Uganda, in alliance with Congolese armed political groups, have systematically plundered the region on a vast scale . . . The ambition of all these combatant forces to exploit eastern DRC's mineral and economic wealth has been the biggest single factor in the continuing violence. The major beneficiaries have been senior members of the Ugandan and Rwandese armed forces, foreign businesses and leaders of armed political groups.

The eastern DRC is a prospector's wet dream, rich in gold, diamonds, coltan (columbo-tantalite), cassiterite, copper, cobalt, wolfram, zinc and oil, as well as timber, coffee and palm oil. For all that the local people have benefited from this, they might as well have been living in a resourceless desert. Until independence in 1960, the then Belgian Congo was milked by its colonial masters. As Amnesty observes: 'King Leopold II accrued vast personal wealth without ever setting foot on Congolese soil.' And then came Mobutu. If his American benefactors were looking for anti-socialist credentials, then the new president had them by the bucketful. There were state-owned mineral companies, true, but the cash from them flowed reassuringly straight into the bank accounts of the president and his cronies. Later, the Rwandan government would set up a special Congo Desk in its Department of External Security, specifically to oversee the exploitation of the eastern DRC. The insurgent forces within the country would fight over anything they could turn to profit: not just minerals but farm produce, land and even tax revenues.

The town of Kisangani, formerly Stanleyville, in diamond country near Stanley Falls on the Congo River, was the real 'Inner Station' of Joseph Conrad's *Heart of Darkness* and the setting for V. S. Naipaul's *A Bend in the River*. Its recent history is darker than anything even Conrad might have imagined, and stands as a paradigm of the modern African experience. For six days in June 2000, Rwandan and Ugandan forces fought each other for control of the town, shooting at each other with no concern for residents caught in the crossfire. The cathedral area was shelled, and Rwandan soldiers used people's homes as firing positions, leaving the occupants to take the return fire as they moved on. More than 1,200 civilians were killed and thousands more wounded. In the following year, 2001, 3.8 million dollars' worth of diamonds were exported to Antwerp from Uganda – a country which has no diamond production of its own, but one which is often held up as an example of 'good governance'. The UN's 'Panel of Experts on the Illegal Exploitation of Natural Resources and Other Forms of Wealth of the Democratic Republic of the Congo' noted, too, that gold exports from Uganda were far in excess of its own national output.

Rwandan and Ugandan-backed groups also seized control of the coltan mines. *Coltan?* It is one of those strange commodities upon which much of modern life depends, but about which we who benefit from it know shockingly little. It combines two precious metals – niobium (aka columbium) and tantalum – and is more properly known as columbo-tantalite. Tantalum, which has a high melting point, is widely used in the manufacture of capacitors for electronic equipment and mobile phones. Without knowing it, we've all got some. To get it to us, armed forces in the eastern DRC killed and tortured local people, drove them from their homes or forced them to work at gunpoint. According to Amnesty:

The Rwandese army's extraction and transfer of coltan and other natural resources to Rwanda was a carefully managed military operation ... Checkpoints on roads in the mining areas deterred civilian coltan traffic. In major towns and airstrips, coltan and other materials were stockpiled for onward transport by air or road. Airstrips in the mining zones were created or extended to accommodate larger aircraft. Army helicopters and contracted air-freight companies ... regularly transported coltan ... to Rwanda, where state-owned facilities were reportedly used to warehouse the material. Return flights brought in arms and equipment.

They were not doing all this for the simple pleasure of collecting the stuff. Its destination, via the international market, was our mobile phones and computers. In October 2002, the UN Panel of Experts blamed 'functionaries, companies, banks and individuals' for the perpetuation of the trade. The Belgium-based Peace Information Service reported the involvement of one American and several European companies in bringing stolen Congolese coltan to a phone near you. As explained in Chapter 7, corruption in Africa does not happen in a vacuum. Criminal businesses and governments, no less than legitimate ones, need trading partners, and what better than a free market to provide them? For all the complexity of their fiscal ducking and diving, their smokescreens of economic jargon, the secret tunnels between public corporations and offshore banks and the worldwide mycelium of financial interconnectedness, markets at base are uncomplicated beasts, driven like hyenas by raw instinct. They smell profit like other predators smell blood, and their response is just the same. Amnesty puts it bluntly:

The international traders and the tantalum-processing companies worldwide that purchased coltan directly from the Rwandese army and RCD-Goma [Rassemblement Congolais pour la Démocratie, a Rwandan-backed rebel force] sources or their proxies in eastern

DRC or Rwanda are complicit in the human rights abuses by these forces in the region. Their business deals have paid for the 'war within a war' in eastern DRC that has claimed hundreds of thousands of civilian lives and subjected millions of others to an associated humanitarian catastrophe.

Every global and national organization with an audible voice – the UN, G8, World Bank, IMF and almost every national government – has declared war on corruption. Countries have signed up to long-winded but good-sounding initiatives designed to prevent banks and other financial institutions from laundering the proceeds of corruption, deny safe haven to the guilty and return stolen assets to their owners. Congolese miners are not holding their breath. Nor is any dispossessed farmer, bankrupted businessman or starving child anywhere in the developing world. The conditionalities imposed by the IMF have nothing whatever to do with the institutionalized, people-eating corruption of western business, and everything to do with ensuring that the corruption continues. As the environmental campaigner George Monbiot put it in the *Guardian*: 'When the finance ministers say "good governance" and "eliminating impediments to private investment", what they mean is commercialization, privatization and the liberalization of trade and capital flows. And what this means is new opportunities for western money.'

Two-thirds of the world's poorest people live in resource-rich countries leaking wealth into the world economy. The IMF's army of PhDs wants us to believe that liberalized markets will put all this right, but it is an idea that has all the aerodynamic lift of a pregnant pig. Is it really the ambition of rich countries to surrender their advantage – to give the poor a level field to play on? They have every incentive to do the opposite, to squelch competition, seize control of public utilities and buy raw materials and labour at the lowest possible prices. Indeed, this is the duty that corporations legally owe to their shareholders. Debt relief, like loans, goes to those who do as they are told, and it creates exactly the same conflicts of interest. It is the IMF and World Bank that set the criteria and decide whether or not they have been met. But it is also the IMF and World Bank that advanced the money in the first place, and which now must adjudicate on the cancellation of debts owed to themselves. 'They have a vested interest,' says Monbiot, 'in ensuring that debt relief takes place as slowly as possible'. He went on, 'Attaching conditions like these to aid is bad enough: it amounts to saying "we will give you a trickle of money if you give us the Crown Jewels". Attaching them to debt relief is in a different moral league: "we will stop punching you in the face if you give us the Crown Jewels". The G8's plan for saving Africa is little better than an extortion racket.'

This puts in admittedly extreme terms a view which is shared by most aid agencies working in developing countries as well as by those who bear the debt. The home page of the Jubilee Debt Campaign displays this endorsement from former president Benjamin Mkapa of Tanzania: 'I encourage you in your advocacy for total debt cancellation because, frankly, it is a scandal that we are forced to choose between basic health and education for our people and repaying historical debt.'

This is no exaggeration. Despite the universally held belief that primary education, for girls and boys alike, is essential to the future development of impoverished countries, the Washington axis wants indebted states to follow the example of their own corrupt officials (cf Chapter 7) and charge school fees. Thus is an already difficult situation made impossible. Dirt-poor parents take a lot of persuasion to enrol their children for classes even when they are free, especially in the case of daughters. When payment is required, the disincentive is total. The same applies to health. Uganda introduced 'user fees' for basic healthcare in the late 1980s, when a survey ordered by the World Bank came up with the counter-intuitive finding that people were willing to pay.

To the surprise of no one but the ideologues, the finding turned out to be false. The hatred of health fees in Uganda reached such a pitch that every candidate in the 2000/1 presidential election (won eventually by Museveni) pledged to abolish them. After abolition in 2001, attendance at outpatients' clinics rose overnight by between 50 per cent and 100 per cent. And yet not even this could dent the World Bank/IMF conviction that the best medicine for sick Africans was a stiff dose of market realism. The economists didn't want 'patients'; they wanted 'customers'. People who paid for a service, they reasoned, would value it more highly and demand better service. They complained that a potentially valuable source of revenue had been thrown away, and denounced the Ugandan health ministry as 'a bad investment or bottomless pit'.

User fees for primary education in Uganda similarly were introduced in the late 1980s, with the result that millions of poor children, particularly girls, were withdrawn from school. Again the World Bank had commissioned a survey that predicted the opposite. Again the Ugandan government preferred the mundane evidence of its own eyes to the mountaintop theology of the economists. It abolished primary school fees in 1997, and enrolment for primary education more than doubled, from 2.5m to 6m. To record all the ways in which the IMF and World Bank have impacted negatively on poor people would require a book all on its own. Joseph Stiglitz's *Globalization* probably is as good an account as any, but even that is not comprehensive (not least because it dates from as long ago as 2002 and he concentrates his fire on the IMF alone).

The idea that conditionality kills corruption is as risible as the idea that it promotes social justice. Consider for example the period of economic transition that followed the fall of the Berlin Wall in 1989. For Russia, facing its second great economic upheaval of the 20th century, the fruits of capitalism were as mouldy as the fruits of Marx. The IMF came bustling in with its low-inflation agenda and wrecked the economy by insisting that the overvalued rouble should not be devalued (not until devaluation in 1998 did the economy begin to grow). For ideologues of any political stripe, full-strength 'democracy' – the right of the people to choose – is a monstrous inconvenience. Voters cannot be trusted to make the right call and must be duped or coerced. In the case of the IMF's 'conditionalities' they may be duped and coerced simultaneously. Conditionalities are terms of surrender that remove strategic decision-making not just from electorates but from the governments that represent them. For many people this sticks in the craw like poisoned meat. But Russians of course were wholly accustomed to the iron claw of centralized power, and democracy by *diktat* was hardly a shock to the system. Just as Brezhnev had imposed his five-year plans, so Boris Yeltsin could impose the market system by *fiat*.

Each new boss, as The Who proclaimed in their anthem to political cynicism, 'Won't Get Fooled Again', is much like the old boss. Stiglitz is hardly less acidic: 'It is as if the market Bolsheviks, native true believers, as well as the Western experts and evangelists of the new economic religion who flew into post-Socialist countries, attempted to use a benign version of Lenin's methods to steer the post-communism, "democratic" transition.'

Vladimir Illich himself must be spinning inside his mummified corpse. Stiglitz in *Globalization* expends a great deal of ink on the IMF's Russian adventure – what was intended, what actually happened and why it went wrong. He explodes the fiction that IMF-led market liberalization reliably does for corruption what DDT once did for the mosquito. Public ownership is anathema to free-market purists, who see it as a barrier to competition and growth. Privatization of nationalized companies therefore is one of the Washingtonians' highest priorities – so high, in fact, that they want it done without delay. Even in developed economies, privatization can be of dubious benefit to taxpayers. The two most notorious recent examples in the UK were the railways, which made multi-millionaires of former middle managers at the expense of service reliability and passenger safety, and the defence research company Qinetiq, which let go a valuable public asset at a knock-down price and all but drowned the fat cats in cream. (Their wealth was guaranteed by a £5.6bn government contract signed on the very day that the US private equity giant the Carlyle Group paid £42m for a 31 per cent stake – an investment which, after flotation, increased in value to over £350m.) The former stank of incompetence; the latter just stank.

Both these scandals occurred in a well-regulated country where good corporate governance hedged by legal safeguards is the bedrock of the economy. The corporate dogs may be greedy and on a very long leash, but at least they are under some restraint. That is the theory, though the banking crisis of 2008 proved that greed cannot be regulated out of the system and that moral bankruptcy is a vacuum to be filled with other people's money. Where no safeguards exist at all, the rush to privatization is a race between wolves. The sons and daughters of Lenin had no more idea of 'good corporate governance' than they had of the laws of cricket, and no legal framework to make sure they got it. 'Property is theft' (*La propriété c'est le vol*), wrote the socialist thinker Pierre-Joseph Proudhon in 1843. One hundred and fifty years later, the post-revolutionaries of Yeltsin's Russia did their best to prove him right. Managers of national enterprises suddenly became owners of companies. Property was stolen; assets stripped; and swags of Soviet industry fell into the hands of private banks that had lent money to a chum-packed government which declared itself suddenly unable to keep up the repayments. *Oh dear, what a shame! Never mind! Have an oil well.* Billionaire oligarchs sprouted like fungi on dung. There was no hanging about for the regulated mechanisms of a free market, or for the election of a government that might have a different idea of what constituted economic propriety. The newly minted fortunes were over the border and into foreign banks before the oligarchs had finished toasting the IMF. Such was the damage to the country's economy that some Russians believed it was a deliberate act of sabotage by the Americans.

Something very similar was happening in Uganda, whose conditionalities also involved privatization of state-owned companies. In 1992, giving in to pressure, it embarked on the sale of no fewer than 142 of them, a policy which was expected to yield a return for the national exchequer of 500m US dollars. Like Russia, however, Uganda had no effective mechanism for overseeing the transition and making sure taxpayers received their due. It found itself caught between the pincers of local and international greed, and the 500m was squeezed down to nearer 2m. In *New Strategies, Old Loans*, a report published with the support of ActionAid in 2002, Warren Nyamugasira, national co-ordinator of the Ugandan National NGO Forum, and Rick Rowden, researcher for the Washington-based RESULTS Education Fund, explained how it happened:

Several factors contributed to the failure of Uganda to realize the expected $500m, particularly asset stripping prior to finalized sales, influence-peddling, failure or refusal of buyers to make full payments on purchased assets (this has been an extremely common problem in which buyers offered a small deposit at the time of sale and later never paid the rest of their scheduled payments), and the initial overvaluing and over-pricing of public enterprises. The government poorly managed its privatization programs and failed to involve public workers and citizens' groups in these processes, while existing regulatory mechanisms have proven ineffective at ensuring adequate oversight.

The most significant factor was the IMF/World Bank's conviction that the *fact* of privatization, and the speed of its accomplishment, was more important than the *means*. No surprise, the air is thick with bluebottles. Like most abstract nouns, 'corruption' has no single definition that is universally recognized. Its meaning on the Arabian Gulf is not the same as its meaning in the Home Counties, which is different again from its meaning on 19th Street. But this only inspires the evangelists of the free market to raise the volume of their sermons. They are not only richer than thou, but holier too. The leaders of the G8 have signed up to a range of initiatives designed to ensure the victory of (their own) virtue over (other people's) vice. These include the OECD Convention on Combating Bribery of Foreign Public Officials, the UN Convention Against Corruption, and the Extractive Industries Transparency Initiative (EITI). All are meant to achieve what it says in the title. The OECD Convention is supposed to eliminate bribery from international business. The UN Convention expects member states not only to prevent, detect and prosecute bribery and extortion but also to return stolen cash and property. The EITI prescribes open and honest management of the mining, gas and oil industries. Members of the G8 have also pledged to deny guilty individuals access to financial institutions. But of course pledging is the easy bit. Run this sort of stuff up any flagpole, anywhere in the world, and everyone will come out and salute it. They might as well buy woggles and whistles and sign up to the seven principles of the Boy Scout Law. They make for a pretty comprehensive moral blueprint:

A Scout is to be trusted.
A Scout is loyal.
A Scout is friendly and considerate.
A Scout belongs to the worldwide family of Scouts.
A Scout has courage in all difficulties.
A Scout makes good use of time and is careful of possessions and property.
A Scout has self-respect and respect for others.

The UN or G8 could hardly do better. Back in the days when

Scouts wore shorts and carried knives on their belts, they were sworn also to be 'clean in thought, word and deed', be 'kind to animals' and 'smile and whistle under all difficulties'. They were, of course, just like any other boys – grubby-minded, evilly intentioned, foul-mouthed and carnivorous. The same might be said for ministers of government and their officials. In principle they would sign up to all seven of scouting's virtues – trustworthiness, loyalty, friendliness, racial tolerance, courage, thrift, respect – but in practice they would be hung with so many caveats that you could hardly see them for the 'what-ifs'. What if corrupt practices are creating employment for our people? What if there are parts of the world where bribery is integral to the procurement process and no deal is possible without it? What if our fiercest competitor will pay the bribe if we don't? What if it's necessary to keep foreign governments onside in the 'war against terror'? Of course we're all for virtue but – hey! we're pretty straight kinda guys and we all have to live in the real world, don't we?

So it goes, as the late Kurt Vonnegut might have said. In July 2008, on the eve of the G8 summit in Japan, Transparency International published its *2008 G8 Progress Report – an Assessment of G8 Action on Anti-Corruption Commitments*. There was some good news. France, Germany and the US had all taken action against bribers, including many powerful multinationals. France alone had gone after the defence contractor Thales, the oil company Total and the engineering giant Alstom. Germany had taken on Siemens. Among many others targeted by the US were three subsidiaries of the UK oil services company Vetco International, which had been fined a record $26m for bribing Nigerian customs officers. In fact at the time of the TI report, the US with 103 prosecutions to its name had a far better enforcement record than any of its G8 partners. Germany scored 43, France 19 and Italy 2. TI conceded that Italy's cases were 'few in number' but was encouraged by the fact that they were 'both against major multinationals with the potential to have a profound and broad impact'. Canada and Japan got a slap for each having brought only one minor case, and Russia . . . Well, Russia is Russia. Technically, not being one of the world top eight developed economies, it ought not to be in the G8 at all. *Realpolitik*, however, recognizes that the world's geographically largest and far from least belligerent nuclear-armed country needs special treatment and exceptional tolerance. 'To date,' said the TI report, 'promised anti-corruption commitments have not materialized, but the new president has indicated that a national anti-corruption plan is forthcoming.'

That left only one member of the G8 unaccounted for . . . The UK's record on bribery has been pitiful. At the time of writing (August 2008), not only has it failed to bring a single foreign bribery case but, immune to its own stink, it has actually halted the Serious Fraud Office's (SFO's) investigation into allegations of bribery by BAE Systems in the notorious £43bn Al-Yamamah arms deal. It did so, by its own admission, because the Saudi government had threatened to withdraw its co-operation on anti-terrorism. This flagrantly breached the OECD Convention which, TI reminds us, 'expressly prohibits consideration of national economic interest or the potential effect on relations with another state to influence decisions whether to investigate or prosecute (Article 5). The UK action threatens to create a dangerous precedent for others seeking to avoid their commitments.'

It was an unedifying spectacle. In April 2008 the High Court upheld a challenge by anti-corruption campaigners and ruled that the SFO had acted unlawfully when it suspended its investigation. In the opinion of Lord Justice Moses and Mr Justice Sullivan, the SFO and the government had 'abjectly surrendered' to the Saudis, whose action amounted to a 'successful attempt by a foreign government to pervert the course of justice in the United Kingdom'. 'No one, whether within this country or outside,' said Lord Justice Moses, 'is entitled to interfere with the course of our justice. It is the failure of government and [the SFO] to bear that essential principle in mind that justifies the intervention of this court.'

But the government would not back off, and in July the Law Lords overturned the verdict. Allowing the SFO's appeal against the High Court, their lordships ruled that the SFO's former director, Robert Wardle, had acted within his authority when he stopped the investigation. Nicholas Hildyard of The Corner House, one of the campaign groups that petitioned the High Court, summed up the implications of the legal climb-down:

Now we know where we are. Under UK law, a supposedly independent prosecutor can do nothing to resist a threat made by someone abroad if the UK government claims that the threat endangers national security. The unscrupulous who have friends in high places overseas willing to make such threats now have a 'Get Out of Jail Free' card – and there is nothing the public can do to hold the government to account if it abuses its national security powers. Parliament needs urgently to plug this gaping hole in the law and in the constitutional checks and balances dealing with national security. With the law as it is, a government can simply invoke 'national security' to drive a coach and horses through international anti-bribery legislation, as the UK government has done, to stop corruption investigations.

Law 8: A Scout knows which side his bread is buttered. Virtue is not absolute. Motherhood may be universal, but there is more than one recipe for apple pie and more than one recipe for debt relief. Your opinion of the current formulation will depend on how hungry you are. The Heavily Indebted Poor Countries (HIPC) Initiative, which is the principal international scheme for relieving debt, was set up by the IMF and World Bank in 1996 and has been criticized ever since. One of its most persistent opponents in Britain has been the Jubilee Debt Campaign, a coalition of more than 80 national organizations as diverse as Christian Aid, Comic Relief, the WI and the TUC. Its message could not be simpler. It wants '100 per cent cancellation of unpayable and unfair poor country debts', and its reasoning is familiar: 'The world's most impoverished countries are forced to pay over $100 million EVERY DAY to the rich world in debt repayments, while poverty kills millions of their people. Meanwhile, creditors use their power over indebted countries to force them to privatize their services, open up their markets or cut essential spending.'

The word 'poor' in the initiative's title is defined by economists to mean countries with an annual per capita income of not more than $905 and debts of more than one and a half times their annual earnings from exports. For 'poor' read 'very poor indeed'. To earn relief from IMF or World Bank debts, they must first follow IMF economic guidance for three years; then they must accept the conditionalities that open their markets to multinational corporations and charge primary schoolchildren for their education.

Countries get some initial relief on acceptance into the HIPC, but it might take many years to reduce their debts to the 'sustainable' level of one and a half times export earnings. In the meantime, enforced cuts in spending will reduce the number of doctors and teachers, and the privatization of water and energy will mean higher prices and reduced access for the poor. Inflation, balance of payments and interest rates might tick the boxes on a Washington desktop, but they don't put dispossessed farmers back into work, or sick people back into health, or make illiterate children read.

Twelve years after the initiative began, only 23 countries have completed the course. These are Benin, Bolivia, Burkina Faso, Cameroon, Ethiopia, Gambia, Ghana, Guyana, Honduras, Madagascar, Malawi, Mali, Mauritania, Mozambique,

Nicaragua, Niger, Rwanda, São Tomé and Príncipe, Senegal, Sierra Leone, Tanzania, Uganda and Zambia.

Nine more – Afghanistan, Burundi, the Central African Republic, Chad, the Democratic Republic of Congo, the Republic of Congo (Congo Brazzaville), Guinea, Guinea Bissau and Haiti – have qualified for initial relief, and Liberia has qualified but not yet joined the process. Another eight – Comoros, Côte d'Ivoire, Eritrea, Kyrgyz Republic, Nepal, Somalia, Sudan and Togo – have a chance to join, but must first serve their three-year probation and show obedience to the IMF. It is easy to guess the Jubilee Debt Campaign's objections to all this, but here they are just the same:

> HIPC takes too long: more than 10 years for 23 countries so far.
>
> HIPC offers far too little – total cancellation of all unpayable and unjust debt is needed.
>
> HIPC is too limited – many more countries need and deserve debt cancellation.
>
> HIPC comes with damaging and unfair strings attached.
>
> HIPC does not include all debts: debts are only partially cancelled, and some countries, banks and companies refuse or fail to take part in the HIPC process at all.
>
> HIPC is entirely controlled by creditors: they do not accept responsibility for their part in creating and maintaining the debt crisis, or allow poor countries to have a say.

People become disillusioned with politics because they are tired of polarized debate with its paralysing orthodoxies of left and right. We distrust economists for much the same reason that we distrust astrologers – the only things they are right about are the things we can see for ourselves. Unlike the theorists, we value substance over process, and we suspect that experience may be a better teacher than Harvard Business School. What experience shows us is that debt cancellation works. On average in the countries where it has applied, spending on education has gone up by 40 per cent and on healthcare by 70 per cent. Tanzania got 2,000 new schools in three years; Malawi is training 3,600 new teachers; Mozambique has a free children's immunization programme; Zambia has abolished user fees at rural health clinics; 2.2m more people in Uganda have access to clean water; 60 per cent of births in Mauritania and 70 per cent in Bolivia are now attended by health professionals – up from 40 per cent in both cases. By western standards these are small steps up the lower rungs of civilization's ladder – stuff that we take for granted. But this is why it matters. Globalization should not be about undermining national sovereignty or overriding democracy. Nobody wants to live in what Joseph Stiglitz has described as 'dictatorships of international finance'. Relief programmes should not be Trojan horses filled with western bankers and multinational corporations. The word 'people' should not be confused with 'economic units'. Africa, Asia and South America should not be expected to swallow policies that would be unacceptable in Europe or the US. Economics is the only belief system in which a human life in Kisangani is of lesser value than a human life in Washington. Only a man in a suit, in an air-conditioned office a very long way off, could look at ravaged people on a ravaged continent and see only a market.

10

Winner Take All

When I was younger and limber, I played a bit of squash. A couple of times a week for 30 minutes or an hour, a cathartic stress-busting thrash followed by a pint in the pub with whoever I'd just beaten or been beaten by. Opponents were drawn from a group of friends, four or five moderately competent players of similar ability who liked a hard game and fought for every point, but in whom the result aroused little in the way of exultation or depression. We won, we lost, we had a beer. It was fun. We were jolly nice chaps, so it was typical that one of our number should bring along his new neighbour. This man had never played squash before, but he was a goodish tennis player, physically fit and eager to turn his racket skills to new and more vigorous purpose.

He was at first a joke, and then a thoroughgoing pain in the arse. Joke because he turned up wearing the latest high-tech kit and swinging a ridiculously flash, highly expensive professional racket. Pain in the arse because every missed point was like a red-hot dagger twisted in his bowels. He would yell abuse at himself, throw down his racket and clasp his head in his hands as if he had just come fourth in the Olympics. Afterwards in the pub he would draw diagrams of rallies on the backs of beer mats, and theorize about tactics and techniques. 'Best-case scenario, you score a backhand nick. Worst-case, you lob.' To our considerable relief he learned quickly, improved his game and started to win.

The relief was short-lived. It was a toss-up which was worse – losing a point to him, or winning one. In the former case he would shout – *Yesss!* – pump his fists and declaim the score. In the latter he would do much the same – *Come ON!* – though in this case the score might be overlooked. There were occasional variants, usually when he was far enough ahead to feel secure – *Oh, good shot!* if you fluked one past him, *Bad luck!* if you hit the tin. He never conceded a let, even when the point was plainly lost. We tried to laugh him off, but found ourselves corrupted by his example. *He had to be beaten*, even if it meant exploiting a two-stone weight advantage in 'accidental' collisions and not putting our hands up for double bounces. The game turned sour and lost its point, ruined by an idiot.

And yet he was not stupid. He held a good degree from the University of Cambridge and a well-paid job in the upper-middle management of a large national company, through whose ranks he was rapidly being promoted. I asked him what his ambition was.

'To be a managing director.'

Just that. He wanted to run a company. It didn't matter whether it made paint, shoes, invalid buggies or intercontinental ballistic missiles – it had to be a brand leader, and he had to have the power. Thirty years ago this struck me as deranged. How could he not care what industry he was in, what his product was or how it might affect the environment or people's lives? He dealt with this like a slow, waist-high ball in mid court. *Whup!* It was people like me, wet-lettuce liberals with guilt in their veins and no lead in their pencils, who people like *him*, energetic red-blooded wealth creators, had to carry on their backs along with all the hippies, homosexuals, arts graduates, commies, poets, pacifists, welfare scroungers, women and folk singers who squatted on the economy like toads in a garden. In the context of the generation to which we belonged – the love 'n' peace-mongers of the Sixties – he had the germ of a point. Our rejection of 'business', the belief that management training, like the church in earlier centuries, was a grey haven for intellectual second-raters, was as unworldly as our belief in the healing power of rock music. I do believe we caused harm, funnelling the best brains into 'the media' and away from politics and business. The world still bears the scars.

But they are as nothing compared to the scars now being inflicted by my squash-playing friend and those who think like him. One kind of craziness has been replaced by another. In my own brief time as a Cambridge fellow commoner, and in my sons' rather longer experience of an English public school, I saw all the dangers of institutional madness. People in enclosed worlds are like sub-species on an island, unconscious of any values except their own. They may fight among themselves (and how!), but never at the cost of their shared assumptions. Their codes are the law, their objectives sanctified, their superiority unquestionable. If Darwin could return and demonstrate his theory by reference to humans, then they would be Exhibit A.

The prime example is the world of international business. Like a wasp, high finance knows where to lay its eggs. They hatch and swarm through the body politic, and make sure that legislatures know what is expected of them. The mechanisms were discussed in Chapter 9. For an insight into the corporate mindset there is no place quite like Harvard Business School, the world-leading madrassa of capitalism whose students are told their destiny is to rule the globe. 'We educate leaders who make a difference in the world,' it says. The promise of its fabled two-year Master of Business Administration (MBA) course is 'a lifetime of leadership', placing graduates among a worldwide community of 70,000 business leaders in 150 countries. 'Decisive moments define a Harvard Business School education. Here, everything from Section life to case studies, from field-based learning to international Immersions, culminates in one larger lesson – what it means to assume leadership within an ever-growing, ever-changing world.'

I like that 'assume'. Leadership by this definition is exactly what my squash fanatic understood it to be – a virtue in its own right, to be cherished for what it gives to those who have it. It is the abstract idea that underpins the meatier concepts of private jets, Floridian beach houses and dinners with the president. Harvard MBAs are not called upon to serve the world. They are called to possess it. Every year the school takes on 900 new keenies, mostly in their late twenties and early thirties. Many of them already will have enjoyed fast upward trajectories in business and finance, and come to Harvard for the booster stage that will fire them deep into the upper stratospheres of venture capital, hedge funds, investment banking and entrepreneurism. You do not need to be conventionally intelligent (George W. Bush was admitted to the school) or conventionally honest (so was Kenneth Lay, chief executive of Enron), but you do need to be eyeballs-out, 24/7 ambitious. Diffidence is for wimps.

Serendipitously as I begin this chapter there falls into my hands a wonderfully entertaining book, *What They Teach You at Harvard Business School*, by the former *Daily Telegraph* journalist Philip Delves Broughton, describing his own two years as a student at 'HBS', as everyone seems to call it. To him I owe the knowledge that the school's alumni include the president of the World Bank, the mayor of New York and the CEOs of General Electric, Goldman Sachs and Proctor and Gamble. 'HBS alumni,' he writes, 'filled 20 per cent of the top three jobs at the Fortune 500 companies. The newly fashionable private equity and hedge fund industries were stacked with Harvard MBAs, who were received like gods when they returned to campus.'

The 'Fortune 500' are America's top public corporations, ranked by revenue, which between them tots up to 9.1 trillion dollars. If they banded together and called themselves a state, the economy of Fortuneland would be bigger than the combined economies of the UK, Germany, France and Japan. We are talking *major* political clout here. In 2006 when President Bush needed a new treasury secretary the job did not go to a career politician. It went to Henry Merritt 'Hank' Paulson, chairman and CEO of the investment banking giant Goldman Sachs. Needless to say, Paulson is a Harvard MBA. Needless to say, too, his influence reaches far beyond the seaboards of the United States. With the job comes a seat on the IMF board, where the US power of veto gives it unparalleled influence over the lives of billions, many of whom will never have heard of it, let alone had an opportunity to vote for its officers. Democracy for export is weapons-grade. But at least Paulson was a public figure whose name was out in the open. Others wield just as much influence without any kind of public scrutiny. You don't need public office to have political influence or global power – the free market will do the job just as effectively, and it is the free market that the trainee economic war-lords at HBS are drilled to command. It is not just Harvard. HBS may top the rankings, but it is one among many dozens of business schools in the US. Behind it in close order come Wharton, Stanford, Chicago, Columbia, Stern, Yale, Tuck . . . There are dozens more in the UK, and hundreds across the world, all teeming with 'winners'. As befits the champions of market economics, it is a growth industry. I learn from Philip Delves Broughton that 5,000 MBAs graduated from American universities in 1960. Forty years later it was 100,000. 'Business schools,' he writes, 'no longer produce just business leaders. MBAs determine the lives many of us will lead, the hours we work, the vacations we get, the culture we consume, the health care we receive, and the education provided to our children.'

The HBS MBA, Delves Broughton says, is 'the calling card of the global financial elite'. But perhaps we should not be too frightened or indignant. Everything we value or enjoy – education, the arts, science, architecture, fashion, cookery, sport, politics, the law – throws up elites, and we have much to thank them for. The stage needs leading actors. Even wild landscapes are *managed*. Without the benign interference of experts, moors, marshes and hills would lose most of their beauty and all of their usefulness. They would become impenetrable, ungovernable, hostile to humans. Why should business and finance be any different? Why should we not be glad that so many people are being trained as wardens of the global economy? Do we want it run by *amateurs*? Do we heck!

But the analogy is weak. Landscape managers are working transparently for a visible public benefit. What they appear to be doing is what they *are* doing. The thing that matters is the *product*, a well-cared-for, healthy and sustainable landscape which everyone can enjoy. MBAs are not taught to think like that. Unless it's cash, the product is immaterial. Most of these people will never see or handle a product; they will certainly never make one. All they see is strings of digits; risks worth or not worth taking; profit projections; assets to be grown or offloaded; currencies to be bought or sold; businesses to be acquired and stripped; taxes to be avoided; buyers and sellers to be bluffed or played off against each other. Criminal masterminds think in much the same way, but they face the awkward impediment of a society hostile to the practice of robbery. Company masterminds have no such worries. Their influence in government means that finance and trade law is drafted to suit them. Allowing the odd Enron-type exception, they can make their killings without acting illegally. The line they tread is a thin one, but it's a line nonetheless. As Philip Delves Broughton puts it: 'No matter how hard it tries, business can never escape the fact that it is the practice of potentially thieving, treacherous, lying human beings. Its challenge is in reining in the thieving, treachery and deceit sufficiently that the entire edifice of business and society does not dissolve into a medieval vision of hell.'

That is the oligarchs' first line of defence. Public morality is defined by the law, and they take very good care to keep within it. The second is on the boggier ground of economic theory. Thus we are invited to believe with Dr Pangloss that all is for the best in the best of all possible worlds. Specifically, we have to believe that free trade brings benefits to all, from Boston to Bangladesh, company president to Congolese peasant. You would need a very special kind of evidential filtering system to stand this up in court. You would have to rule as inadmissible the evidence of increasing Third World poverty; the widening gap between rich and poor; the protectionism and market manipulation by the first world against the third; the vast salaries awarded to themselves by the managements of global corporations. To reach such a verdict you would have to be either an MBA on the make, a fool, or perhaps the president of the IOC, Jacques Rogge, who announced that the commercial success of the Beijing Olympics 'fully justified' his organization's decision to overlook Chinese repression. Who in the world wants leaders who believe this kind of thing? Who in the world thinks the best qualification for a leader is the ability to turn a buck?

In 1998 David Glass, chief operating officer of Wal-Mart, famously spelled out his ambitions: 'First we dominate North America, then South America, then Europe and Asia.' Way back in 1968 the president of Nabisco, Lee Bickmore, told *Forbes* magazine that he was looking forward to 'one world of homogeneous consumption . . . the day when Arabs and Americans, Latins and Scandinavians will be munching Ritz crackers as enthusiastically as they already drink Coke or brush their teeth with Colgate.' In 1999, the *Financial Times* quoted the then CEO of Burger King, Dennis Malamatinas: 'The solution is to make people stay hungry. The killer instinct always prevails and you're after market share. If you're going to be successful, you've got to have that attitude.' Were these the authentic sounds of altruists determined to make equatorial Africa a nicer place?

The power of brands can express itself in unlikely ways. Americans now are naming their babies after them – a survey in

2000 revealed, for example, L'Oreal, Chevrolet, Armani, Chanel, Del Monte and Canon. When their time comes, they should be first in line for top grades at HBS. In the opinion of Cleveland Evans, the psychology professor who carried out the survey, product-labelling your child 'is no different from the 19th century when parents named their children Ruby or Opal ... it reflects their aspirations'. So watch out: Monsanto and Wal-Mart will be along very shortly with their swinging sister Syngenta. But that word 'aspirations' ... It's so often a weasel – a harbinger of deceits, a subtle softener of grasping ambition, a legitimizer that sends greed to the party dressed as sweet reasonableness. You won't find an MBA without aspirations. Arriving at business school without them would be like a violinist enrolling without an instrument. Aspirations in corporate-speak are 'the vision'. And the vision in multinational corporate-speak is the one spelled out for us forty years ago by Lee Bickmore – 'one world of homogeneous consumption'.

We are well on our way towards it. In a campaign briefing published in early 2005, the global anti-poverty agency ActionAid International reports that just 30 retailing corporations now account for a third of all worldwide grocery sales; five companies control 90 per cent of the grain trade, and 75 per cent of the pesticides market is shared between six. At their mercy are the world's poor, 70 per cent of whom live in rural areas and depend on food production for their living. MBA courses do not spend much time on the economics of small-scale farming. But they spend a very great deal of time on the virtues of entre-preneurship and growth. Big is beautiful, but biggest is best. Even in the developed world this is at most a half-truth. We might look, for example, at supermarkets. In the UK, where business is dominated by five superbrands led by Tesco, we have paid a high price for the car-dependent, one-stop 'convenience' these retail powerhouses have blessed us with. Big branches now stock 40,000 product lines – eight times more than they were doing

30 years ago. For every kind of competitor from corner shop to milkman, the effect has been ruinous. Specialist shops have been put out of business, local supply lines severed and food production and processing concentrated in the hands of a few operators big enough to cope with the supermarkets' demands for huge quantities at rock-bottom prices. In 1998 the British Retail Planning Forum calculated that a major supermarket opening in a town would create a net loss of 276 jobs. High streets lost their character, communities lost their heart and local economies faltered. When shops closed, their suppliers went with them; so did the decorators, carpenters, electricians, accountants and others who had helped to keep them running. Instead of circulating locally, customers' money was sucked out of their cash-cards straight to head office, whose record profits each year would make headline news. Economic contrarians opposed to biggism worked out that £10 spent on a vegetable box scheme would generate £25 worth of benefit to the local economy – £11 more than the same money spent in a supermarket.

The justification for supermarkets' purchasing policies is that by screwing their suppliers they can offer handsome deals to their customers. The likelier truth is that they are spilling more cream into the already brimming bowls of their shareholders and executives. The 1990s, for example, saw severe cuts in the prices paid to lamb and milk producers, but no commensurate cuts at the checkout. In a single year, farm prices fell by 9.6 per cent while the retail price index climbed by 15 per cent. When a local community does manage to fight off a new supermarket, the news is reported in terms of David and Goliath, as if Doncaster Rovers had beaten Real Madrid. These vast megaliths are what Ernst Stavro Blofeld would have dreamt up if ever he'd thought of going into the retail trade. Against Leviathan, the planning system has the penetrative power of a wounded haddock.

Now imagine . . . If this is what happens in a judicially independent, financially robust and highly regulated country like the UK, what happens when the same pressures are applied in judicially weak, financially enfeebled and poorly regulated countries in the Third World? Universities lure business management and economics students by promising to lift the fog; to blow away the misconceptions and unravel the complexities of what they like to call TNCs (transnational corporations). Let's wish them luck. The complexities are real enough, but they are the kind of sleight-of-hand, small-print duckings and weavings that the financially slick use to outflank the financially naive. 'Outflank'? Why did I not just say 'rob'? Behind the complexity is one simple truth, its propelling force the same that puts cuckoos in dunnocks' nests; the same that allows the biggest boy in the playground to fix the rules of the game; the same that forever makes large entities gobble up small. Some would call it 'aspiration'. Let us call it greed.

In 2003 the US food retailing giant Wal-Mart, owner of the UK Asda chain, made pre-tax profits of 12.3 billion dollars – bigger than the combined economies of Mozambique and Ghana. Fifty-one (by some accounts 52) of the world's 100 biggest economies are corporations, not countries. The 49 (or 48) others are bound, in theory if not in practice, by a slew of treaties and conventions which together add up to 'international law'. They are a bit like the rules of chess – not guaranteeing fair play exactly, and certainly not abolishing winners and losers, but sufficient to restrict the scope for abuse. Heads of state may sign such things, but not heads of corporations. On the windswept plains of multinational business, where the gale of competition blows hard and cold from other continents, human rights take their chance with the price of bananas.

You could choose as exemplar any internationally traded commodity you like, but let us stay with foodstuffs. Every link in the supply chain, from seed to shelf, is now dominated by a handful of transnationals of vast power and infinite reach. This applies as much to sellers (the seed companies) as it does to buyers (the retail chains). At the seed and agri-chemical end we find Syngenta, Monsanto, DuPont and Bayer. At the supermarket end are the likes of Wal-Mart, Carrefour, Metro and Tesco. In the middle are the traders and processors – ADM, Louis Dreyfus, Bunge, Cargill – and the manufacturers – Nestlé, Kraft, Unilever, PepsiCo. One thing that all MBAs learn about at business school is horizontal and vertical integration. Horizontal integration means buying or merging with another company in the same line of business – dog eats dog, one supermarket buys another, and, as deal follows deal, Rover turns into Cerberus. Vertical integration means buying companies at different points along the supply chain. A food processor, for example, might buy a seed and fertilizer company, thus creating a pincer movement against growers who must sell to the former and buy from the latter. And it doesn't have to be either/or. Corporations can integrate in both directions simultaneously. Or they can simply forge alliances with other corporations in the same supply chain and achieve what MBAs call 'vertical co-ordination'. The accounting is different, but the effect is the same – a supply chain entirely owned and controlled by global corporations. Just as lions in the Serengeti will spot the cheapest sources of supply – the wounded animal, the juvenile easiest to catch – so the corporations are drawn to the cheapest labour markets and the weakest administrations. There can be horizontal co-ordination too – for example, when corporations in an advanced form of reciprocal altruism share technologies to help each other consolidate their market strength. To understand what co-ordination can achieve, you have only to read this big-boy's boast from the transnational commodity trader Cargill: 'We are the flour in your bread, the wheat in your noodles, the salt on your fries. We are the corn in your tortillas, the chocolate in your dessert, the sweetener in your soft drink. We are the oil in your salad dressing and the beef, pork or chicken you eat for dinner. We are the cotton in your clothing, the backing on your carpet and the fertilizer in your field.'

You won't see Cargill's name on anything in the supermarket, but there is only a vanishingly small likelihood that you've bought none of its products. The networks of wholly owned, partly owned and interrelated companies that have spread across the world from America and Europe are the major cause of the complexity that the professors promise to unravel. But again the truth is simple. The concentration of corporate power, forcing producers to sell to a smaller and smaller circle of buyers, can have only one effect, which is to drive down farm prices. In defiance of what free markets are supposed to achieve, the result is anti-competitive. Buyers are not bidding against each other. They are creating and exploiting monopolies. Savings made by forcing down prices either swell the corporation's profits or, if its end product is in a particularly competitive market, cut its price to the consumer. As the author of the ActionAid report, Dominic Eagleton, puts it: 'Agrifood TNCs are therefore using concentrated buyer power to transfer wealth from farmers and rural communities to company owners and urban consumers – and from poor countries to rich countries.'

This is wholly in accordance with the rule set down in *Capitalism and Freedom* by the Nobel economics laureate Milton Friedman in 1962, and which remains the guiding principle of market economists nearly half a century later. The sole responsibility of a private firm, said Friedman, was 'to use its resources and engage in activities designed to increase its profits so long as it stays within the rules of the game'. Yet again the outcome is easy to predict. ActionAid offers the example of the Côte d'Ivoire, where 95 per cent of the country's cocoa processing, and 90 per cent of its cocoa exports, are controlled by transnationals, and where farm gate prices account for just 5 per cent of the retail price of chocolate. Bananas are another example, though in this case the power is concentrated at the retail end of the chain. ActionAid explains:

[A UK supermarket] used its bargaining power over suppliers to negotiate price cuts for bananas in 2002, and then brought the UK retail price for bananas down from £1.08 to £0.94 per kg. Other supermarkets followed suit and demanded deep price cuts from their suppliers. By 2004 bananas were retailing at £0.74 per kg in UK supermarkets. The fruit is a crucial source of livelihood for millions of producers and workers in Latin America and the Caribbean. But research from the campaign group Banana Link shows that with a retail price of £0.81 per kg it is impossible for growers in Costa Rica to be paid the legal minimum price for a box of bananas, and in turn impossible for growers to pay plantation workers the legal minimum wage.

Despite the fact that, unlike cocoa and coffee, bananas need next to nothing in the way of processing, only 12 per cent of the retail price stays in the country of origin and only a fraction of that finds its way into workers' pockets. 'For every £1 that shoppers in the UK spend on loose Ecuadorian bananas,' says ActionAid, 'around 40p goes to supermarkets, while plantation workers receive just 1.5p.'

Third World farmers are also squeezed by corporate *selling* power. Before the opening up of poor countries' markets ordained by Washington, many farmers received government support for their agri-chemicals, and harvested their own seed for each succeeding crop. To the Washington consensus this was not so much blasphemy as devil worship. Government subsidies blocked free access to the agri-chemical market, and seed-harvesting breached the intellectual property rights of the bio-engineers who had bred the varieties. In the face of overwhelming economic fire-power, governments backed off, the corporations had their victory and farmers paid the price. Let us for a moment ignore the illegal price-fixing cartels which are such a regular presence in the market, and assume for the sake of argument that no law has been broken. We can certainly say that Milton Friedman – let us not forget, the most influential economist of the late 20th century – will be sleeping easily in his grave, for this is the free market exactly as he prescribed it. Yet times have changed since 1962. The true test of a theory is not how good it sounds in debate, or how well it reads in textbooks, but what actually happens when it is put into practice. Is this the outcome its proponents envisaged? If not, what is the justification for persisting with it? Is it even morally defensible? Let me repeat the quotation from Joseph Stiglitz: 'Modern high-tech warfare is designed to remove physical contact: dropping bombs from 50,000 feet ensures that one does not "feel" what one does. Modern economic management is similar: from one's luxury hotel, one can callously impose policies about which one would think twice if one knew the people whose lives one was destroying.'

Television news footage gives us a filtered glimpse of the world's poor. But we do not empathize well. These people are not *us*. Their experience of life is so remote from our own that, even if we try, we cannot imagine what it is like to be them. We buy what they grow – bananas, coffee, cocoa, cotton, tea, rice, palm oil, sugar – and have no idea of the true cost, or of who has had to pay it. Under market pressure, prices for coffee, cocoa, rice, palm oil and sugar fell by 50 per cent in the last two decades of the 20th century, and others dropped almost as steeply. By one calculation, the failure of tropical commodity prices to keep pace with inflation over the previous 20 years cost producer countries 242bn dollars in 2002 alone. In that same year UNCTAD's (United Nations Conference on Trade and Development's) Least Developed Countries Report declared that extreme poverty

is pervasive and persistent in most LDCs [least developed countries], and . . . the incidence of extreme poverty is highest in those LDCs that are dependent on primary commodity exports. The incidence of poverty is so high because most of the LDCs are caught in an international poverty trap. Pervasive poverty within

LDCs has effects at the national level that cause poverty to persist
and even to increase, and international trade and finance relationships are reinforcing the cycle of economic stagnation and poverty
. . . the current form of globalization is tightening the poverty trap.

So there we have it. It's official. The prices that smallholders
receive for their crops often are less than the cost of producing
them, with dire effects on their families and livelihoods. The
charity Save the Children reports that nearly a third of children in
undeveloped countries are stunted or underweight as a result of
chronic malnutrition. Every day 850m people go hungry, and the
problem is at its worst in countries whose GDP leans most heavily
on agricultural exports. The textbook pattern of vertical
integration and co-ordination in the market means that farmers
are subjected to the financial equivalent of medieval torture –
progressively crushed between two great weights. Low prices for
their produce, grinding against high prices for their seeds and
fertilizers. Just as the drug companies protected their patents at
Africa's expense, so bio companies do the same. Patents on crop
varieties can last 20 years, and in some cases may allow 'ownership' of an entire plant species. This is particularly galling for
native growers who may have developed varieties of their own,
which they then see whisked away to be genetically tweaked,
patented and price-inflated by a transnational corporation. The
new commercial seeds are often more expensive than the
traditional varieties they displaced, but not always more productive. And they are routinely tied in with costly agri-chemicals
– pesticides, herbicides and fertilizers – without which they will
either not grow at all or will produce an inferior yield. Oxfam
reports that rice farmers in Costa Rica are having to pay an average 16 per cent of their production costs on agri-chemicals, and
that banana-, coffee- and potato-growers are being hit for even
more. Small farmers unable to afford this from their incomes
must take out loans which, at best, they struggle to repay.

The enforced dependence on pesticides is harmful in other ways too. There is increased risk not just of environmental damage but of poisoning. Developing countries do not have the kinds of health and safety laws that encourage safe handling of dangerous substances in countries such as the UK. Very often safety training is not provided; nor are protective clothing or safety gear for those working in hazardous environments; nor are there environmental safeguards to prevent poisons leaching into groundwater or streams. Many of the people using agri-chemicals speak only tribal languages and cannot read the instructions. They inhale droplets of spray; they eat without washing their hands; they drink from polluted wells; sometimes they even consume poisons directly (24 children died in Peru after an illiterate woman mistook pesticide for powdered milk). The UN Environment Programme calculates that between 1m and 5m cases of pesticide poisoning occur every year, and that 20,000 farmworkers die. Others suffer from respiratory problems, reproductive diseases and cancers. There is often no medical insurance, and no available healthcare for people made ill. Developing countries between them use only 25 per cent of the world's pesticides but suffer 90 per cent of the injuries.

For many reasons – the unwillingness of corporations to accept responsibility, the ineffectiveness of local legislation, the high cost of going to law, the fear of persecution – victims of corporate negligence seldom achieve legal redress. For these reasons and more, UNCTAD has called for 'increased and more effective aid and debt relief, a review and recasting of international commodity policy, and policies which recognize the interdependence between the socio-economic marginalization of the poorest countries and the increasing polarization of the global economy'. This might seem a rather obvious conclusion, but it is good to see an official body coming to it.

The UN, too, has recognized that maltreatment of workers and their communities by transnational corporations can amount to human rights abuse. In July 2005 Secretary General Kofi Annan appointed an American academic, Professor John Ruggie, as his special representative on business and human rights. In June 2008 the professor duly delivered his report to the UN Human Rights Council (HRC). He is not a police force, and not a judicial authority (though he was able to review cases brought by others), so no one was convicted of anything and many of the allegations remained unproven. But the sheer volume and seriousness of what Ruggie reported should make even the most passionate of Friedmanites listen to their inner voices. He told the HRC: 'By now we have analysed nearly 400 public allegations against companies; we have followed dozens of court cases; and I have met personally with victimized indigenous peoples' groups and other affected communities, with workers in global supply chains, and with labour leaders whose colleagues were killed by paramilitaries protecting company assets.'

In an addendum to his main report he listed all the human rights which transnational corporations were said to have breached. It is a long list, but it deserves to be given in full. Violations were alleged against:

Freedom of association.
The right to organize and participate in collective bargaining.
The right to non-discrimination.
The abolition of slavery and forced labour.
The abolition of child labour.
The right to work.
The right to equal pay for equal work.
The right to equality at work.
The right to just and favourable remuneration.
The right to a safe work environment.
The right to rest and leisure.
The right to family life.
The right to life, liberty and security of the person.

Freedom from torture or cruel, inhuman or degrading treatment.

The right to a fair trial.

The right to self-determination.

Freedom of movement.

The right of peaceful assembly.

The right to marry and form a family.

Freedom of thought, conscience and religion.

The right to hold opinions, freedom of information and expression.

The right to political life.

The right to privacy.

The right to an adequate standard of living (including food, clothing and housing).

The right to physical and mental health; access to medical services.

The right to education.

The right to participate in cultural life, the benefits of scientific progress, and protection of authorial interests.

The right to social security.

Many of the abuses infringed more than one human right and were reliable harbingers of wider malpractice. Corporations that treated people badly were equally unworried about damage to the environment, and were likely to conceal, destroy or falsify their records in order to escape blame or hide the truth during factory inspections or audits. A quarter of all complaints involved corruption. The most heavily abused part of the world, source of 28 per cent of the allegations, was Asia and the Pacific, followed by Africa, 22 per cent, and Latin America, 18 per cent. In 60 per cent of the cases, the abuses were committed directly by corporations against workers or communities. In 40 per cent the abuses were indirect – ie a corporation benefited from violations committed by other companies or states. The most obvious examples were the forced displacements of indigenous peoples by states clearing land for corporations to exploit – in some cases affecting as many as 60,000 people. Such incidents confound the commonly held belief that workers alone suffer the ill-effects of predation. In fact 45 per cent of the cases involved workers, and 45 per cent the communities they lived in or had displaced. The other 10 per cent involved abuses of customers or 'end users' – mostly by patent-obsessed pharmaceutical firms preventing access to essential medicines. Specific examples of malpractice described by Professor Ruggie included:

Mining companies in South Africa refusing to allow subcontractors the use of medical facilities, including HIV/AIDS medication.

The same companies discriminating against women (a common complaint worldwide), thus forcing them into prostitution; accommodating workers in shacks with no electricity, sewerage or water, and not providing masks in a dust-laden atmosphere.

Drinks companies forcing Muslim women to promote and sell alcohol. To secure orders and meet sales quotas, some of them were expected to have sex with clients.

Electronics companies employing children and enslaving adults by taking and keeping their identity papers, enforcing 90-hour working weeks, withholding pay and refusing to accept resignations.

The same companies denying workers access to their families and making up to 12 men sleep in the same small room with no access to water. Documents were falsified, and workers told what to say when interviewed by inspectors.

Mining firms in Asia employing security firms to beat, torture and kill unauthorized workers.

Firms supplying UK supermarkets from Bangladesh, India and Costa Rica denying workers the right to organize, firing and rehiring workers at lower pay and discriminating against women.

Footwear factories with a 90 per cent female workforce discriminating against men by charging fees for jobs, paying piecework rates that caused workers to receive less than the minimum wage, and refusing leave even for childbirth or bereavement.

The same companies not training workers in the safe use of toxic chemicals and failing to provide insurance against accidents.

Managers in the same companies harassing, intimidating and performing 'intrusive' body searches of female employees who were forced to sleep 10 to a room and share a bathroom with 100 others.

A utility company failing to pay compensation after causing a gas explosion that killed eight people and destroyed 10,000 homes.

A mining company not seeking permission before entering private land, where indigenous people were forcibly removed from their homes, dissenters arrested and in one case shot.

The same company failing to rehouse the people whose homes it had demolished.

A construction company benefiting from state oppression. Fifty thousand people were forcibly displaced to make way for a dam, with no adequate compensation or resettlement plan. Objectors were arrested and two of them killed. Normal planning procedures were bypassed, raising suspicions of corruption.

A large financial institution lending money for a project that expelled indigenous people from their homes and farmland, and failed to rehouse them.

Other banks lending to corrupt governments with long histories of human rights abuse, and manufacturing companies supplying the physical tools of oppression.

For most impoverished people who stand in the way of the free-trade juggernaut, the idea of legal redress is an off-colour joke. Cash-strapped governments hesitate to prosecute wealthy corporations that provide jobs, taxes and/or bribes, and individual claimants do not have the resources to challenge companies in court. Of course it is not supposed to come to this. 'The corporate responsibility to respect human rights,' Professor Ruggie told the

HRC, 'is the baseline expectation for all companies in all situations.' Perhaps there are Friedmanites who agree with this – maybe it's part of what the great man meant by 'the rules of the game'. And yet Friedman himself in 1970 was still telling the *New York Times* that 'the social responsibility of business is to increase its profits'. More profit means more tax and more jobs, so society will get its reward and justice is satisfied. That is the theory, but offshore tax havens, smoke-and-mirrors networks of client companies and an accountancy profession playing hide-and-seek with tax law have dented this old verity's armour. The rules of the game may survive in the letter, but they are very different in spirit. Ruggie concluded that many corporations literally did not know what they were doing: '[How do they] know they respect human rights? Do they have systems in place enabling them to support the claim with any degree of confidence? In fact relatively few do.'

Where they exist, such systems are known as corporate social responsibility (CSR) codes. Even though there is a large and varied number of these, and although they enjoy more lip service than Wagner, they are voluntary and restrict themselves to general statements of principle rather than rules to be followed. They are also rather thinly spread. ActionAid reported in 2005 that only between 1,500 and 2,000 out of an estimated 64,000 transnational corporations were producing annual CSR reports, and that very few of these were in the agricultural and food industries where the worst abuses were taking place. With or without codes, companies have little difficulty in avoiding accountability. Even where local jurisdictions *are* willing to prosecute, they cannot hit moving targets. Like deer at twilight, companies vanish into the legal thickets and leave barely a shadow. The rules of the game are a corporate veil behind which lawyers are able to sustain the fiction that parent and subsidiary companies are unconnected. If the subsidiary has to take the rap, then at least the other companies in the corporate chain will avoid liability. Where fines *are* imposed, they are often so low that it is cheaper for the offender to pay up and risk repeat fines than it is to change its *modus operandi*.

ActionAid's report was published in January 2005, and so reflected the world as it was in 2004. The situation may have improved since then, though the evidence of the Ruggie report is that it has not done so by very much, least of all in the areas where people are most vulnerable. Among legislators, NGOs and the best company managements it is being recognized that good behaviour needs to be more than an optional extra bestowed by voluntary codes. The rules of the game need to change, and they need the force of law. Without it, fair trade and free trade will remain as distantly related as free love and rape.

For the rest of us meanwhile, all the old dilemmas and paradoxes remain. If you buy a banana, you can feel pretty certain that someone, somewhere will have suffered for it. Cocoa, coffee, tea, handbags, sports shoes, rice, electronics . . . Anything grown or assembled in the developing world brings with it the risk that our cut-price purchase is at the cost of another person's health, education or liberty. Morally we are all in Joseph Stiglitz's 'luxury hotel', taking tea while economic bombs are dropped in other continents. Yes, I go on buying bananas. For the man on the plantation a fraction of very little is better than a fraction of nothing, and what principle would be served by denying him that? For the British in particular, bananas have a strange symbolism. We do not grow them here; they are not essential to health (though of course they are nutritious) and they are a luxury which we could easily forgo. As befits a luxury, they were the very last commodity to come off ration after the Second World War, later even than sweets and sugar, yet in 1996 they overtook apples as the country's favourite fruit. Greed cheaply indulged at someone else's expense. If that doesn't peel our consciences, then nothing ever will.

This has not been quite the book I set out to write. I had planned something a bit more just-fancy-that, a bit more celebratory of the pleasures of indulgence, perhaps even a bit more confessional. Well, let me confess this. Not many weeks ago I flew in a jet aircraft at low cost to an island in the Aegean where I enjoyed a two-week holiday of supreme indolence and extravagant gluttony. By 'enjoyed' I mean loved every minute. Barbecued fish, stewed goat, grilled lamb, wine, fruit . . . all dished up whenever I fancied them and digested cat-like in the sun. A warm refreshing sea; mountains to walk among; the perfect companion; good books; cocktails at six. If I were god, this would be my blueprint for heaven (though I'd leave out the mosquitoes and the bloke with the Northumbrian pipes). Guilt? No, not for a moment. I had earned a holiday.

It is now late August, and the Norfolk countryside wears muted colours – the toning greens of wood and field, the scuffed gold of straw and stubble, the bitter chocolate of newly turned earth. Gardens and orchards bulge with surfeit – so many apples that the portion left for the birds will hugely exceed what goes to the kitchen. The talk on the radio is of economic downturn, plummeting house prices, distant wars. The chancellor of the exchequer, dour at the best of times, now makes Eeyore sound like Jiminy Cricket. In Bihar, India, two million people have been flooded out of their homes, thousands are missing and the best/worst guess is that 2,000 have died. In Russia, one of Putin's goons has threatened to nuke Poland. In Carlisle, the owner of a Chinese restaurant refuses to allow an eight-year-old boy and his 11-year-old brother to eat from the children's menu because they are 'too tall'. 'It's not the money,' says their father. 'It's the principle.' The fashion editor in a weekend magazine tells us that 'berry tones add a flash of colour to autumn's sober palette'. Half a dozen pages away, Keira Knightley is photographed wearing the trademark lips-apart expression someone once must have told her was sexy but which has turned her into a human sardine. 'Manipulation is something women do a lot,' says the cover line.

'Keira Knightley speaks out.' Jacques Rogge has spoken out too, commanding London in 2012 to 'put the bar even higher' than Beijing 'so that we can have consistent improvement and evolution of the Olympic Games'. In Norfolk, I chair a debate on globalization during which a Conservative MP declares his faith in 'the law of comparative advantage' (which holds that countries at different stages of economic development can benefit equally in a free market). He also says he does not believe in utopias, but nobody spots the contradiction. A well-educated young man tells me he doesn't give 'jack shit' for Africa. It doesn't affect him, so why should he care? Ownership of a television set has been made worthwhile again by the BBC Proms, where the performances of the National Youth Orchestra and Daniel Barenboim's West-Eastern Divan rekindle flames across a wide spectrum of hope – hope for youth, hope for music, hope for art as a force for good. In a local deli I buy the best pork pie I have ever eaten, made apparently by two women in a barn. In India there are food riots. Doctors in the UK report that the obesity epidemic is causing a rapid increase in tendon damage, osteoarthritis and various other torments of the foot. The National Consumer Council complains that supermarkets' response to the credit crunch has been to increase the number of special offers on cheap sugary and fatty foods. In the Caribbean, the old island of Hispaniola, now divided between Haiti and the Dominican Republic, is smashed by Hurricane Gustav. In Monaco, contesting the European Super Cup against Zenit St Petersburg, the Manchester United midfielder Paul Scholes is sent off for deliberately palming the ball into goal. South Africa's cricketers announce that they will not take part in the Champions Trophy if it is held in Pakistan – an example which England, Australia and New Zealand are expected to follow. In the US, the Democratic presidential candidate Barack Obama taunts George W. Bush for his failure to find Osama bin Laden. A team of scientists publishes a new theory about the ability of flies to avoid swatting . . .

If this was a soundtrack, it would now fade to birdsong. Such is life. There is no end to the story; no conclusion to be reached. We are, and always will be, a work in progress, prompted by our genes into expressing our natures in ways that we cannot always predict or control. We cannot decide what we want; we just *do*. Our weakness is that we are inherently, incurably and insatiably greedy. Our strength is that we know we are.

But our biologically unique intelligence also brings us the gift of discretion. We have willpower. We know we cannot have everything we want, and we know that restraint in the short term can be for our greater good in the long. We can learn from our mistakes. We can be patient. The outcome of Harvardian hubris, the conviction that men and women with business degrees were uniquely fitted to prescribe our destiny, was the 'age of irresponsibility' from which politicians now rush to dissociate themselves. As the banks fell and share prices tumbled, so the political left piped up with hope in its heart, proclaiming the death of capitalism. It was wrong. The monster has had its nose stung, but it has not lost its appetite. We need to nurse it back to health, but never again should we allow it to slip its leash. Greed may pump saliva to its jaws, but we must be deaf to its bark and very, very careful about its diet.

Acknowledgements

Sometimes I wonder if I am the only person who reads acknowledgements in books. I understand why others don't. The catalogues of books read and experts consulted can look more like boasting – 'Just look how hard I've worked!' – than proper humility.

My own solution wherever possible has been to acknowledge books and papers in the text. (By 'wherever possible' I mean when I actually remember where I learned something.) I would like to mention in particular Joseph Stiglitz's *Globalization and Its Discontents* (Penguin, 2002) and John Kenneth Galbraith's *The Economics of Innocent Fraud* (Houghton Mifflin, 2004), from which I learned not only how economists view the world but also that there were bigger brains than my own that despaired of the consequences. I had also hoped here to acknowledge the kindness of the copyright holder in allowing me to quote ten words from Woody Guthrie's hymn to freedom, 'This Land Is Your Land', but they wanted £500. If Guthrie's shade is anywhere stalking the land, I hope it has a taste for irony.

Otherwise all I wish to add here is that without a vast quantity of other people's work to draw upon there would have been no book. Ranging from genetics through biology to macroeconomics has taken me far outside my comfort zone and I needed all the help I could get. To all those authors, campaigners and researchers therefore I offer my thanks, and commend their work to anyone who would like to know more. Beyond that, I have to thank only the usual suspects – my agent Karolina Sutton, editor Susanna Wadeson and copy editor Deborah Adams. The idea for this book (I don't know whether to thank or blame her) came from Caroline McGhie, for whose company and insights I have to confess feelings of insatiable greed.

Index